D1607526

Excluded Within

Excluded Within

The (Un)Intelligibility of Radical Political Actors

SINA KRAMER

OXFORD
UNIVERSITY PRESS

OXFORD
UNIVERSITY PRESS

Oxford University Press is a department of the University of Oxford. It furthers the University's objective of excellence in research, scholarship, and education by publishing worldwide. Oxford is a registered trade mark of Oxford University Press in the UK and certain other countries.

Published in the United States of America by Oxford University Press
198 Madison Avenue, New York, NY 10016, United States of America.

Library of Congress Cataloging-in-Publication Data
Names: Kramer, Sina.
Title: Excluded within: the (un)intelligibility of radical political actors/Sina Kramer.
Description: New York, NY: Oxford University Press, [2017] |
Includes bibliographical references and index.
Identifiers: LCCN 2017011887| ISBN 9780190625986 (hardcover : alk. paper) |
ISBN 9780190840013 (epub)
Subjects: LCSH: Equality. | Political rights. | Political science—Philosophy. |
Marginality, Social. | Intersectionality (Sociology) | Political participation—Case studies. |
Social action—Case studies. | Social movements—Case studies.
Classification: LCC JC575.K73 2017 | DDC 320.01/4—dc23
LC record available at https://lccn.loc.gov/2017011887

9 8 7 6 5 4 3 2 1

Printed by Sheridan Books, Inc., United States of America

For A. D.

CONTENTS

ACKNOWLEDGMENTS

In *Precarious Life*, Judith Butler writes, "I am not fully known to myself, because part of what I am is enigmatic traces of others." This work is largely a contribution toward thinking through that insight, and without the friendship, support, and work of the following persons (and to be sure many others besides), traces of all of whom I carry within myself, this work would not have been possible. In the production of any intellectual work, but especially in the production of a first book, across four institutions and some twelve years, I have accumulated many debts. It is my great joy to do my best to acknowledge them here, in full knowledge that such accounting is always incomplete, begging forgiveness for this, and with assurances that all shortcomings of the finished product are entirely my own.

My first thanks is to my first teacher, my mother, JoAnne Kramer. Thank you for your fierce insight, for your curiosity, for your sacrifice, and for your faith. Thanks also to my father, Kris, to my brother, Aaron, and my sister, Courtney. Thanks to my other family, the Diltses: Anne, Jon Paul, and Chris. Thanks to all of the extended Kramer and Snyder and Dilts clans, and especially to Alverta, Joe, Leonard, and Riet, for making me who I am and for the gift of your love.

Many thanks to my editor at Oxford University Press, Angela Chnapko; it is a joy to work with an editor so supportive of her authors and who is bringing so many great voices to print. My thanks as well to Princess

Ikatekit at Oxford and to my indexer, Suzanne Sherman Aboulfadi. I am grateful to two anonymous reviewers for their close reading and commentary, as well as their excitement and encouragement. An earlier version of Chapter 2 was published in the *Southern Journal of Philosophy* (52:4), December 2014; earlier versions of portions of Chapters 1 and 6 were published in *philoSOPHIA: A Journal of Continental Feminist Philosophy* (5:1), Winter 2015, and in *Returns of Antigone: Interdisciplinary Essays*, edited by Tina Chanter and Sean Kirkland, SUNY 2014, respectively. I am grateful to these publications for their kind permission to reprint this work here.

I am immensely grateful to the intellectual communities in which I have had the great good luck to find a home, to all of the generous commentators and patient audiences that I have had for this project over the years at the Society for Phenomenology and Existential Philosophy, the Western Political Science Association, the Radical Philosophy Association, the DePaul Graduate Philosophy Colloquium and the Manfred R. Frings Colloquium, the Collegium Phaenomenologicum, the Pacific meeting of the Society for Women in Philosophy, the UCLA Political Theory Workshop, and the philoSOPHIA Feminist Philosophy Society. Thanks especially to Libby Anker, Paul Apostolidis, Libby Barringer, Cristina Beltrán, Emanuela Bianchi, Sara Brill, Anita Chari, George Ciccariello-Maher, Joshua Dienstag, Peter Gratton, Megan Gallagher, Sarah Hansen, Yves Hersant, Roni Hirsch, Lynne Huffer, Anthony Kammas, Jimmy Casas Klausen, Michelle Larson Rose, Fred Lee, Mary-Beth Mader, Robyn Marasco, Naveed Mansoori, James Martel, Kirstie McClure, Marina McCoy, Ladelle McWhorter, Chris Meckstroth, Eduardo Mendieta, Elaine Miller, Shannon Mussett, Anthony Pagden, Melvin Rogers, George Schulman, Holloway Sparks, Falguni Sheth, Althea Sircar, Giulia Sissa, Fanny Söderbäck, Shannon Sullivan, Dianna Taylor, Sarah Tyson, Laura Werner, Shannon Winnubst, Emily Zakin, and especial thanks to James Flannery, formerly of Bloomington High School South.

I am grateful for the support of and the friendship of my colleagues at Loyola Marymount University, where the Women's and Gender Studies Department continues to model feminist solidarity in all our work within the department and the college. Thanks to my colleagues, Mairead Sullivan,

Traci Voyles, and my chair, Stella Oh. This book was kindly supported by the Bellarmine College of Liberal Arts Fellowship. My thanks to the BCLA Scholarship/Research Committee members, to Dean Robbin Crabtree, and to Associate Dean Michael Horan for their support of this project. And thanks as well to my colleagues and friends across the college and the university, especially Marne Campbell, Gil Klein, Jessica Langlois, John Parrish, Richard Fox, Eliza Rodriguez y Gibson, Mona Seymour, Faith Sovilla, Dan Speak, Brad Stone, Traci Tiemeier, Brian Treanor, Thomas Ward, and Robin Wang. Special thanks to the coordinators for my three departments over the years at LMU: Elizabeth Faulkner, Michelle Larson Rose, and Alexis Dolan.

I am grateful for invitations from friends to come speak to their colleagues and students, including Kunitoshi Sakai and the audience at Chicago Theological Seminary; Chris Buck and the audience at St. Lawrence University, especially Mary Jane Smith and Amir Jaima; Ed Kazarian and the audience at Rowan University, especially Kim Wilson and David Clowney.

Thanks to Fordham University's philosophy department and the New York City crew, especially Samir Haddad, Crina Gschwandtner, Shiloh Whitney, Aaron Pinnix, Kyoo Lee, Emmanuela Bianchi, and Hernando A. Estévez, for making NYC home for nine months.

I am immensely grateful for my training in continental philosophy at DePaul University, and for my teachers there, faculty as well as fellow students, from whom I learned so much. Thanks especially to Tina Chanter, Kevin Thompson, Darrell Moore, and Rick Lee. Thanks to my DePaul colleagues Ali Beheler, Jeremy Bell, Marie Draz, Rick Elmore, Azadeh Erfani, Dilek Huseyinzadegan-Bell, Robin James, O'Donovan Johnson, James A. Manos, Jeff Pardikes, Amanda Parris, Rosalie Siemon Lochner, Anthony Paul Smith, Molly Sturdevant, Sam Talcott, Robert Valgenti, Robert Vallier, Joe Weiss, Robin Weiss, and Perry Zurn. Special thanks to Mary Amico and Jennifer Burke. I am especially grateful to my cohort: Jana McAuliffe, Kristen McCartney, Heather Rakes, Holly Moore, and Andrew LaZella. For a discipline with so few women in it, to be in philosophy classrooms with so many talented and brilliant women was a remarkable experience, and it took a while for me to really grasp how special it was. I have never let go of the promise in that naïvité. Thank you for building with me an expectation of what this world could be, and may yet.

I am grateful for my other Chicago home in Hyde Park, my friends in political science at the University of Chicago, for making me a better and more responsible thinker. Thanks especially to Patchen Markell, Andrea Frank, Deva Woodly, Lauren Duquette-Rury, Neil Roberts, Emily Nacol, and Rafi and Anna Youatt. Thanks especially to Harper House: Chris Buck and Emily Meierding. Thanks for the long nights, the late nights, and the gift of your friendship.

Thanks to my faculty and friends at Earlham College in philosophy, for giving me a start down this path, and for creating in me the ideal I strive each year to meet in my own classrooms. Thanks as well to my faculty and friends in the theater for making me a good teacher, keen to the significance of performance in and out of the classroom. Special thanks to Charles Holmond, Ferit Güven, Peter Suber, and Lynne Knight.

Also, for those most material of supports, my thanks to Soma, Java Jazz, Istria, the Bourgeois Pig, the Grind, Beans and Bagels, Intelligentsia, Metropolis, Darling, Cafecito Organico, and Dinosaur. Growing Home, and the South Central Farm. Bear's Place, especially John and Jeremiah. Jimmy's, especially Vito. The Pub. The Local Option, especially Tony and Dox. The Red Lion, especially John and Colin. The Grafton, especially Jen, Jenny, Jen, James, and Kelly. Indian Road Café. The Inwood Local. Jay's. The Faculty, especially Mike, Mikey, Mauricio, Colin, Derrick, and Trevor.

Also, and finally, to Andrew Dilts. Andrew, who has read countless drafts of this project over the years, who always had the insight to make me a better writer than I ever thought I could be, and who always had faith in my voice. Andrew, from whom I have learned so much, and who teaches me new things every day. Andrew, who gave me the space to write. Andrew, who let me go on about the Kantian a priori at midnight at Denny's at eighteen, and who has been my enthusiastic interlocutor at every step since. Words fail me. You never have.

Excluded Within

1

Constitutive Exclusion

I begin with three scenes.

The first scene features the figure of Antigone. We are familiar with the story: Antigone appears in the eponymous play by Sophocles, at the end of the Oedipus cycle.[1] She is the daughter of Oedipus and Jocasta, but because of the curse on her family line, she is also her father's sister; her mother and sister are also her aunts; her brothers are her uncles. Oedipus has died and Antigone's brothers have killed each other in contest for the throne. Her uncle Creon has taken it and forbidden burial for her brother Polyneices as an enemy of Thebes. Antigone, against the counsel of her sister Ismene, breaks the law and buries her brother anyway; moreover, she defends her right to do so in public, in the face of the king. She insists upon her right to mourn her brother, refusing to subordinate her rights to the rights of the state. In challenging the authority of the king and his state, she calls into question the borders that secure that authority, finally and especially the border between man and woman. In doing so, she appears insurrectionary and monstrous, her claims unintelligible as political claims. Condemned to a living death by Creon, shut away in a cave, Antigone takes her own life. Though her contestation ends in her death, the play has inspired a whole history of reproductions, a proliferation of adaptations to fit new political circumstances, from Nazi-occupied Paris to apartheid South Africa to Ireland in the midst of the second Iraq War.[2]

What about *Antigone*—and Antigone—inspires this history of repetitions and re-articulations of this insurrection from within, both in the history of performances of the play and in the history of modern thought? How does the figure of Antigone seemingly both secure and trouble the distinctions between private and public, between family and state—indeed, between woman and man—upon which the political body of ancient Thebes and political agency in the city is grounded? Why does Antigone's defiant contestation result in her death, and why does it continue to haunt our political life?

How is Antigone excluded within?

The next scene features two figures who occupy either side of the reconstitution of political agency in the United States in the middle of the twentieth century: Claudette Colvin and Rosa Parks. The latter name is familiar to us: Rosa Parks, the quiet middle-aged woman who refused to give up her seat and move to the back of the bus; Rosa Parks, who sparked the Montgomery bus boycott with her arrest in December 1955; Rosa Parks, patron saint of the civil rights movement of the mid-century United States. Less well known is the story of the arrest of a teenaged Black girl, Claudette Colvin, nine months before Parks. Colvin was arrested for refusing to give up her seat on a Montgomery bus on her way home from school; the police passed the time they spent booking her guessing her bra size and referring to her as a "whore."[3] She was charged with violating the local segregation ordinance, disorderly conduct, and assault. Local leadership of the Women's Political Council and the Montgomery chapter of the National Association for the Advancement of Colored People (NAACP), including E. D. Nixon, Jo Ann Robinson (the Reverend Dr. Martin Luther King Jr. was to arrive later, at Nixon's request), and Rosa Parks herself, had been looking for an opportunity both to legally challenge bus segregation in Montgomery and to organize a boycott of the public bus system.[4] With the arrest of Colvin, Robinson felt that their opportunity had arrived. Other NAACP activists, particularly Nixon, were not so sure that Colvin was a good candidate for a figurehead; nine months later, they chose to rally a boycott around the arrest of Rosa Parks instead. NAACP activists at the time were concerned about Colvin's youth, her outspokenness, her poverty, and her fierceness. Their concerns were solidified when, after her arrest, Colvin wore her hair in cornrows and she discovered that she was pregnant by an older, married man.[5]

In the national narrative of the civil rights movement in the United States, Colvin's story has been buried. Meanwhile, Rosa Parks's story has been whitewashed: rather than the tireless Black nationalist activist she actually was—the secretary of the Montgomery chapter of the NAACP who cut her teeth organizing against the trial of the Scottsboro boys and the sexual assault of Black women around the South, who always kept guns in her home—the nation continues to celebrate Parks as a shy, retiring middle-class woman whose private decision made a public fuss she herself never sought.

Why has it taken us so long to hear Colvin's story? And are we so sure that we "know" Rosa Parks? Why did the organizers of the Montgomery bus boycott choose to organize around Parks rather than Colvin? And most important, what effects did this choice have? Who is intelligible as a political agent in this choice, and who is not? How does our understanding of political agency shape the very "we" of the political body that Colvin and Parks helped to reconstitute through their efforts?

How are Colvin and Parks excluded within?

The third scene features a fragmented collective figure: the 1992 Los Angeles Riots/Rebellion. On April 29, 1992, just shortly after three in the afternoon, the jury in a Simi Valley courtroom acquitted four police officers—Stacey Koon, Lawrence Powell, Timothy Wind, and Theodore Briseno—of the multiple charges against them, including assault with a deadly weapon and filing a false report. Just over a year earlier, on March 3, 1991, these officers responded to an apparent traffic violation in the San Fernando Valley and, after a lengthy high-speed chase, brutally beat the suspect, Rodney King, while seventeen other police officers looked on. The video captured by George Holliday, who lived near the scene of the beating, went viral, broadcast first on KTLA and then on news programs around the world. When the four officers were acquitted the following spring, the response mounted in some quarters of the city—South Central, Pico Union, Koreatown, Hollywood, and parts of West Los Angeles (LA) and the San Fernando Valley—similarly went viral. The riots, or the uprising, or the rebellion—the contestation over its name already indicating the contestation over the meaning of the event itself—lasted from six to ten days, and resulted in the deaths of between forty-five and fifty-four people, the loss of about $1 billion in property, the arrests of about 1,600 people, and the deportation of an unknown number of others. It was the largest urban uprising since the Watts riot in 1964. The response to the Riots/Rebellion was characterized by a deep ambivalence: on the one hand, a bewilderment; and on the other hand, a refusal. The 1992 LA Riots/Rebellion remains an ambiguous event in the life of the United States: the rioters were unintelligible in making a political contestation of political conditions and instead were figured as the threat of a wild criminal mob. This ambivalence is reflected in the contestation over its very naming, as the term "riot" invokes aimless, disorganized madness, wildness, or criminality, whereas "rebellion" or "uprising" marks a directed response to political repression.[6] The Riots/Rebellion is in a certain sense unintelligible as a political event, providing a blueprint for the unintelligibility of similar uprisings to come.

What was the 1992 Los Angeles Riots/Rebellion, and what bearing does it have on us? Are riots ever intelligible as political claims? How does the foreclosure of the claims of the rioters construct the citizenship of others in the United States? How do the claims of the rioters continue to remain unintelligible to the larger political body, and what are the continuing effects of this unintelligibility?

How is the 1992 Los Angeles Riot/Rebellion excluded within?

These figures, I argue, mark the limit between several distinctions that put intelligible political agency into play. Antigone—especially as she has been taken up in modern and contemporary thought—figures the distinctions between the family and the polity, between private and public, and ultimately between woman and man that ground political agency. Claudette Colvin and Rosa Parks figure either side of the transition from unintelligible to intelligible political agency, which renders Parks less a political subject than a reified political object, while Colvin remains unintelligible as neither. And the fragmented collective of the Los Angeles Riots/Rebellion figures the distinction between the wild, threatening criminal mob and the law-abiding citizen, respectful of property.

Yet none of these figures are absolutely excluded from the space of intelligible political agency. Instead they lie ambiguously both within and without that space, paradoxically both grounding and troubling the distinctions that structure political bodies and the terms of political agency. They are excluded *within*. How is this possible? How are *they* possible?

My answer, as I will argue in this book, is that this paradoxical grounding and troubling of political bodies and the distinction between intelligible and unintelligible political agency on which they rest, is effected through *constitutive exclusion*.

Rather than a simple or absolute exclusion, constitutive exclusion describes the phenomenon of *internal* exclusion, or those exclusions that occur *within* a philosophical system or a political body. Constitutive exclusions occur when a system of thought or a political body defines itself by excluding some difference which is intolerable to it. This excluded difference nevertheless remains within the system or body that has excluded it; it continues to do that defining or constituting work from within, but under an epistemological block. This book offers an analysis of the concept of constitutive exclusion and the contestations of concrete exclusions, to better articulate how we know what counts as a *political action* and who counts as a *political agent*. It is undertaken for the sake of imagining a future beyond constitutive exclusion.

The movement of constitutive exclusion is logically (though, as we shall see, not temporally) twofold: first, a philosophical system or a political body constitutes itself by producing an excluded element or figure that nevertheless remains within it; second, this remaindered element is covered over, repressed, or disavowed. This constitutively excluded figure is therefore both the condition of *possibility* and the condition of *impossibility* of that constitution. The exclusion of the figure makes the constitution of these philosophical systems and political bodies possible, but the fact that the figure remains within that space makes these constitutions impossible: it therefore occupies what Jacques Derrida refers to as a "quasi-transcendental" position with regard to the bordered, delimited space whose boundary it draws. Such figures are excluded in order to draw the borders of intelligible political agency, but these figures and exclusions remain inside, marking differences that threaten those borders as well as marking modes of resistance to and paths of flight out of or beyond the delimited space drawn through their exclusion. Rather than marking the "eternal irony of the community," they mark its insurrection from within.[7] However, because these excluded figures also draw the borders of intelligible political agency, contestations of their exclusions are unintelligible as political claims. These contestations of exclusion thus demand a reconstitution of the political body and of political agency on new terms, terms no longer settled by means of constitutive exclusion.

Constitutive exclusion cuts through ontological, epistemological, and political levels, often marking the border between these levels. This is because maintaining the fantasy of a bordered, delimited, and intelligible political agency depends upon casting these excluded figures into an a-, extra-, or pre-political space, despite (or perhaps because of) their persistence within those borders. The border is often drawn through making some contingent difference—gender, or race, or sexuality—the basis for exclusion, and then rendering that difference, and that exclusion, a matter of necessity. Because their exclusion secures the fantasy of a fully intelligible political agency on the "inside," if those who are excluded contest their exclusion, their claims are unintelligible as political claims and instead appear as wildness, madness, criminality: a diffuse threat. Translating the claims that come from these quarters into intelligible political agency is difficult; frequently this translation is managed through mere inclusion, in the form of a forced or coerced assimilation to already established terms (a dynamic at work to a certain extent in the politics of respectability in the case of Rosa Parks: we can hear you, we can include you, if only you erase your difference from us—or who we imagine ourselves to be). To do justice to the excluded, to render those claims intelligible as political claims, instead requires the reconstitution of the political body on new terms.

Constitutive exclusion helps us think about race, class, gender, and sexuality all together. It can help us better understand how these identity categories constitute each other and how they are reinscribed over time. In this sense, constitutive exclusion is closely related to intersectionality.[8] But whereas intersectionality's dominant metaphor is spatial, in that it names the *location* where identities meet and redefine each other, constitutive exclusion adds the dimension of time, articulating the *historical sedimentation* of these identities. It can show us how the histories of multiple exclusions and strategic choices build upon each other, layer by layer, shaping the "ground" of politics on which we presently "stand," but of which we are usually ignorant. And it can help us to become sensate to those epistemological blind spots without assimilating or appropriating their critique in advance, and in the hopes of a constitution that no longer relies upon these disavowed exclusions.[9]

CONSTITUTIVE EXCLUSION IN CONTEXT

Though the concept of constitutive exclusion has never really received its own treatment, in the past twenty years or so, something like it (sometimes referred to as the "constitutive outside") has emerged as an important framework for understanding various forms of political and social exclusion. These frameworks generally take four forms. The first stems from critical theory and the radical democratic strain of political theory, especially work influenced by Jacques Derrida, and Ernesto Laclau and Chantal Mouffe. The second is work in feminist theory, especially as it draws on either the work of Derrida, Mouffe, or Judith Butler (or all three). The third is queer theory, especially as it draws on the work of Lacan and Butler. And the last is critical race theory, especially those race theories influenced by queer and sexuality studies, and especially Afro-pessimist work. While each of these schools of thought makes use of the concept of constitutive exclusion or something similar, none of them make the concept the explicit focus of their analyses, nor do they explore its full implications or potential as an analytical tool. None focus on the operation of constitutive exclusion across ontological, epistemological, and political registers. Likewise, none focus specifically on the effects of political unintelligibility in the concrete contestations of exclusion. As such, they are ill-equipped to avoid the reinscription of the very exclusions within that they are meant to critique. *Excluded Within* does this work for the first time. In this section, I briefly describe these approaches, where they have influenced my own, and where I depart from them.

The first is the constitutive outside or constitutive exclusion in critical and political theory. Much of this work is specifically indebted to deconstruction, and thus to the work of Jacques Derrida. In fact, Chantal Mouffe makes specific reference to the concept of the constitutive outside as developed by Derrida.[10] Laclau and Mouffe rely on this principle of the constitutive outside to develop their radical democratic political theory. While antagonism is central to their *Hegemony and Socialist Strategy*, its relationship to the constitutive outside is clearest in later works such as Mouffe's *The Return of the Political*, or in Laclau's *New Reflections on the Revolution in Our Time*.[11] In *The Return of the Political*, Mouffe treats the constitutive outside as a political ontological principle, seeing it as the source of antagonism and the impossibility of the arrival of democracy. She argues that since there can be no creation of a "we" without the creation of a "them," or no inclusion without exclusion, antagonism will always mark politics, and democracy can never finally be realized.[12] In *New Reflections on the Revolution in Our Time*, Laclau treats the constitutive outside as central to the "pure facticity" of antagonism, which paradoxically blocks identity and constitutes it.[13] If Laclau and Mouffe attribute the constitutive outside to Derrida, it is a peculiarly Schmittian and Heideggarian Derrida, in that it comes close to equating the constitutive outside with Schmitt's friend/enemy distinction, and attributing to it a pure facticity. They use the constitutive outside to advance the thesis that antagonism is irreducible to political life, as the establishment of any identity is predicated on exclusion. Following the work of Lacan, Laclau and Mouffe argue that the relation between identity and exclusion is a reflection of the "lack" at the heart of identity itself, indicating an essential incompleteness to identity. This implies a fundamental negativity to the social and the political, and thus the constitutive failure of totality.[14]

Second, the language of constitutive exclusion has been taken up by feminist theorists, in particular those working in critical political theory. These tend to be poststructuralist and deconstructive critiques of certain strains of political theory, especially Jürgen Habermas's democratic political theory.[15] Feminist theorists such as Carol Pateman, Nancy Fraser, and Iris Young argue that women's exclusion from the public sphere—the central concept of Habermas's early political theory—is in no way accidental or contingent to its development.[16] For these theorists, women's exclusion from the public sphere has gendered the norms of communication and political activity as masculine. Simple inclusion into the public sphere is therefore not sufficient; the terms of the public sphere itself must be altered. For instance, Jodi Dean's *Solidarity of Strangers* follows the radical democratic bent to the work of Laclau and Mouffe but departs from their tendency to reify the "them" against which a plural "we" is defined by situating the enemy or the stranger inside our own selves. In that work, Dean develops a notion of constitutive exclusion, which she takes to mean an element inherent to the categories of civil society that requires the creation of an excluded other.[17]

Like feminist political theory, feminist philosophy that works from a concept of constitutive exclusion also draws on the work of Derrida and Butler as well as on the tradition of "French" feminist philosophers, such as Julia Kristeva or Luce Irigaray. For instance, Alison Stone fleshes out Irigaray's method as one of reading texts and cultures for their constitutive exclusions.[18] Penelope Deutscher develops an understanding of constitutive exclusion in Derrida, Irigaray, and Butler, while Lynne Huffer develops an Irigarayan concept of constitutive exclusion identified with a "forgetting of the other" and develops an ethics adequate to respond to it.[19]

Feminist philosophy that works from an Irigarian concept of constitutive exclusion grapples with the common critique that Irigaray privileges the exclusion of the feminine in ways that occlude other exclusions, such as those that cut along class, race, sexuality, or disability. In this sense, one could read Irigaray as a stand-in for the history of feminist thought: women of color, and women who are queer, trans, poor, and/or disabled have frequently critiqued feminism for taking the concerns of white, middle-class heterosexual women as universal or normative, or for presuming a grounding subject taken to be universal but in fact reflecting the lived experiences of a particular subset of women. This has had the effect of excluding those women who do not share this experience. Grappling with the dialectics between universal and particular, and between inclusion and exclusion, is precisely what is at stake in the feminist theorization of constitutive exclusion. Judith Butler offers such a critique of Irigaray in the introduction of *Bodies that Matter*, where she asks, "Is it not the case that there is within any discourse and thus within Irigaray's as well, a set of constitutive exclusions that are invariably produced by the circumscription of the feminine as that which monopolizes the sphere of exclusion?"[20] If identities are predicated upon exclusions (as Laclau and Mouffe argued), can we avoid making further exclusions in our critique the exclusion of some women from the grounding concept of feminism? Are constitutive exclusions inevitable? If so, what does this mean?

Recent work in queer theory and critical race theory also draws on the concept of constitutive exclusion and extends its implications. Lee Edelman employs the concept to flesh out the precise negativity at work in the anti-social turn in queer theory, identifying "the queer" with a constitutive exclusion that he calls "the limit point of ontology," a "No" that marks a radical negation of being.[21] Edelman's approach is similar to Irigaray's in that his Lacanian ontological approach tends to situate the queer as the originary difference, at the exclusion of other axes of difference.

A richer, more complex approach is offered by Afro-pessimist critical race theorist Jared Sexton, who combines critical race theory and queer theory in his *Amalgamation Schemes* to analyze the occluded nexus of anti-Black racism, compulsory heterosexuality, and gendered sexual violence at work in the history of multiracialism and the new valorization of the multiracial child. For Sexton, Blackness is the limit point of ontology: the constitutive outside against which good forms of multiraciality are distinguished from the bad.[22]

While all of these approaches make use of the idea of constitutive exclusion or the constitutive outside, there has been no thoroughgoing account of this concept. These approaches thus leave unexplored and unanswered several important questions: Is constitutive exclusion an absolute outside? Does it operate at the level of ontology, or at the limit of ontology? Is it flexible and specific enough to account for multiple interlocking or intermeshing identities and oppressions? Does the critique of something like the constitutive outside necessitate making further exclusions or occlusions, or laying down one form of difference as original or foundational to all of the others? Is constitutive exclusion an essential lack, common to all, and thus the basis for political solidarity? Or does it draw a binary between them and us, between excluded and included, a friend/enemy distinction that defines the political? Can we ever be without constitutive exclusions? And can we, in our critique of exclusions, avoid making them ourselves as we go?

In *Excluded Within,* I offer both a diagnosis and a critique of the concept of constitutive exclusion. I argue that constitutive exclusion can be both a useful tool for reading the structure of philosophical systems and a useful analytic for understanding operations of hegemony and oppression—specifically those that render some claims unintelligible as political claims or some persons unintelligible as political agents. This analysis is rooted in critical theory and the critique of hegemony or ideology. These sorts of critiques usually operate by means of taking ideology or hegemony's claim to totality seriously and trying to turn its force against itself, or by means of putting the lie to that claim of totality by pointing to the multiple ways that totality has failed. By interrogating the very distinction between inside and outside, the critique of constitutive exclusion I mount here requires both tactics. The vigilant negativity of the critique of constitutive exclusion, as well as the multiplicity and materiality of constitutive exclusions, indicates that this analysis remains on the side of the concrete rather than the abstract. This forestalls the risks both of installing even further exclusions as we make our way and of determining the meaning and the force of the contestation of exclusions in advance. And the political epistemological and historical character of the critique of constitutive exclusion indicate the sedimented layers of exclusions structuring political agency in the present, of which political agents themselves are typically ignorant. Finally, attention to the contestation of constitutive exclusion helps us to redeem those shards of radical potential buried in the sedimentation of the political present, pushing us toward a reconstitution of the political field and the terms of political agency it animates.

THE "CONSTITUTIVE OUTSIDE" AND THE POLITICS OF RECOGNITION

Most of the foregoing approaches have their root in the work of Judith Butler, the thinker who has made most extensive use of the concept of constitutive exclusion or the constitutive outside, and who has developed its implications most widely. As *Excluded Within* likewise takes many of its political and theoretical clues from Butler, it is necessary to spend some time with her work here in order to specify both where my conceptualization of constitutive exclusion draws on and takes its distance from her thought. Butler's contributions to the development of constitutive exclusion raise three major questions that this work addresses: the question of the role of constitutive exclusion in political epistemology, or how the intelligibility of political claims is rooted in constitutive exclusion; the question of the persistence of foundations in feminist thought; and the question of the peculiar temporality of constitutive exclusion. I take up the political epistemology of constitutive exclusion and the politics of recognition as a possible response to it in this section. I describe how my account builds on and moves beyond Butler's in the next.

In her most recent work, Butler gives a rich political epistemological analysis of the constitutive outside (specifically in her analysis of the construction of political bodies and political agency) and how some lives are rendered unintelligible or unlivable through those constructions. She does this work most explicitly in *Frames of War*, which treats the political epistemology of life by means of who is rendered unintelligible as a life.[23] Butler argues that this unintelligibility is produced through what she calls "the frame." Within the frame, political agents are present, represented, and representable: they are intelligible and recognizable as political agents. But who appears within the frame? Who is recognized? Butler argues that to question who can be recognized presupposes that recognition is conditioned, and she identifies this prior condition as "recognizability."[24] Recognition is then a practice or a scene that takes place between subjects, but these subjects *must count as subjects* in order for such a scene to take place. This condition of "recognizability" thus describes who counts as a subject. Since recognizability is also constituted or conditioned, she argues, this indicates that some persons are not recognized by recognition; our ability to recognize recognizability, so to speak, indicates a way of knowing outside of or beyond recognition.[25]

That recognition is conditioned in advance is already an indication that it is insufficient as a response to the unintelligibility of political claims. In political theory, the struggle with unintelligibility has frequently been cast as a struggle for recognition.[26] Since at least Hegel, this points to the underlying sociality of individual agency: if "to act" means "to bring about something new in the world," in order for this newness to have an effect, or in order for newness to arrive, it must be received and taken up by others. This is not the same thing, however, as recognition. Recognition is insufficient as a framework for dealing with the problem of (un)intelligibility because recognition tends to assume the subject positions it produces, and it tends to enforce inclusion within already established terms—terms already established by those in power. Hegemonic power—power that operates through various ideological forms, rather than through the bare exercise of force—produces the subjects it then recognizes. This logic receives perhaps its richest theoretical account in the work of Luce Irigaray, who treats the category "woman" or "the feminine" as the mirror produced to reflect the hegemonic order of phallogocentrism back to itself.[27]

In *Bound by Recognition*, Patchen Markell argues that the politics of recognition is misguided for two reasons. First, he argues that the ideal of mutual reciprocal recognition, in its pretensions to settle the terms of social and political life, misunderstands and even erases the fact of human finitude and the radical contingency of the future. Second, he argues that recognition is insufficient as a solution to relations of domination, which often treats sovereign agency as something to be enjoyed at the expense of others, whose sovereignty and complexity are undercut by being "recognized," not as *who* they are, but as *what* they are.[28] On Markell's account, recognition is thus perfectly compatible with reification, with a contingent identity category rendered into a necessary basis for exclusion or domination.

Similarly, in *Red Skin, White Masks*, Glen Coulthard develops a critique of the politics of recognition as it has operated in reconciliation projects between the state of Canada and First Nations/Indigenous peoples. In a subtle and powerful analysis of Hegel and Fanon, Coulthard argues that struggles over recognition take place between equals: one does not struggle to be recognized by a woman or a slave. He writes,

> Although the issue here is an obvious one, it has nonetheless been critically overlooked in the contemporary recognition literature: in relations of domination that exist between nation-states and the substate national groups that they "incorporate" into their territorial and jurisdictional boundaries, there is no mutual dependency in terms of a need or a desire for recognition. In these contexts, the "master"—that is, the colonial state and society—does not require recognition from the previously self-determining communities upon which its territorial, economic, and social infrastructure is constituted. What it needs is land, labor, and resources. Thus, rather than leading to a condition of reciprocity the dialectic either breaks down with the explicit *non*recognition of the equal status of the colonized population, or with the strategic "domestication" of the terms of recognition leaving the foundation of the colonial relationship relatively undisturbed.[29]

While I want to preserve the specificity of Coulthard's analysis within the political conditions from which it emerges and to which it responds, this central theoretical problem at the heart of recognition can, I think, be taken up more generally. That colonial power has no need to recognize Native peoples indicates that recognition is entirely consistent with domination. Where it must, it will render politically unintelligible claims intelligible by means of assimilation and reification—that is, by disavowing the insurgent ways of being and knowing of unintelligible political actors. Ultimately, this is why recognition cannot be the axis upon which the translation from unintelligibility to intelligibility turns.

Taken together, these critiques of the insufficiency of recognition serve to underscore Butler's insight that recognition is conditioned by a previous recognizability. For Butler, these conditions of recognizability are norms. Following the Foucauldian strain in Butler's thinking, such norms are themselves operations of power. These norms furnish the frames that establish the conditions of recognizability, framing subjects as intelligible and recognizable. Insofar as the norm is always an operation of power, it is always therefore political, though it also functions ontologically and epistemologically. That is to say, norms produce subjects as real and existing, as well as intelligible and recognizable. Butler explains this dual function of the norm by arguing that frames both produce the idea of life itself and delimit the appearance of lives *as* lives. She writes, "In this way, the normative production of ontology thus produces the epistemological problem of apprehending a life, and this in turn gives rise to the ethical problem of what it is to acknowledge or, indeed, to guard against injury and violence."[30] Thus frames shape both the conditions of the recognition of lives and the material support of those lives.

This normative production of ontology that produces the conditions for intelligible lives, however, also produces lives that are unintelligible or unrecognizable. This is because the norm for Butler always produces the specter of its own failure, its ontological double, ambiguously both inside and outside, unintelligible and monstrous. This specter is the "figure." In *Frames of War*, Butler argues that the figure is made to bear precarity, which she argues is the differential political distribution of precariousness, or the fundamental vulnerability common to living things. The figure is made to bear precarity in order to secure the fantasy that those subjects within the frame are individual, independent, and autonomous and that their lives are fully intelligible and under their own control.

If we cannot exactly recognize recognizability and the norms that frame it, we can catch a glimpse of it: Butler argues that we can *apprehend* the figure and the frame that produces the figure as its outside when the frame is broken. And frames can break because they are iterable—they only operate as frames if they circulate, and their circulation depends upon their iterability. If norms always produce the specter of their own failure, this is due to the iterability of the frame, and the fact that iterability takes *time*: "what is taken for granted in one instance becomes thematized critically or even incredulously in another. This shifting temporal dimension of the frame constitutes the possibility and trajectory of its affect as well."[31]

Thus intelligibility is produced at the cost of rendering some lives unintelligible as lives, and on the basis of producing those lives as precarious, or forcing them to bear precarity. This account of the epistemological character of the constitutive outside is very close to my own interest in constitutive exclusion in this book. But my account departs from and builds upon Butler's in two specific ways. First, while Butler gestures toward a pre-political foundation on which to ground a politics, constitutive exclusion as I articulate it here avoids this by means of closer attention to method. And second, Butler invokes but does not take on directly the specific ways that time operates in these exclusions. *Excluded Within* addresses the peculiar temporality at work in constitutive exclusion, by analyzing its retroactive character.

FEMINIST FOUNDATIONS AND TEMPORALITY

The first problem I take up is the question of the persistence of foundations in feminist and political thought. We can see this persistence in two readings of Butler's recent work. Lynne Huffer argues that Butler's ethics in *Frames of War* and *Precarious Life* refer us to a pre-political concept of "life itself."[32] As I noted above, in *Frames of War*, Butler argues that those outside the frame are made to bear precarity, the political distribution of a fundamental precariousness, which she seems to take as a universal: the precariousness of "life itself," which cannot be recognized or appear within the frame. This precariousness of life itself cannot be recognized, but nevertheless it exerts an ethical force on us to which we must attend and which ought to orient our politics. Huffer's concern here is that Butler (along with several other feminists involved in the project of renaturalization, such as Elizabeth Grosz, Hasana Sharp, and Karen Barad) refers us to a notion of "life itself" that operates prior to political forces or frameworks.[33] For Huffer, "life itself" operates dangerously close to what Foucault identified in *The History of Sexuality* as "sex itself": an invisible, imaginary axis around which the truth of life was ordered, measured, mapped, and controlled.[34] That is, the concept of "life itself" operates as a new term of biopolitical investment. It becomes the truth of our lives now, a new incitement to discourse, without an attendant analysis of the political emergence and political uses of the term. Bonnie Honig and Miriam Leonard make a similar critique of Butler's recent work, but from a slightly different direction; rather than an appeal to "life itself," they see in *Frames of War* and other works an appeal to a new kind of humanism—an appeal to the universality of human mourning and grievability.[35]

While these critiques are (as I argue elsewhere) somewhat overstated, there does seem to be a problem here.[36] Whether an appeal to life itself or to a universal grievability, Butler seems to institute an a-, extra-, or pre-political ground for politics—an ethical or an ontological foundation to which politics should be oriented in response. In earlier works such as "Contingent Foundations," Butler argues that the recourse to a foundation—something that stands outside politics that can act as a ground for politics—is one of the "most insidious ruses of politics."[37] This is because the foundation—the concept of nature, the concept of the human, or the purported universality of the concept of woman—is effectively shielded from political critique, contestation, and transformation. Of course, this is hardly news to Butler; the whole of *Gender Trouble* is devoted to the project of denaturalizing the concept of "woman" as the supposed foundation of feminist politics. Nevertheless, this reference to the precariousness and the vulnerability of life itself sounds like an appeal to a pre-political ground—whether ethical or ontological—for politics.

The problem is not exclusively the relationship between ethics or ontology and politics per se. The problem is whether feminist theory or critical theory can entirely do without an appeal to foundations. Butler herself gives the beginnings of an answer in "Contingent Foundations": "the point is not to do away with foundations, or even to champion a position that goes under the name antifoundationalism. . . . Rather, the task is to interrogate what the theoretical move that establishes foundations *authorizes*, and what precisely it excludes or forecloses."[38] But the question remains: Can one entirely avoid making such a theoretical move oneself? Can one avoid setting up such a foundation, even with the knowledge that in doing so, one may be producing unforeseen exclusions and foreclosing possibilities? If such an appeal to foundations is unavoidable, then how can these foundations be made more emphatically contingent?

The appeal to foundations renders some difference an a-, extra-, or pre-political ground for politics, shielding that difference from political critique. In constitutive exclusion, this has taken the form of rendering some contingent difference necessary, by means of that exclusion, to establish the coherence of the borders of politics and the intelligibility of political agency on the "inside." It is taken as the fundamental difference, either the root of the others, or at least the essential rather than the accidental difference. In other words, this difference is essentialized. In order to forestall these risks of essentialism, these foundations will have to be more emphatically marked as contingent. In other words, if recourse is made to an outside of politics—either in the form of ethics or in the form of ontology—then this ethics or this ontology would have to be understood as provisional. However, Butler has never been very clear about the method proper to this provisional ontology or to the contingency of foundations. A better account of the relation between the concrete and the abstract—that is, a better articulation of *method*—would be necessary to forestall the dangers of appealing to foundations, even contingent ones.

A more self-consciously dialectical method, one that preserves the tension between the concrete and the abstract, between the immanent and the transcendent, or between politics and its conditions, would help us to better understand the problem of the relation between politics and ethics or ontology. Rather than reifying the distinction or opposition between politics and the extra-political space of either ethics or ontology, a more dialectical approach that would emphasize the relation between a delimited field of politics and its conditions allows for thinking the irruption of the transcendent within the immanent sphere of politics. It also requires us to interrogate the specific relation between politics and its conditions at each step; in other words, it requires us to specify the terms of contingency for each establishment of a contingent foundation. Such a method is negative, dialectical, and ultimately genealogical, as it requires a more specific account of the conditions of this provisional ontology in each instance.

Second, this provisionality of ontology or the contingency of foundations turns our attention toward the past, or toward history. This is due to the peculiar temporality of constitutive exclusion. As we have read, Butler argues that the iterability of the frame is how the frame operates, and that breaking the frame of drawing attention to the work of framing is possible because iterability takes *time*. But how does time operate through the constitutive outside? Rather than the tragic repetition of the exclusionary function of the frame, Butler argues that we should understand the temporality of iterability as a limit to the power of discourse, ideology, or hegemony, and that we should instead approach the constitutive outside as a critical resource. In *Bodies that Matter*, she puts it this way:

> The task is to refigure this necessary "outside" as a future horizon, one in which the violence of the exclusion is perpetually in the process of being overcome. But of equal importance is the preservation of the outside, the site where discourse reaches its limits, where the opacity of what is not included in a given regime of truth acts as a disruptive site of linguistic impropriety and *unrepresentability*, illuminating the violent and contingent boundaries of that normative regime precisely through the inability of that regime to represent that which might pose a fundamental threat to its continuity. In this sense, radical and inclusive representability is not precisely the goal.[39]

While I take seriously the caveat that "radical and inclusive representability" cannot be the goal, predicated as it is upon a colonialist dynamic between a dominating will to knowledge and a demand for assimilation to the already existing terms of representation, I am unsure that an orientation toward a future horizon is sufficient as we make our way through the critique of exclusions. Without an account of the temporality peculiar to constitutive exclusion, an orientation toward the future will only be an extrapolation of current conditions and will reinscribe the disavowal of the radical potential buried in those shards of exclusion within. Instead, a richer account of temporality—one that will orient us to the past rather than the future and will open up the radical reconstitution that the critique of constitutive exclusion is meant to effect—will be necessary.

As I will show in later chapters, constitutive exclusion is both *multiple* and operates through a *retroactive temporality.* Constitutive exclusion determines the difference that makes a difference: exclusion from politics and the terms of political agency is predicated on turning a contingent difference into a necessary one. But this distinction between a contingent and a necessary difference is achieved retroactively. This retroactive temporality erases its own trail, so to speak, and we act *as if* time works in the normal linear way that assures the straightforward operation of causality. Similarly, attention to the retroactive temporality of constitutive exclusion reveals the multiplicity of exclusions buried beneath what seemed a singular foundation. Because of this retroactive temporality, and because of the multiplicity of exclusions, our political present is sedimented with constitutive exclusions. Our political present is the sedimentation of past exclusions working on us now, shaping who we are—both our political bodies and our selves as political agents—by means of these exclusions. This requires a materialist historical method for the critique of constitutive exclusion. This method shows us that rather than an inclusion achieved on the basis of assimilation to already existing terms, responding justly to the contestation of constitutive exclusion requires a *reconstitution* of our political body and the terms of political agency on which it operates.

Spelling out the details of a method for critique, and orienting our attention toward history—as a radical history of the present, or, as genealogy—returns us to the scenes with which I opened the chapter. The retroactive temporality of constitutive exclusion helps us to understand how the contingent difference of gender was rendered a necessary difference for the exclusion of Antigone from the terms of political agency, despite the work she does for the political body. Antigone thus occupies a "quasi-transcendental" position, acting as the condition of possibility, as well as the condition of impossibility, for the polity of ancient Thebes. Her constitutive exclusion renders her contestation of that exclusion unintelligible as a political critique. However, the radical potential of her refusal of that exclusion, her insurrection from within, lies in the history of reinterpretations of the play.

The focus on method and materialist history helps us to see the multiplicity of constitutive exclusion at work in the model of Rosa Parks and Claudette Colvin. Here we see the operation of multiple exclusions and the strategy and effects of playing one mode of exclusion off the others. This has rendered Colvin almost entirely unintelligible as a political agent, burying the subversive potential of her fierceness. It has limited the intelligibility of Parks's contestation as well, in that the national hagiography of Parks remembers her not as a savvy political organizer and Black nationalist freedom fighter, but instead as the Madonna of Montgomery. The complex knot of forces surrounding the choice of Parks over Colvin—class, gender, sexuality, respectability—has rendered both Parks and Colvin politically unintelligible, though in different ways.

In the case of the 1992 Los Angeles Riots/Rebellion, the contestation takes place at the level of intelligibility itself. In this case, several factors—multiplicity, retroactive temporality, materialist history, and the negative dialectic between the delimited field of politics and its internally excluded conditions—are in play. The analysis of constitutive exclusions in the 1992 Los Angeles Riots/Rebellion accounts for the refusal of intelligibility that met the riots and requires us to think how that refusal has constituted us. Who are we now because of what we could not see, hear, or understand then? How does the political unintelligibility of the Los Angeles Riots/Rebellion figure whose lives—white lives, Latinx lives, Korean lives, poor people's lives, women's lives, young people's lives, Black lives—matter[40]?

PLAN OF THE BOOK

Excluded Within moves through three different moments, treating three different levels of analysis: ontology, epistemology, and politics, though as we will see, the distinctions between these will be called into question by the analysis itself. Part One diagnoses the structure and operation of constitutive exclusion in drawing the distinction between ontology and epistemology. Part Two treats the work of critique and shifts to a more political epistemological register, and Part Three returns us to concrete models of political contestation. While this structure appears to bring the abstract concept of constitutive exclusion down to concrete events, the method of critique of constitutive exclusion operates as the point of contact between the two registers, bringing the concrete political insights of Part Three backward as well as the philosophical insights of Part One forward. This is in keeping with the fundamental ambivalence of constitutive exclusion, requiring a both/and method of critique, and a way of reading for what lies in the margin, outside the frame, whether in the text or in the world.

Part One of the book is a diagnosis of the structure and operation of constitutive exclusion in philosophical systems. I take up the apotheosis of systems thinking in Chapter 2, in the work of G. W. F. Hegel, and in particular his *Science of Logic*. I argue that the operation of the dialectic in the *Logic*, and by extension the rest of the Hegelian system, is predicated on the constitutive exclusion of multiple negativity, a subtextual negativity that is necessary to but excluded from the supertextual negativity of the dialectic: determinate negation. While Hegel means for being and knowing to be coextensive in the *Science of Logic*, and thus reserves ignorance of nonknowledge for the level of the empirical or mere understanding, I argue that the constitutive exclusion of multiple negativity indicates an epistemological blind spot at the heart of Hegel's speculative system. The very distinction between the register of the speculative and the register of the empirical is thus subtended by this more radical negativity. Chapter 3 investigates the character of constitutive exclusion as quasi-transcendental. Drawing on an analysis of the quasi-transcendental in Derrida's *Glas* and in his 1971–1972 lecture course, "*La famille de Hegel*," I argue that the constitutively excluded figure occupies a quasi-transcendental position, the simultaneous condition of possibility and impossibility of the delimited field whose boundary it draws. This quasi-transcendental character gives us insight into the economy of difference and the retroactive temporality according to which constitutive exclusion operates.

Part Two marks the hinge of *Excluded Within*, bringing the levels of ontology and epistemology more fully into contact with politics. It makes the case for a critical theoretical method proper to constitutive exclusion, by taking up its *quasi-transcendent* character, or the emergence of a transcendent element from within an immanent political field. Drawing on an analysis of Adorno's "nonidentity," Chapter 4 shows how the method of the critique of constitutive exclusion must be both dialectical and negative. Chapter 5 turns us more fully toward the political by arguing that our method of critique must be materialist and historical. Relying here on the work of Adorno and Benjamin, I argue that since our political present is sedimented with constitutive exclusions, our critique must seek to unearth them for the sake of a reconstitution of politics and the terms of political agency that would no longer operate by means of it.

Part Three turns explicitly to the contestation of exclusions, returning us to the models of Antigone, Parks and Colvin, and the 1992 Los Angeles Riots/Rebellion. Chapter 6 treats the singular figure of Antigone, articulating the risks of contesting her exclusion in a language of sovereignty that is predicated upon it. It then turns to the twin figures Claudette Colvin and Rosa Parks to understand the dynamic of political unintelligibility—in this case, the occlusion of Colvin and the reification of Parks. Relying on Holloway Sparks's analysis of strategic straightness in the Montgomery bus boycott, I argue that this model shows us that constitutive exclusion functions multiply, allowing figures to play one form of exclusion (such as gender or class or sexuality) off of another (such as race) in their contestation. This strategy has the effect, however, of reinscribing other exclusions, making contestation along those lines more difficult for those relegated to them. Chapter 7 treats a more complex figure, the fractured collectivity of the 1992 Los Angeles Riots/Rebellion. This chapter parses the complex operations of race, gender, sexuality, and geography at play in the riot and argues that the refusal of intelligibility of this contestation of constitutive exclusion has lasting effects on our political present.

Finally, the Postscript returns us to the interlacing of ontology, epistemology, and politics with which the book begins. Drawing on women of color feminist thought and the Black Lives Matter movement, I sketch out a pluralist political ontology as a response to the critique of constitutive exclusion and as a way of doing justice to our multiple exclusions by means of illuminating our multiple constitutions.

PART ONE

Diagnosis

2

Multiple Negativity: Negativity and Difference in Hegel's *Science of Logic*

Hegel's philosophy is the highest modern expression of the tension that characterizes constitutive exclusion: the tension between a radical, open-ended, heterogeneous movement in which nothing is finally settled or certain and in which no moment is ultimately pure, and a closed system in which that movement comes to rest in an absolute, totalized whole. These two Hegels—the totalizing, absolutist Hegel, and the Hegel of radical difference and openness—occupy the same oeuvre, and yet they do not seem to be able to see, to hear, or to recognize each other. It may seem strange to begin an analysis of constitutive exclusion with the work of Hegel, especially given the claim that I want to develop the concept as a tool that is responsive to and useful for political, feminist, antiracist, queer, and critical theories. But this contradiction—the co-existence of these two opposed Hegels, occupying the same text simultaneously—is a symptom of constitutive exclusion. Tracking the emergence of this symptom here, in the heart of philosophical modernism, serves to sharpen the concept as a tool.

The undecidability between the metaphysical, totalizing Hegel and the non- or anti-metaphysical Hegel of difference and change is a marker of the specific negativity at work in constitutive exclusion, a negativity exhibited in Hegel's philosophical system for the first time. Moreover, that specific negativity at work behind the back of the concept—a rhythmic, multiple negativity, in tension with the determinate negation that secures the operation of sublation, or *Aufhebung*, the dialectical negativity by which the concept operates—will help us to better understand constitutive exclusion as the relation between the delimited field of politics and its repressed, yet internalized, conditions. Even as constitutive exclusion helps to secure the fantasy of a closed political field or a closed philosophical system, it gives us the resources to trouble that field or system, to alter or abolish it, from within itself.

Hegel's philosophy is also useful in understanding the structure and operation of constitutive exclusion because Hegel thinks ontology, epistemology, and politics together, often at the same time. By locating a single symptom of constitutive exclusion in Hegel, then, we can trace its operation across these different registers (a task that extends into Chapter 3, via Derrida's treatment of the brother/sister dialectic in the *Phenomenology*). This is ultimately what makes Hegel's thought such a rich resource for diagnosing the structure and operation of constitutive exclusion (and why his thought is at the root of so much of critical theory). Moreover, given its privileged position in Hegel's system, the *Science of Logic* is the best place to locate this symptom, and trace it across these different registers.

Kimberly Hutchings and Tuija Pulkkinen argue that there are three modes of reading Hegel in the contemporary scholarship: the closed readings (which emphasize Hegel's systematicity), the open readings (which emphasize Hegel's plurivocity), and the deconstructive readings (which emphasize those levers in the system which work against the system).[1] While my interpretation tends toward the third, deconstructivist, mode of reading Hegel, I extend this claim: the constitutive exclusion of multiple negativity underpins the distinction between the open and closed readings of Hegel. That is, Hegel's system is *both* open and closed, a contradiction posed and managed by the constitutive exclusion of multiple negativity in his work and never entirely resolved, putting both Hegels into play simultaneously, in the same system and often in the same text.[2]

This tension between these two modes of reading Hegel—Hegel open, Hegel closed—is as old as the *streit* between the left Hegelians and the right Hegelians, older, even, as this tension already exists in Hegel's work itself. Both are correct: Hegel is both a thinker of totality, and a thinker of the radical negativity that dissolves every totality—even his own. The contradiction between these Hegels is never resolved but only held in tension, subtended by the operation of constitutive exclusion in his texts.

The tension in interpreting Hegel maps onto the tension between two methods of critical theory. On the one hand, there are those methods that take seriously hegemony's tendency toward totality, and so seek resources within the force of hegemony to overthrow it in its entirety. On the other hand, there are those methods that put the lie to hegemony by showing its cracks and failures, showing us multiplicity where hegemony claims unity. Both strategies have their benefits: the latter shows us that hegemony never actually succeeds at what it claims, while the former tries to ensure that we are not unconsciously miming hegemony in our critiques or just opening up new markets for the totality machine. Both have their roots in Hegel's thought: historically, in that the Marxian adaptations of Hegel are at the root of tradition of critical theory, and theoretically, in that both the diagnosis of the totalizing tendency in capitalism and other ideological forms as well as the methods of immanent critique that seek to undermine or overturn totality from within have their theoretical roots in this tension in interpretations of Hegel.

In Part Two of the book, I make a case for both of these strategies as a method for critiquing constitutive exclusion. In order to get to the one, however, I must go through the other. While the peculiar negativity of constitutive exclusion uncovered in this chapter allows for both Hegels, or allows for a both/and interpretation of Hegel's texts, the closed reading makes up the supertext of negativity, and the open reading the subtext.

While the constitutive exclusion of multiple negativity makes both the dialectic and the totality of Hegel's system possible, it cannot be recognized by that same system. Put another way, multiple negativity is both the condition of possibility of the Hegelian dialectic as well as its condition of impossibility. The constitutive exclusion of multiple negativity is thus the quasi-transcendental of the Hegelian system (as I will argue in Chapter 3). My reading of Hegel is thus a deconstructive one, but I argue that this deconstructive reading subtends both the open and closed readings of Hegel, making both readings possible and impossible. It thus requires a particular way of reading. Part One of *Excluded Within* seeks to develop this way of reading by diagnosing the structure and operation of constitutive exclusion in philosophical systems, taking the Hegelian system as its apotheosis.

In this chapter, my focus is on the diagnosis of the structure and operation of constitutive exclusion in the ontological and epistemological registers. In further chapters, I will explore more explicitly the political epistemology of constitutive exclusion. This chapter examines how the constitutive exclusion of multiple negativity subtends the distinction between ontology (the register of being) and epistemology (the register of knowing) in Hegel's thought. It aims to show that the level of ontology cannot be so easily shielded from the epistemological, and that the constitutive exclusion of difference subtends the distinction between the two. This is important for understanding the consolidation of multiple contingent differences into a single necessary difference, as in the case of Antigone: how do the contingent differences of sex, gender, sexuality, and class, get translated into a necessary difference, one that marks the borders of political authority and intelligible political agency in the dramatic scene of ancient Thebes? And it is important for understanding how this operation of translating empirical differences into ontological difference—into the difference that makes a difference—gets covered over, disavowed, and erased.

In part one of this chapter, I describe the epistemological "blind spot" at the heart of Hegel's *Logic* and argue that the constitutive exclusion of multiple negativity subtends the distinction between being and knowing that structures Hegel's system. In part two, I treat the negativity side of multiple negativity. There I look at three different moments, or three different rhythms, of negativity. I argue that none of them are reducible to any other and that they cannot ultimately be reduced to determinate negation, the form of negativity that is the "motor" of the dialectic in the *Science of Logic*. In part three, I treat the multiplicity side of multiple negativity. As negativity cannot be reduced to determinate negation, so too difference as multiplicity in the *Science of Logic* cannot be reduced to contradiction, which is the central form of difference operative in the *Science of Logic*. Difference as opposition and contradiction are intimately involved with determinate negation, so I take up difference explicitly in part three. There I analyze Hegel's treatment of the term *Verschiedenheit*, which marks diversity, plurality, or multiplicity. I argue that though Hegel wishes to control the multiple meanings of the term *Verschiedenheit* according to the distinction between speculative and empirical thought, he fails because the constitutive exclusion of *Verschiedenheit* both founds and troubles this distinction in the first place. Finally, in part four, I articulate what is at stake in the diagnosis of multiple negativity for understanding the structure and operation of constitutive exclusion.

BEING AND KNOWING IN THE *SCIENCE OF LOGIC*

In the Hegelian system, ontology (the register of being) is identical to epistemology (the register of knowing). Hegel's speculative idealism claims to resolve the gulf between the two registers that Kant had left behind in his systematic thought. For Hegel, reality is characterized by reason, or by the movement in the concept of the world, whether in the natural world or in the human worlds of politics, history, art, or religion. Each of these spheres is a movement in the self-development of the concept, a progression that has its end in absolute knowing. Our ability to know this reality is dependent on the historical development of the concept, as we can achieve "absolute knowing" only when reason has reached its historical apex. Absolute knowing as self-knowledge is possible only in principle, however: it does not ensure that any individual human knower has achieved absolute knowledge, though it is the condition of that possibility. It only ensures that the gulf between being and knowing has been in principle resolved, opening up the possibility of the retrospective knowledge of the whole (the whole being for Hegel the true) through philosophy.

Because Hegel's ontology is rational (that is, since what *is* is essentially reason), what *is* will have been determined by structures of thought. Or in other words, ontology will have been logic. Hegel argues that all previous forms of logic fail to describe the ontology that he is in a historical position to articulate: rather than the seemingly unjustified Kantian categories, or the dead static logic of Aristotle, Hegel developed a logic that moves—a dialectical logic. The *Science of Logic* thus describes Hegel's onto-logic.

Insofar as being and knowing are identical for Hegel, and insofar as we have achieved the historical possibility of absolute knowing, then it would seem that there is no place for non-knowing in Hegel's thought. While this is true in one sense, it is not the case that all humans are all-knowing creatures, free of error and ignorance. So where does Hegel make room for non-knowledge, or ignorance, in his system? In his influential commentary, *Logic and Existence*, Jean Hyppolite argues that non-knowledge or ignorance in Hegel's thought is merely relative, the particular failures of any single human consciousness, or the perspective of the understanding (as opposed to the concept), which grasps things as essentially positive.[3] The level of reason, of the concept, and of philosophy, however, grasps the "identity of being and knowledge," and the negation that is essential to this identity.[4] At this level, Hyppolite writes, "absolute knowledge means the in principle elimination of this non-knowledge, that is, the elimination of a transcendence essentially irreducible to our knowledge."[5] Hyppolite associates absolute knowledge with the *Science of Logic* and what he terms "speculative thought," and non-knowledge with the ordinary, everyday consciousness of the *Phenomenology* with what he terms "empirical thought."

While Hegel's thought unites being and knowing in the unity of the system, he reserves a place for relative non-knowledge at the level of the understanding or with "empirical thought." The level of speculative thought, the level of the science of absolute knowing, has no place for non-knowledge. However, non-knowledge or ignorance *does* occur at the level of speculative thought. This is because an epistemological blind spot exists in the *Science of Logic*, where being and knowledge are united, and where non-knowledge ought to have no place. In other words, the *Science of Logic* is structured by an epistemology of ignorance, symptomatic of the structure and operation of constitutive exclusion.[6]

The distinction between the empirical and the speculative so important for the operation of Hegel's logic is subtended by a multiple negativity that both troubles and manages that distinction. Multiple negativity is constitutively excluded in the Hegelian system. It is thus both necessary for and impossible within the operation of the Hegelian dialectic. Multiple negativity is necessary in that multiple rhythms of negativity are in fact operative in the text and are not accidental to its operation: rather, they tie these different moments of the dialectic together. Multiple negativity is however impossible to the dialectic in that the recognition of the work that it does would fundamentally alter the way that the Hegelian dialectic operates. This more diffuse, more responsive, more radical negativity—tied to a multiple, material difference—operates behind the back of the concept. It operates in and through an epistemological blind spot, or an epistemology of ignorance: its disavowal, repression, or abjection is central to its operation.

Ignorance of multiple negativity is thus necessary to the Hegelian system, and in particular to the hegemonic form of negativity—determinate negation—that structures the operation of the dialectic. To explicitly include multiple negativity would necessitate a redefinition of the Hegelian system by new terms: it would mean an end to the Hegelian dialectic as we know it, but not, perhaps, an end to Hegel, or an end to dialectics as such.[7] The inclusion of what is constitutively excluded, if it is to be true inclusion and not merely assimilation, would be a reconstitution. While this reconstitution may take place by means of another exclusion along a different axis, the radical hope that motivates this analysis is a future in which no constitution would necessitate an exclusion, or that such exclusions, whether in thought or practice, be approached democratically rather than by means of disavowal. The conditions of this impossible possibility I therefore take to be a political problem as much as an epistemological one, as will become clear in what follows.

NEGATION AND NEGATIVITY: THREE MOMENTS

Negativity is central to Hegelian thought; it is its very *via negativa*, the "self-moving soul, the principle of all spiritual life."[8] Despite or perhaps because of its centrality, it never really receives its own treatment in Hegel's work. The supertext of negativity in Hegel's work operates as determinate negation [*bestimmte Negation*], the negation of the particular content of a moment. Through the activity described in the verb *aufheben* (translated most usually as "to sublate"), this negated content becomes the positive content of the next moment. Hegel describes determinate negation in a few key places in his work, such as the introduction to the *Science of Logic* and in the preface to the *Phenomenology* (which Hegel was editing at around the same time that the *Logic* was written).[9]

Determinate negation therefore describes the operation of the motor of the dialectic through *Aufhebung* or sublation. Here I follow Hyppolite, who writes in *Genesis and Structure of Hegel's* Phenomenology of Spirit that "the result of an experience of consciousness is absolutely negative for that consciousness; in point of fact, however, negation is always determinate negation."[10] This is a productive logical negation, or a generative movement of relationality. In this movement, one moment truly becomes itself by means of its self-othering or self-diremption, by reaching beyond itself and returning to itself. One moment is negated by another moment, but it comes to truly be itself, or rather only finds that it truly *is* itself, by means of this negation. The movement of the dialectic thus guarantees a return from this self-alienation, but this does not make the process any less difficult or deadly. The moment with which the movement begins dies during the dialectical process: it dies as what it was, but it becomes something new. This is the movement of determinate negation that makes up the supertextual form of negation within the Hegelian dialectic.

While the work of negativity is everywhere in the *Science of Logic*, Hegel has very little to say about the concept or the operation of negativity itself. Given the vital role it plays, not just in the *Logic* but in the whole system, it merits close consideration. This task is not without risk: trying to adequately describe the dialectic is a tricky business. As a philosophy of movement, a philosophy that moves, to capture it or to pin it down is necessarily to do it a kind of injustice. It is to trade a picture for a process. I offer here three stills or three gestures, as it were, to discern the differences between each one that allows or enables the movement between them. These three gestures, taken together, are meant to negatively demonstrate the multiplicity of negativity at the heart of the dialectic.

Negativity in Being: Negativity as Nothing

The first moment in this multiple rhythm is the first mode of negativity we encounter in the *Logic* in its opening scene, on being. Here we encounter the movement of being and nothing into becoming. Hegel begins with being and nothing, not because they are the origin or the foundation of his system; on the contrary, Hegel's system is foundationless, or as Stephen Houlgate describes it, it is a wholly free, self-determining system of thinking without presuppositions.[11] Rather, Hegel begins from being and nothing because they are most abstract, immediate, and indeterminate.

The form of negativity at work in this moment is thus the abstract negativity of nothing [*Nichts*], the absolutely empty thought or intuition of nothing as such. Empty of all determinations, nothing is found to be essentially the same as being [*Sein*], which is equally abstract and empty of all determinations. Yet the two moments are not identical and do not collapse into each other; there is instead a kind of oscillation between them, a movement of sameness and distinctness that Hegel calls a vanishing or a passing-over-into. This establishes the movement of coming-to-be and passing-away, the two sides of which constitute becoming.

Being and nothing—the two moments (or perhaps a moment split in two, a doubled moment) that begin the *Logic*—lack the kind of progressive movement into the ground that is typical of the dialectic. The movement between these two moments instead seems to be a kind of peaceful oscillation back and forth between the two of them. While being and nothing are meant to be equally both the same *and* distinct from one another, Hegel emphasizes their unity: they are the same insofar as they are both equally indeterminate. This unity is the first picture of the absolute, although completely lacking in the concreteness or determination with which the progression of the *Logic* will fill it. Hegel thus writes in the introduction to the *Science of Logic* (in a passage famous for confounding its readers) that "the analysis of the beginning would thus yield the notion of the unity of being and nothing—or, in a more reflected form, the unity of differentiatedness and nondifferentiatedness, or the identity of identity and nonidentity. This concept could be regarded as the first, purest, that is, most abstract definition of the absolute."[12]

Hegel writes that the movement between being and nothing is characterized by a passing-over-into or a vanishing-into each other. Being not only passes over into nothing, but has already done so. On what basis does such a movement within a unity take place? What makes it possible? It does not seem to be possible on the basis of mere nothing [*Nichts*] itself, for this makes up only one side of the movement of passing-over-into. Nothingness [*Nichts*] is not of being, yet it is also the same as being; they are the same, yet they remain distinct. This paradox makes it easier to understand what Hegel means when he writes in the essay at the opening of the Doctrine of Being, "With What Must the Science Begin," that we take up the beginning, these two moments of being and nothing, "as something unanalysable, taken in its simple, unfilled immediacy."[13]

Because the supertextual negativity, determinate negation, is most usually associated with mediation, differentiation, and relation, what is most interesting in this moment is the movement between being and nothing. As we shall see, this movement is unlike most others in the *Logic*, which already makes it worthy of attention: if the movement of negativity changes from place to place in the *Logic* without Hegel making this explicit, then this already points to the kind of subterranean work that the subtextual, multiple negativity performs within the dialectic. My point here is simply that the negativity of abstract nothing [*Nichts*] does not on its own seem to be enough to establish this strange relationship between being and nothing, nor is there anything to account for the movement of oscillation. Instead, some other kind of negativity seems to be at work in this moment.

There seem to be two possible ways to think of the movement between being and nothing. The first possibility would be that becoming is already implicit within being and nothing, and that being and nothing are essentially already the movement of becoming. This would be to affirm the supertextual form of Hegelian negativity, that of determinate negation, as already existing within the opening moments of being and nothing. However, this would also be to impart a *telos* to the opening moments of the *Logic*, despite Hegel's insistence that no such teleology is at work in the progressive self-determination of thought that takes place there. This interpretation seems to me to be unjustified, if we want to take seriously Hegel's own claims about the immanent unfolding of his system.

The second option is a movement of some kind between being and nothing, which puts them in relation or allows them to touch, so to speak, and would shepherd them into the movement of becoming. This negativity would allow being and nothing to be the same and yet distinct, and would impart a kind of movement—a distanced nearness—between them. Without this distanced nearness, what would keep them from collapsing into each other and into a stable, stale, ossified, and ultimately dead unity?[14] That the oscillation between being and nothing moves beyond oscillation and beyond being and nothing itself indicates a different kind of mediation or negativity at work already within or between being and nothing, as their unity possesses already what Hegel calls an "inward unrest," one of the names that mark negativity in Hegel's texts. Hegel denies any relation between being and nothing, as relation rests upon determination, and being and nothing are entirely empty. However, in order for oscillation to be something more than back and forth, in order for a path to open beyond being and nothing, there must be something a little more at work. Perhaps "inward unrest" acts as a kind of double marking: if this phrase marks the supertextual form of negativity in Hegel's work—determinate negation—it seems also to point to a negativity not yet accounted for in Hegel's system.

Negativity in Actuality: Absolute Negativity

The second gesture of negativity comes in Book Two of the *Logic*, the Doctrine of Essence. The section on actuality leads us to the closing moment of the Objective Logic; it is here, in the chapter on actuality, that the rupture between being and essence begins to heal, the result of which will be the concept [*Begriff*]. In this moment, Hegel accounts for possibility and contingency within the necessity of the system and its dialectical movement. It is a difficult argument, but my focus will be exclusively on the *kind* of negativity at work here. Though this form of negativity seems to be the most destructive and abyssal, what Hegel calls "absolute negation" is in fact nothing more than the supertextual negativity of the Hegelian system, determinate negation. Rather than the root of all negativity in the *Logic*, however, I see it as a negativity distinct from, if not all the forms which precede and follow it, at least from the negativity at work in the movement between being and nothing, and that at work in the totality of the concept (which I will treat next). As absolute negativity, determinate negation is in one sense the only negativity at work in the *Logic*, and in another sense, a negativity among others.

In the chapter on actuality in Hegel's *Science of Logic*, absolute negativity is described in terms of death and destruction, making it seem absolutely destructive and even dangerously abyssal. Yet if negativity is the way that the dialectic mediates between two opposed or seemingly contradictory terms, the way that one thing relates to its other and relates to itself through that other, then absolute negativity is the beginning of a kind of self-realization or a self-recognition of these powers of mediation and relation. Hence, Hegel also refers to it as "self-mediation," "determinateness . . . in truth," and "negative self-relation."[15]

Hegel calls absolute negativity "a blind destruction in otherness."[16] As the truth of becoming, it is the necessity of passing-away, the necessity of every being to pass into nothing and every actual thing to become merely possible. The language of destruction makes this form of negativity sound particularly dangerous, as that destruction would seem a threat to the careful logic of any system, and perhaps any discourse. This negativity of breaking-apart is, however, at the same time a "union-with-self" [*Zusammengegehen*], or a coming-together with itself. It sounds like determinate negation, in which identity is achieved through a movement of self-othering. The "blind destruction" of this negativity would seem to be balanced, then, by an equally blind "creation," or a coming-to-be to match that passing-away.

The movement of negativity in actuality, though it seems to introduce the danger of disruption in its "blind destruction in otherness," is also a negativity that assures the mediation or the transition of one thing into another. Thus, it is a prime example of the logic of determinate negation. Absolute negativity is not the merely empty abstract negativity of nothingness; nor is it an ultimately destructive force. It is the cold necessity of death, but it is just as much the cold necessity of life. Everything that comes to life, which manifests itself, necessarily must also die. This reciprocal movement, absolute negativity as absolute identity, as absolute self-relation, will develop into the concept [*Begriff*], which Hegel will say is characterized by that "absolute mediation which is, precisely, the negation of the negation or absolute negativity."[17] This phrase, the negation of the negation, is the very definition of determinate negation. Here we see the language of *determinate* negation at work to recapture the deployment of a potentially disruptive and destructive negativity and bring it into relation with its opposite, both of which are sides of absolute negativity.

Though this picture of negativity seems extreme in its presentation, it is in fact the same movement of determinate negation that ensures for Hegel the speculative closure of the whole. In what follows, I will examine one further still picture of the movement of negativity, and argue that it is fundamentally different from and not reducible to this operation of determinate negation, even in its most extreme appearance.

Negativity in the Concept: Negativity as Boundless Blessedness

Our final single gesture of negativity is found in the first chapter of the subjective logic, the concept. The focus here becomes the movement of the dialectic itself; the development of the concept is particularly important here, because it is in the concept that the process of self-othering is finally taken as given in a self-mediating totality. The concept is thus defined as essentially self-othering, and yet it retains its self-identity. This should sound familiar by now: this is of course the language used to describe absolute negativity, and Hegel's early chapter on the concept is punctuated with references to absolute negativity. The negativity at work in this moment, however, seems distinct from the absolute negativity that we just examined, and constitutes a third kind of negativity at work in our overall rhythm of multiple negativities.

The ground on which the concept operates here (at least initially) is the relationship between universality, particularity, and individuality. The negativity at work in this final scene rests in the relationship between universality and particularity in the concept [*Begriff*]. The conception of universality that Hegel develops here should be contrasted with the Kantian conception of universality as a relation of subsumption, or a category under which certain particulars are subsumed. That relation is not immanent to those particular things themselves and so does a kind of violence to them. Hegel claims instead that his universal concept does not relate to particular things by subsuming them under itself, but rather by "embracing" those particular things. He characterizes this form of universality as an "absolute power," but one that is without any violence, as the universal relates to itself in and through the particulars. This unique relation between the universal and the particular things it "embraces" makes up the totality of the concept.

The universal has this strange ability to remain what it is through its interaction with particular things; Hegel writes that the universal "is not dragged into the process of becoming, but *continues* itself through that process undisturbed and possesses the power of unalterable, undying self-preservation."[18] This is because the universal concept is initially characterized by absolute negativity, or is an absolute self-relation; it is "the absolute self-identity that is such only as the negation of negation, or as the infinite unity of the negativity with itself."[19] The universal concept is not, however, empty; it "possesses *within itself* the *richest content*" of difference or determinateness.[20]

The negativity at work in this moment is thus also different from every other moment of negativity in the *Science of Logic*. The familiar story of negativity as determinate negation was one of the emergence of identity through a movement of self-othering or self-alienation, in which a thing moves out from itself, goes beyond itself, and through this process comes to be what it truly is. This involves struggle and loss, the death of each moment in the birth of the next. But this movement of negativity in the universal concept is instead characterized by what Hegel calls a "peaceful communion," a "free love and boundless blessedness."[21]

Here the universal returns to itself from its relation with its other, or particularity, but it does not suffer any loss in doing so. Negativity here bears the character of abundance; the model here is one of agapic love. It does not suffer the violence of destruction or the suffering of becoming. While it retains its work as relation and mediation, negativity achieves this "peaceful communion" through the movement of embracing the other and coming to rest in itself through the other, but without having done any violence to the other, or suffering any violence itself in the process.

How is this possible? Insofar as the universal concept already contains all determinateness within itself, the particulars to which it relates are merely externalizations of the content of the universal itself. Particular things are therefore not foreign to the universal, but belong to the universal itself: the universal is the truth of the particular things that it externalizes. The particulars are externalized in such a way that they are not a limitation upon the universal but rather a manifestation of the identity of the universal; as such, the universal concept, "as absolute negativity . . . is the shaper and creator."[22] It is a power without force, a creation without destruction.

Negativity in the universal concept then must pick out particular determinations from the universal concept, but in doing so it does not limit the concept. Instead it "*continues* itself through that process undisturbed."[23] The universal concept seems to remain placidly identical throughout its particularization. Hegel writes that, "in particularity, therefore, the universal is not in the presence of an other, but simply of itself."[24] In this sense, there is little if any mediation or relation for negativity to do, as it would be relating the universal concept to something already essentially itself. It is difficult to understand what drives the absolute negativity in the universal concept to be the "shaper and creator," when it is defined by absolute self-identity, not as immediate, but as wholly determined and self-related. This explains why negativity here is related to agapic love: negativity as relation, as mediation, and moreover here as *creation* takes on the form of a divine gift. This moment calls to mind the closing leap of the *Logic*, the moment in which the idea "*freely releases* itself" from the shadow-world of the *Logic* into the existent world of nature, a material world which has already been prepared by spirit, so that it encounters nothing alien to itself.[25]

This gesture of negativity does not take the form of a peaceful oscillation back and forth, a distanced nearness that allows for the play of sameness and distinctness. Nor does it take the form of the seemingly destructive force of absolute negativity, in which the painful alienation of passing-away is balanced by the certainty of coming-to-be in the process of determinate negation. Here negativity is characterized as an overflowing, divine gift, which comes from the universal to the particular things it peacefully embraces, but to particular things that are not essentially any different from the universal.

Each of these three moments of negativity is distinct from the other. None seems to resolve into the other, and they do not seem to resolve into the second form, absolute negativity—that form of negativity that defines the movement of determinate negation, the form that makes up the supertext of the dialectic. Taken together, these three modes of negativity point to a different rhythm, a multiple rhythm or a rhythm of multiplicity, which runs through the center of the contentious discussion in Hegelian philosophy between dialectic and system, between negativity and totality. If determinate negation makes up the supertext of the Hegelian system, this multiple negativity is its subtext—operating behind the back of the concept, an epistemological blind spot at the heart of Hegelian ontology.

Given this, I now turn to an analysis of multiplicity in the *Science of Logic*, in order to argue that the multiplicity of multiple negativity cannot be so easily relegated to the register of the empirical but is in fact also operative on the register of the speculative. In other words, this subtextual multiple negativity troubles the very distinction between the empirical and the speculative—and between philosophy and politics.

HEGELIAN DIFFERENCE: *VERSCHIEDENHEIT* AS MULTIPLICITY

I have argued that in order for the dialectic to operate in the way expected, it needs to operate according to the stable logic of determinate negation. Multiple negativity must be excluded from the dialectic and the totality of the system in order for it to operate as a whole. Nonetheless, multiple negativity does in fact operate in the dialectic: it ties together various different moments, responding to each moment differently, marking a rhythm between them. Though multiple negativity operates in the dialectic, Hegel does not, and in fact *cannot*, recognize it because the dialectic in the Hegelian system operates by means of excluding it. This shows us the centrality of ignorance to the operation of constitutive exclusion, in that the inability to see what is constitutively excluded is precisely what allows it to operate, to constitute the body that it is excluded from and in which it nonetheless operates. This disavowal at the heart of constitutive exclusion thus makes up the kernel both of fetishism and of ideology.

Given that negativity marks the relation between *and the distinction from* one thing and another, difference is wrapped up in it. A certain mode of difference, then, one that is rooted in the empirical rather than the speculative, subtends the operation of the dialectic. This mode of difference marks the more radical possibilities on which the dialectic relies, but which it cannot recognize. As we will see in Chapter 3, these include gender—a difference that, since Hegel takes it to be natural (though it also structures his politics), is excluded from the *Logic*. However, Hegel never entirely succeeds in ridding his speculative system of the "empirical" difference of gender, which operates behind the back of the concept. The difference that makes a difference—that mode of difference central to the operation of determinate negation—is achieved through the unjustified disavowal of the work these other modes of difference do for the system. They mark shards or moments that point beyond the totality of the system, insurrections or subversions from within. At the same time, they mark the border between the empirical and the speculative in Hegel's system. Like the drawing of most borders, this is a political operation.

Determinate negation is central to the operation of difference in Hegel. This pair—determinate negation and difference—is bound up in the *Science of Logic*, as determinate negation, the activity of *aufheben*, operates through the specific form of difference identified as contradiction. It is the operation through which one thing comes to alienate itself in another, and then returns to itself, changed, having become truly itself. It is the motor of the dialectic. It is the supertextual difference of the dialectic: it is what allows Hegel to claim that all difference is essentially contradiction. However, a different kind of difference does make an appearance in the *Science of Logic*: the difference described as *Verschiedenheit*. Just as a certain negativity must be excluded to secure the operation of determinate negation, so a certain multiplicity—*Verschiedenheit*—must be excluded to secure the operation of contradiction in Hegel. The two sides of multiple negativity are bound up in this relation of negativity to difference.

In what follows, I argue that Hegel distinguishes between two senses of *Verschiedenheit*: one he takes to be indeterminate, associated with the empirical, and one he takes to be determinate, associated with the speculative. At stake in this distinction at the heart of multiplicity is the difference that makes a difference: what is squeezed out of multiplicity such that it is rendered a symmetrical opposition put to work for determinate negation? What is remaindered in this operation? How is a contingent difference—such as race, gender, sexuality, ability—rendered necessary, the basis for exclusion? And what justifies this?

Determinate Difference: From Identity to Contradiction

In the Essentialities of Reflection chapter, Hegel describes *Verschiedenheit* as a moment in the movement from absolute identity and absolute difference to contradiction. There, Hegel argues that absolute identity *is* absolute difference, inasmuch as identity is different from, distinct from, difference ["*die Identität sei verschieden* von der Verschiedenheit"].[26] Determinate difference *is* its own negativity: it is not merely different from some external other, but is its own other. It is therefore itself and its own difference. But, Hegel writes, "that which is different from difference is identity. Difference is therefore itself and Identity."[27] Difference constitutes an absolute whole, just as identity does, because each contains itself *and* its other. Being both itself and its other, difference has therefore two moments. When we take these two moments *as* two, this moment shows itself to be diversity [*Verschiedenheit*], in which the two parts "subsist as indifferently different towards one another because each is self-identical."[28]

Difference as *Verschiedenheit* is thus an indifferent difference between two distinct self-identical parts. Hegel conceives of difference here as two singular and distinct objects that can seemingly exist with or without the other and are therefore indifferent to each other. As diverse, these distinct monad-like objects do not determine each other as different; instead, each object contains within itself both identity and difference, and each therefore constitutes a whole. As each one is self-identical and only self-related, each is not in itself different, but rather its difference is external to it. Therefore, their difference is not determinate, but mere difference in general, "indifferent to one another and to their determinateness."[29] This is the basis of difference as *Verschiedenheit.*

Like any other moment in the dialectic, however, *Verschiedenheit* does not stay *Verschiedenheit* for long. The indifferent difference of diversity resolves itself into opposition and contradiction, such that Hegel can state that difference is essentially contradiction. Hegel explains this movement in the *Logic* in this way. The determinate difference of these indifferent and therefore diverse objects is not found in the objects themselves, because they are considered wholly identical in and of themselves. Their difference is therefore defined from a viewpoint external to them. Both their identity and their difference, as independent wholes, are based on "externally posited determinations, not determinations in and for themselves."[30] From this external perspective, identity and difference are rendered as similarity [*Gleichheit*] and dissimilarity [*Ungleichheit*]. Any difference these objects have from each other is posited, and the result of an external reflection, which is not related to the objects taken in themselves, but belongs to a third term external to them. Their difference is then merely a posited one, and they can be said to be alike in that they are different. The negativity of difference, the *determinant* of difference in these indifferent objects, belongs to that third term which is external to them and compares them, which is a subjective reflection.[31]

This third term—the subjective reflection—Hegel calls the "negative unity" of both sides, of similarity and dissimilarity.[32] As a comparative term, it stands outside them both. But Hegel asserts that this separation cannot be maintained, and that this "negative unity" belongs essentially to the two terms themselves, as independent wholes that are self-relating. As terms external to the third term of reflection, similarity and dissimilarity are both unlike that external third which compares them. Similarity and dissimilarity are alike in that they are different, but they are different in that they are distinct from that third term, the "negative unity" which compares them. Therefore, the two terms transcend the determinate difference that was external to them. Diversity then, as it has transcended its external difference and now contains this difference in one negative unity, becomes opposition [*Gegensatz*].[33]

But each side still contains its own relation to the other, and in this regard, each side is self-subsistent and indifferent. Each side of the relation is both independent of *and* dependent on the other side. The two terms are mutually constitutive and yet opposed. Hegel writes that each side determines the other and that "therefore [they are] only moments; but they are no less determined within themselves, mutually indifferent and mutually exclusive: the *self-subsistent determinations of reflection*."[34] We find the two sides are therefore in a relation of contradiction. Hegel then writes, "difference as such is already *implicitly* contradiction."[35]

Insofar as any two terms are each self-subsistent and self-identical, but are related negatively to each other as each excluding the other, they are in contradiction. Therefore, for Hegel, all relations of difference are implicitly contradictions.

Excessive Difference: *Verschiedenheit* as Multiplicity

So much for the movement of absolute identity and absolute difference into contradiction. But let us focus for a moment longer on *Verschiedenheit*. *Verschiedenheit* describes that indifferent difference between two self-identical parts, both of which contain their own negativity within them, and so are equally whole. This term is consistently translated as "diversity" in Miller's translation of *Science of Logic*. The sense in which Hegel uses it could as well be rendered "distinctness." However, *Verschiedenheit* can also mean multiplicity or plurality, and both senses of *Verschiedenheit* appear throughout the Hegelian system and in the *Science of Logic*. Hegel nevertheless must maintain a strict distinction between these two senses. On the one hand, he identifies the "multiplicity" sense of *Verschiedenheit* as "indeterminate" and associates it with nature, contingency, opinion, the understanding, and representational or pictorial thinking. On the other hand, he reserves *Verschiedenheit* as "distinctness" or "distinguishability" as the determinate and technical sense at work in the *Logic*. The distinction Hegel makes between these two senses of *Verschiedenheit*—indeterminate on the one hand, determinate on the other—maps onto the distinction identified by Hyppolite between empirical thought or the realm of the experience of consciousness as described in the *Phenomenology*, and speculative thought or the realm of eidetic truth in and for itself as described in the *Logic*. Following Hyppolite, therefore, we can identify indeterminate *Verschiedenheit* with empirical thought, and determinate *Verschiedenheit* with speculative thought, as he describes them in *Logic and Existence*. The difference between these two senses of *Verschiedenheit* is the difference that makes a difference for the whole Hegelian system. But how does it work?

As Hyppolite puts it, "negation and distinction imply each other, as Hegel tried to show."[36] At issue in distinctness is negation (there is no word here of negativity). It is only *Verschiedenheit* in its determinate sense that occurs in the movement from absolute identity and absolute difference to opposition and finally to contradiction. The distinction between the indeterminate and determinate senses of *Verschiedenheit* is managed by what Hegel calls the *law of diversity*: that thing which makes a thing distinctive, such that "it can no longer be exchanged with any other."[37] This claim to have distinguished between these two senses of *Verschiedenheit* is complicated, however, by the fact that Hegel expresses multiple laws of diversity—in fact, he already seems to have a certain difficulty distinguishing between them.

Hegel describes the law [*Satz*] of diversity in a remark [*Anmerkung*] to the section on diversity in the *Logic*. However, this law takes two forms whose relationship to each other is not at all clear. The law is stated as follows: "All things are different, or: there are no two things like each other."[38] These two statements of the law are connected in the Miller translation with a disjunctive "or," but also with a colon, which implies their identity; the German contains the disjunctive but not the colon. However, the next sentence begins: "This law is in fact opposed to the law of identity [*Dieser Satz ist in der Tat dem Satzen der Identität entgegengesetzt*]."[39] But to which law does Hegel refer? As we shall see, Hegel tends to associate one side of the law with indeterminate diversity and the other with determinate diversity, but at this moment in the text, the very law of distinguishability itself is already somewhat indistinct.

Hegel defines this first (form of the) law of diversity ("all things are different") by what he calls a "very superfluous proposition": "that everything is different from everything else."[40] This "superfluous" version of the law of diversity belongs to ordinary thinking, or (following Hyppolite) with empirical thought. This indeterminate diversity is associated with the "impotence of nature," or with the ability of spirit as pictorial thinking (or empirical thought) to "run riot in endless variety [*Verschiedenheit*]."[41] Hegel also associates it with the metaphysics that Leibniz taught the ladies at court, by comparing leaves to discover whether they could find any two that were exactly alike. He cites the ability of the concept t abandon its difference" in these ways (in nature, opinion, contingency, in women; all of these will be tied together by *Verschiedenheit*) as evidence of its power. Hegel warns us, however, that we should not take these to be anything more than "the abstract aspect of nothingness."[42]

Hegel wants to correlate "All things are different [*Alle Dinge sind verschieden*]" and "Everything is different from everything else [*alle Dinge sind verschieden voneinander*]" as equally superfluous; however, these propositions are not clearly the same. While the second may refer to the distinction between things even as indeterminately plural things, the first may refer either to distinctions *between* things in this sense, or it may refer to distinctions *within* things. That is, "All things are different" could equally mean that all things are different *from each other*, or that all things are plural or many *within themselves*. This first proposition is a much more ambivalent one, and could refer as much to internal multiplicity as to external multiplicity (or "manyness [*Mehrheit*]"). This would be a violation of the distinction between indeterminateness, which is based upon an indifferent difference between self-identical things, and determinateness, which is based on a negation internal to these supposedly self-identical things, the determinate negation that sets the movement toward contradiction in motion.

The internal multiplicity to which I refer is something slightly different from these: neither entirely indeterminate nor entirely determinate, it is a multiplicity of more-than-two, a plural ontology similar to the one suggested by María Lugones in *Pilgrimages/Peregrinajes*.[43] That all things are different might imply an internal self-diremption, neatly into the two of contradiction; it may, however, also imply something far messier and far richer. I will return to Lugones, to plural ontology and its relation to epistemology at the close of the book. To be clear, however, I am not suggesting a plural ontology as an alternative to Hegel's ontology in the *Science of Logic*; rather, given that multiple negativity is already at work there, plural ontology *is already operative* in the *Science of Logic*.

Determinate diversity is thus defined against this indeterminate, "superfluous" manyness, and associated with the proposition "there are no two things like each other."[44] This sense of *Verschiedenheit* secures the distinction of one thing from another, such that one "can no longer be exchanged with any other." This law is later restated as "things are different from each other through unlikeness" and "two things are not perfectly alike."[45] Hegel marshals the relationality between the two indifferently different things implicit in "likeness" and "unlikeness" to show that determinate diversity in truth is implicitly oppositional and finally contradictory.

Thus, the distinctions between indeterminate diversity and determinate diversity, and likewise between empirical thought and speculative thought, are secured. However, this internal multiplicity or manyness has already infected the determinate sense of *Verschiedenheit*. Hegel wants to make the determinate sense of *Verschiedenheit* distinct from that indeterminate mere manyness. But the multiple presentations of the law of diversity (all things are different; no two things are alike; everything is different from everything else) make the determinateness of this law difficult, to say the least. This mere manyness, which is meant to be restricted to indeterminate diversity in the empirical, creeps into the determinate diversity that Hegel deploys in the eidetic structure of the dialectic.

At stake in this for Hegel is the transition from diversity to opposition, but also the metaphysics in the ability to distinguish one thing from another, which involves an internal negation. One thing is distinguished from another insofar as it is not that other, or not any other. The basis of such a distinction is negation (in the form of *determinate negation*, or difference as implicitly contradictory). Determinate diversity is contaminated with indeterminate manyness, in the form of internal multiplicity. This implies a negativity beyond determinate negation and a difference beyond contradiction, beyond the reflective self-diremption within one moment of the dialectic.

Hegel wants to be able to determine between the two senses of the term *Verschiedenheit*: on the one hand, distinctness, heterogeneity, diversity as distinguishability; on the other hand, plurality, multiplicity, diversity as manyness. Hegel wants to deploy the first sense of *Verschiedenheit* for speculative thought, while he wants to reserve the second sense for empirical thought, for the realm of nature, or the register of mere understanding.

The concept is strong enough, he assures us, to maintain a place for this "blind irrational multiplicity" and "endless diversity";[46] it has the strength to withstand metaphysics being done by ladies comparing leaves, but only insofar as empirical thought or ordinary consciousness has its own place, a place distinct from that of reason, the concept, and speculative thought. However, Hegel is unable to maintain the absolute distinction between these two senses of *Verschiedenheit*, just as he is unable to control the diverse presentations of *Verschiedenheit* under the term "law" or "proposition" [*Satz*]—a strange law, an already multiple law. The multiplicity of *Verschiedenheit* interrupts the distinction Hegel wishes to maintain between the determinate and the indeterminate, between diversity understood as distinction and understood as mere manyness, and ultimately between empirical thought and speculative thought. However, it is not as if Hegel can simply do without it; it is absolutely fundamental to his conception of difference, as well as to the operation of determinate negation, and the specular whole of the system hinges on this point.

Hegel of course does not recognize such an indeterminateness operating within a technical term so vital for determination and distinction. To do so would be to admit of a fundamental problem in his speculative system. It would amount to an admission that the speculative is already determined by the empirical in some way, or that they are mutually implicated in each other, in a way far deeper than the dialectic by means of determinate negation implies. The operation of this ambiguously multiple *Verschiedenheit* is secured by Hegel's ignorance of it in the *Logic*. That is, the constitutive exclusion of multiplicity, an excessive and internally multiple *Verschiedenheit*, operates by means of ignorance of its continued inclusion within the speculative system. It is difficult to pin down the relationship here between the operation of constitutive exclusion and the epistemological blind spot that accompanies it, because constitutive exclusion operates according to a retroactive temporality that makes causality rather murky (a topic I will take up in Chapter 3). The epistemological blind spot in which *Verschiedenheit* operates is not caused by its constitutive exclusion; but rather, its constitutive exclusion operates through Hegel's blindness to it. They are not coextensive, but the separation between these two registers, the ontological and the epistemological, is not so clear and distinct here. This should come as no surprise, since the distinction between the specular and the empirical, between the register of ontology and the register of epistemology, is itself secured by means of a constitutive exclusion: its very terms are set by the exclusion of multiple negativity.

Though this fundamental undecidability of *Verschiedenheit* occurs in the midst of the careful distinctions Hegel makes between one side and the other, it does not, for all that, seem to destroy the system or the dialectic, or even to make these distinctions absolutely untenable. As with the different rhythms of negativity that I located in the *Science of Logic*, the multiplicity of *Verschiedenheit* operates in this strange manner: subterranean, surreptitious, both necessary and dangerous to the operation of the Hegelian system. This is precisely what characterizes the operation of constitutive exclusion. The Hegelian system constitutes itself on the basis of excluding from itself a sense of negativity as multiple, as excessive, as more than the operation of the logic of determinate negation; it also constitutes itself on the basis of the exclusion of an indeterminate multiplicity in *Verschiedenheit*, a form of difference which is not fundamentally reducible to contradiction. Yet these (negativity, multiplicity, multiple negativity) are not "successfully" excluded from the system; they remain within the system. The system maintains itself on the basis of its inability to see, hear, or recognize the remainder it defines itself against. It constitutes itself on this produced blindness to the remnants it has not "successfully" excluded. This remainder continues to "work for" the system, holding that system together, but only under a bar—under the form of denial, disavowal, foreclosure, abjection, or denegation; a negation that is more than a mere negation, but which secures the whole of the system on its basis.

CONCLUSION

Interpretations of Hegel largely tend to take two forms: those that read Hegel as a thinker of totality, who focus on the unity of the system and in particular the *Science of Logic*; and those who see resources for reading

Hegel as a thinker of difference and openness, undoing or upending totalities, who largely tend to avoid the *Science of Logic*. A third, deconstructivist, reading is also available; while this reading is productive (as we shall see in Chapter 3), I go beyond this reading by arguing that Hegel's thought is both open and closed, and that both are at work in the *Science of Logic*. The two Hegels are defined by the two forms of negativity at work in the *Logic*: the supertextual negativity of determinate negation, and the more mobile, more heterogeneous, more radical subtextual negativity of multiple negativity.

Of available interpretations, that of Karin de Boer comes closest to the reading I give above. In her 2010 *On Hegel: The Sway of the Negative*, de Boer seeks a way to resolve the two Hegels by arguing that Hegel's dialectical negativity in the *Science of Logic* relies on but subordinates an earlier mode of negativity, which she identifies as tragic entanglement. She argues that Hegel worked from this form of negativity in his early work on tragedy, as a way of describing how opposed concepts—such as faith and reason, or power and justice, or public and private—remain interdependent and stubbornly in conflict rather than being resolved into a higher determination. De Boer argues that while Hegel initially set out to write a philosophy that would capture the fundamental tensions characteristic of modern human life, he ultimately subordinated this aim to the dialectical logic of his system. While Hegel had to efface the negativity of tragic entanglement for the sake of the absolute negativity of the *Science of Logic*, de Boer argues that it is worth resuscitating this other negativity to put it to the use for which Hegel originally intended it: to understand the fundamental and intractable conflicts that defined his time, and our own. But while de Boer's argument is subtle and powerful, it suffers from two central problems: first, de Boer is unable to locate this other mode of negativity within the *Science of Logic*, and second, her reading of the negativity of tragic entanglement relies on a symmetry between the two opposed concepts that is overstated.

While de Boer herself deftly critiques the "open" readings of Hegel for failing to grapple with the *Science of Logic*, she is ultimately unable to locate the negativity of tragic entanglement within the *Logic*. While she treats the same three moments of negativity I discuss above, rather than reading each as irreducible, she reads them as instances of absolute negativity (the second moment), or in other words, as determinate negation. She thus affirms the totalizing force of the dialectic. But she argues that while absolute negativity required the effacement of the negativity of tragic entanglements, no trace of this other negativity remains in the *Science of Logic*. "Yet nothing prevents us," she argues, from interpreting this dialectical negativity as the result of the effacement of this other negativity.[47] True enough; however, on her reading, nothing seems to require it of us. Without a foothold in the *Logic*, the tragic entanglement de Boer articulates in her reading of negativity is thus too easy to dismiss as belonging merely to the level of the empirical rather than the speculative, a result of particular local failures to attain the concept, rather than a fundamental tension or negativity at the level of ontology itself. Instead, the constitutive exclusion of a multiple negativity that subtends the operation of the dialectic in the *Science of Logic* presents a challenge to the dialectical system at its heart; the included exclusion of this multiple negativity within the *Logic* both allows for and troubles the distinction between the speculative and the empirical, between the ontological and the epistemological; it both allows for and troubles the totality of the system, a totality that is achieved only on the basis of a forced reconciliation.

And even this forced reconciliation is itself achieved only on the basis of rendering a multiplicity into the symmetrical opposition of two sides, a symmetry that is thus subtended by another difference, another negativity. For instance, de Boer argues that tragic entanglement is found in intersubjective relations, such as that between Antigone and Creon, a crucial moment in the *Phenomenology of Spirit*. However, as Chapter 3 will demonstrate, the problem with this moment in the *Phenomenology* is not so much that Hegel mistakenly treats something fundamentally asymmetrical as something symmetrical, but rather that this reconciliation is achieved via force: the tragic symmetry of the opposition between Antigone and Creon can only be achieved by erasing the multiple differences between them—and between the concepts they represent—in order to render them simply opposed. In other words, this determinate difference of opposition is achieved only by erasing the indeterminate differences, or *Verschiedenheiten*, both *between* and *within* Antigone and Creon. But what allows for that? What makes this oppositional symmetry possible? How is diversity, as Hyppolite puts it, pushed up into opposition? What remains when difference has been rendered into opposition?

This problem extends to de Boer's conception of the contemporary condition to which her reading of tragic negativity is meant to respond. She writes, for instance, that "the increasing influence of Christian fundamentalism, especially in the United States, also indicates that pre-modern elements continue to haunt the paradigm of modernity from within, if only by undermining the clear-cut distinction between the private and the public which is crucial to liberal politics."[48] This symmetry necessary to the logic of tragic entanglements thus means that human life is organized by oppositional principles, such as public and private. But the distinction between public and private has been subject to feminist critique for half a century, as it is predicated upon the gendered exclusion of women from the public sphere—an exclusion entirely consistent with modernism and one at the heart of feminist critiques of the modern interpretations of Antigone, such as Hegel's. The exclusion within of women that subtends the distinction between public and private is precisely indicative of the operation of constitutive exclusion.

The negativity of constitutive exclusion is thus a better account of Hegel, but more important, it is a better account of the negativity at work at the level of the political. What is at stake is less the irresolvable opposition between two concepts or categories, and more the parasitic reliance of one concept or category on a difference that it cannot recognize or against which it defines itself. This is the negativity at work in the distinction between the public and private, which is subtended by the domination of the public over the private, and relies on presumption of a gender distinction that is instead its effect—a production that it cannot see, hear, recognize, or understand. This negativity has more in common with the radical negativity in Kristeva's work, especially *Revolution in Poetic Language*, or in the work of Jose Muñoz, especially in *Cruising Utopia*.[49]

Repression or disavowal is thus inseparable from the negativity of constitutive exclusion, from the paradoxical included exclusion it produces. This speaks to the strange epistemological status of the constitutively excluded: it is both determinate and indeterminate, represented and unrepresentable, inside and outside, included and excluded, all at the same time. It has a singular ability to blur the borders, though it simultaneously secures the border by virtue of its "exclusion." It points to a relationality that is based less on the distinction of one thing from another than their indistinction, less on their distinguishability than on their mutual implication, and perhaps less on their independence of than on their vulnerability to each other.

3

On the Quasi-Transcendental: Temporality and Political Epistemology in Derrida's *Glas*

In his 1971–72 lecture course, "*La famille de Hegel*," Jacques Derrida turned his attention to the opening scene of Hegel's *Phenomenology of Spirit*, the ethical world (*Sittlichkeit*) of ancient Greece. Derrida remarked that his analysis of Hegel would be organized around two foci: "The first will be the sepulchre, the motif of the sepulchre; the second will the relation of the brother to the sister. If the whole Hegelian text, in this chapter, turns around these two foci, it is no surprise that Antigone organizes the whole scene."[1] Antigone does this organizational work by figuring a series of motifs in Hegelian thought: sexual difference, guilt and crime, desire and repression, and most important, the relationship between the empirical and the transcendental. To think through the relationship between the empirical and the transcendental, Derrida relies both on Hegel's "transcendental" sister—the figure of Antigone—well as Hegel's "empirical" sisters: Nanette Endel (a young boarder in Hegel's family home) and Christiane Hegel (his own sister). In Derrida's reading, this relationship produces a strange figure, neither entirely empirical nor entirely transcendental, neither both nor neither, a monstrous figure who subtends and animates the *Phenomenology* at this crucial moment: a figure he calls "Antigonanette."[2]

In Derrida's analysis, "Antigonanette" marks the limit of the entire Hegelian system—the moment the whole system falters; a moment that is somehow also necessary to the whole system. This paradoxical moment—both excluded by and yet necessary to the system—is what Derrida describes as *quasi-transcendental*. Following the Kantian sense of the transcendental as the condition of possibility, the quasi-transcendental acts as the simultaneous condition of possibility as well as impossibility of a system, concept, language, or political body.[3] I argue in this chapter that constitutive exclusion produces such a condition of (im)possibility and so has a quasi-transcendental character. The constitutively excluded figure is the condition of possibility in that it defines or constitutes the body that excludes it, while its remaining within that body is a threat that must be managed. In the case of constitutive exclusion, this threat is managed through disavowal or repression—a negativity that, as we saw in Chapter 2, both marks the distinction between the register of being and the register of knowing, and troubles that very distinction.

Turning toward the quasi-transcendental character of constitutive exclusion helps my analysis in several ways. Focusing on its quasi-transcendental character assists in diagnosing constitutive exclusion, both in the text and in the world, as it better attunes us to the contours and effects of constitutive exclusion. It helps to flesh out the distinction between ontology and epistemology, by tracing how this distinction is produced. It identifies the political stakes of constitutive exclusion, by noting the political production of this distinction between being and knowing, and by emphasizing its retroactive operation. That is, the difference that makes a difference—between ontology and epistemology, between empirical and transcendental—is effected retroactively, yet we act *as if* it proceeds linearly. This retroactive character is effaced, erasing its own steps behind it. Since the legitimacy of the distinction between being and knowing, between empirical and transcendental, and between inclusion and exclusion are established through this apparently linear function, the analysis of the quasi-transcendental character of constitutive exclusion calls this distinction into question as a political operation. And finally, the analysis of the quasi-transcendental character of constitutive exclusion helps us to better understand the economy of difference at work in it. Rather than pointing to a prior general economy of pure difference out of which the restricted economy of the dialectic is rendered, constitutive exclusion produces a contingent difference: a specific operation of difference that is neither singular nor general, but rather a difference suspended between particularity and universality, a contingent difference cast in the role of a transcendental difference.

Derrida returns us to Hegel for his analysis of the quasi-transcendental structure of the system because it is Hegel's thought that marks the apotheosis of systems-thinking in modern philosophy and its specific terms: the constriction of difference into determinate, productive difference through the dialectical logic of contradiction. Rather than the *Science of Logic*, however, Derrida turns our attention to Hegel's *Phenomenology of Spirit*. Derrida treats the brother/sister relationship in the opening scene of the Spirit chapter as the quasi-transcendental moment of the *Phenomenology*, and he identifies Antigone, the "transcendental" sister, as our guide, playing the role of an unrepresentable difference in the brother/sister relationship. This quasi-transcendental moment will not be confined to the *Phenomenology*, however, as Antigone guides us through subterranean passageways to the *Science of Logic* and thus to the rest of the system by means of the form of difference she animates, a form that should be familiar to us by now: *Verschiedenheit*. The analysis of *Verschiedenheit* that Antigone guides us through will bring into focus the policing of the border between ontology and epistemology, and thus the politics at work in determining which differences define us, but which we cannot recognize, understand, hear, or see.

This chapter has two parts. In part one, I analyze Derrida's diagnosis of the quasi-transcendental in Hegel's thought in *Glas,* supplemented by the lecture course "*La famille de Hegel*."[4] There I define the relationship between brother and sister in the Spirit chapter of Hegel's *Phenomenology of Spirit*, and its connection to *Verschiedenheit* in the *Science of Logic*. I analyze the quasi-transcendental in *Glas*, and in particular its implications for the relation between the transcendental and the empirical. In the second section, I analyze the retroactive character of the quasi-transcendental, by turning to Derrida's work on the retroactive character of constitutions. There I argue that, rather than restricting the transcendental out of the empirical, or drawing the ethical out of nature as the *Phenomenology of Spirit* would have it, the empirical—the contingent, nature, sex—is posited retroactively, producing an underground economy of resources remaindered through this operation. The retroactive character of the quasi-transcendental indicates that the transcendental is always provisional and is a matter of interpretation in each instance.

The analysis of the quasi-transcendental character of constitutive exclusion thus continues the diagnostic work on the ontological and epistemological levels but will continue to call into question the distinction between these and the political register that is implicitly at work in that distinction between them. Ultimately, this chapter traces how philosophical systems and political bodies tend to define themselves by means of claiming to resolve the very tensions that do that definitional work. Careful attention to the retroactive temporality that claims to draw these borders, and to the economy by which these borders produce the very differences they mean to exclude, opens up new radical potentialities of thinking and acting within and beyond them.

THE DERRIDEAN QUASI-TRANSCENDENTAL

Glas is, without doubt, an impossible book.[5] To begin with, it is not exactly one book. It is more like two: two books in one, split down the middle. The middle of the book, the center of each page, then, is in fact not a middle, but a margin—a blank space, both dividing and linking a "book" "on" "Hegel" from/to a "book" "on" "Genet." To give an account of or to account for such a book—even when the word "book" is itself so inadequate—is obviously impossible.[6] But insofar as an interpretation of some kind is necessary, and insofar as an interpretation necessarily involves some kind of violence, some kind of incision, mine is here—at the heart, or at least its left ventricle—simultaneously of *Glas* and of the *Phenomenology of Spirit*.

The *Phenomenology of Spirit*: "Middle: Passage"

Though it begins elsewhere, *Glas* is organized in a certain sense from the middle, and its left column especially, both its own middle and in what Derrida refers to as the "middle: passage" of the *Phenomenology of Spirit*.[7] Derrida remarks that he opens the book, or opens his reading of the *Phenomenology*, at this "middle: passage" with one stroke [*coup*]. This is a way of referencing the relation between limit and passage that he traces throughout *Glas* and throughout much of his early work.[8] The undecidability between limit and passage could be seen as one way the book as a whole is organized, though as we shall see, whether the quasi-transcendental can organize or be organized into a single structure will remain a question for us. Nevertheless, this undecidable limit/passage, as well as the notion of the stroke [*coup*], is indicative of the quasi-transcendental in Derrida's work. The limit/passage is kin to the quasi-transcendental in that it holds together two contradictory concepts in a way that preserves, rather than overcomes, their tension. The limit/passage especially refers to that which separates two sides, and yet allows them to mediate each other, pass back and forth between each other, or communicate with each other, through or across the cut. Derrida locates this particular limit/passage in the "middle: passage" of the Spirit chapter, at the heart of the *Phenomenology*, in the relationship between the brother and the sister. So what precisely makes the relationship between brother and sister the quasi-transcendental of the *Phenomenology*? And what repercussions does this relationship have across Hegel's larger system?

The relationship between brother and sister in the *Phenomenology* structures the opening scene of the Spirit chapter. Hegel has shifted here from analyzing the movement of Spirit through different shapes of consciousness, to analyzing Spirit as it moves through different shapes of world history. He situates the beginning of this history in what he calls the ethical world [*Sittlichkeit*] of ancient Greece. [9] Hegel treats ancient Greece as the moment Spirit emerges from nature, becoming increasingly more free through the different ages of history. He manages this fraught moment in the emergence of freedom through sexual difference: he argues that the ethical world is split into two, corresponding to the "natural" determination of sex. Men in this world belong to one law—the human law or the law of universality [*Allgemeinheit*]—and women belong to the other—the divine law or the law of singularity [*Einzelheit*]. The human law demands that the duty of men be toward the government and community of the nation (and specifically demands their sacrifice in war), while the divine law demands that the duty of women be toward the household gods and the family (and specifically to burying and consecrating the memory of the dead). The devotion to either law is absolute: it makes up entirely the identity of the people of the ethical world, and it is determined entirely by the "natural" difference of sex.

Here in the opening scene of the movement of Spirit through history, individuals are determined contingently by nature and have no choice as to which law to follow. As the most immediate moment of history, however, the scene is fraught with failure, as Spirit will achieve higher determinations of freedom in its movement through history. Since this is such an early moment in the movement of Spirit, it is no surprise that freedom and ethicality are so closely tied to "natural" determinations. Spirit's measured achievement of freedom from nature in this early moment depends entirely upon what Hegel calls the natural determination of sex; in order for the ethicality of the *Sittlichkeit* to be achieved, men and women must freely choose to do their ethical duty. Like all claims to freedom in Hegel, this freedom depends upon recognition, but in the world of ancient Greece this recognition is unlike any other.

The world of human law and the world of the divine law are sharply separated, and the point at which they meet is in the family, in which boys and girls are raised to be men and women. Men are bound to work for the universal, but first grow up in a family. There they partake in both sides of the ethical world, in the side of singularity and the side of universality.

They then separate from the family, from the side of singularity, and turn toward working in and for the nation, on the side of the universal. Once he leaves the family, the man has not entirely abandoned singularity: he returns to it when he takes a wife and starts his own family. He thus takes part in both universality and singularity, but these remain separate in him. Because he keeps the two sides separate, according to Hegel, the man acquires [*er kauft*] the "right of desire" in his relationship with his wife, but he "preserves for himself freedom from it," because he finds his freedom affirmed in his work for the universal in the life of the nation.[10] Once leaving the family, men find their recognition in other men, not in women.

The woman, on the other hand, does not leave the family: she grows up and leaves the family of her birth to become a wife and mother in a new family, but there is no essential developmental change that takes place in her as a result. Hegel writes, "the sister becomes, or the wife remains, the manager of the house and the guardian of the divine law."[11] She does not, however, partake only in singularity; Hegel writes that the family is an "ethical essence insofar as it does not have the relationship of nature among its members. . . . For the ethical essence is inherently universal."[12] In order for the family to tie together both the divine law and the human law, the family must be both natural and ethical, and as ethical, it must participate in the universal. However, women's experience of the universal in the family is inherent or in-itself [*an sich*] and unconscious. The singularity of the woman is always bound up with universality, but in an immediate, inherent, and unconscious way. For this reason, Hegel argues that a husband's relationship to his wife is very different from her relationship to him. He relates to her as *this particular* woman whom he desires and he is free to do this because his universality is affirmed elsewhere; she, on the other hand, relates to him in both a singular *and* a universal manner, since these are mixed together in her and do not "go asunder."[13] Although she remains determined by singularity, she "remains immediately universal," and is therefore "foreign to the singularity of desiring."[14] Hegel argues that the wife's particular relationship to her husband is thus bound up with the universal; the husband preserves his universality for the work he does in the nation with other men, and he therefore desires his wife in a purely singular way. However, the singularity that determines women is contingent. Taking as his guide Antigone's speech in lines 905–914—in which Antigone argues that she would not have violated Creon's law to bury a husband or a child, because these are replaceable, but because her parents are dead, she can never get another brother—Hegel argues that woman does not relate to *this* particular husband, or *this* particular child, but rather that they are replaceable to her. [15] Because the woman's singularity is mixed with universality, she never knows the particularity or singularity of desire as the man does, and she lacks "the moment in which she [re]cognizes herself as this self in another."[16] She thus never sees herself as *this particular* self in the eyes of the other; it is as if, in relation to her husband and her children, she has no particular self and is instead only a *role*.

As Derrida points out, the ethical world of ancient Greece is not only riven by the contradiction of "natural" sex, but the sides of this contradiction are unequal: men, being bifurcated between universality in the nation and singularity in the family, are self-conscious and are therefore agents of Spirit in a way that women are not.[17] Here Antigone animates Hegel's narrative again, as the split between these two principles comes to a head in the contradictory actions that each side takes, devoted as each is to ethical action for contradictory laws: on the one hand, an unconscious commitment to the divine law that demands the burial of the dead, and on the other hand, the self-conscious commitment to the human law which forbids such burial. This one-sided devotion to an ethical law that is split by the "natural" determination of sex is what makes this moment tragic for Hegel. In this conceptual tragedy, Antigone will come to represent the divine law or the law of the family, whereas Creon will come to represent the human law or the law of the nation—paradoxically making Antigone universal as a representative of the law of singularity (an insight not lost on Derrida).[18]

In order for an act to be ethical for Hegel, it must be at least in part universal, and not entirely determined by nature. In other words, it must be done freely. Freedom for Hegel depends upon recognition, or the subjects' acknowledgment of their intersubjective interdependence. In the ethical world of ancient Greece, ethical action requires that man and woman recognize each other. Since men and women only interact in the family because of women's confinement in it, then this relationship of mutual reciprocal recognition must be found there. Relationships in the family are insufficiently universal according to Hegel, since they are affected by natural feelings of love and desire, with one exception: the relationship between brother and sister.

The reciprocal ethical duties of the brother and the sister, secured by the reciprocal recognition they share, are the key to resolving the contradiction between the two laws, closing the speculative circle of the ethical world. Because they recognize each other, the brother and sister can take up their ethical duties freely, and these duties become truly ethical for the first time. The sister can take up her destiny to bury her fallen brother and, secure in the care of his singular self in the home, the brother can go off to war to protect the nation. But if this mutual reciprocal recognition that allows men and women to take up their ethical duties is so necessary to *Sittlichkeit*, why is this recognition only possible between the brother and the sister?

Hegel argues that recognition is only possible between the brother and the sister because "they are of the same blood, but in them it has come into its calm and equilibrium. Hence, they do not desire one another, and neither one has given being-for-self to the other nor received it; rather, each is a free individuality with respect to the other."[19] The brother and the sister come from the same family and so are of the same blood. But they do not relate to each other as husbands and wives do, or as parents and children do, because they have no natural desire for each other. Instead, "each is a free individuality with respect to the other."[20] Brother and sister approach the relationship between them as equals, free of the natural desires that stand in the way of a purely ethical mode of recognition. They can meet each other as individuals with some natural attachment to each other, but a natural attachment somehow cleansed of its natural-ness.

Hegel writes that the brother is for the sister "the calm and similar essence in general": while the brother and the sister have different roles and take part in the life of their world, and take part in the substance of spirit, differently, they approach each other as "similar."[21] Because the relationship between brother and sister is free of all natural desire, then, they are free in relation to each other: free to exchange the recognition that makes their duties to each other ethical. Once again taking his cues from Antigone, Hegel argues that because it is only as a sister that a woman can experience reciprocal recognition, her duty toward her brother is the highest.[22] Of course, as we will see, relying on Antigone to represent a relationship between brother and sister purified of any incestuous desire puts the role Hegel has her play into question.

To call this freedom and this recognition unusual in the Hegelian schema is an understatement: the eidetic structure of recognition familiar in the master/slave dialectic earlier in the *Phenomenology* indicates that freedom is achieved only through the struggle for recognition. Prior to that confrontation, consciousness is not free—it is consumed with natural desire, a fruitless attempt to consume and negate objects to prove its absolute universality. It is only by being confronted by another consciousness, and by facing death in that confrontation, that consciousness learns that it is not and cannot be absolutely universal. Confrontation with another consciousness proves the particularity of each and results either in the master/slave dialectic or in the acknowledgment of mutual interdependence in reciprocal recognition. But there is no confrontation between the brother and sister, who are "free individualities" before ever even entering into a relationship of recognition; they are never confronted with the realization of their own mutual vulnerability, dependency, and particularity in this exchange. What kind of recognition is this?

The implications of the singularity of this relationship between brother and sister stretch far beyond the scope of the *Phenomenology*. This is due both to the interlocking quality of Hegel's thought and to the particular kind of difference at work between the brother and sister in this early moment in the historical dialectic. That difference is the difference of diversity, multiplicity, or *Vershiedenheit*. In *Glas*, Derrida identifies the relationship between brother and sister with *Verschiedenheit*, which he argues is the "hinge" of the greater logic.[23] Hegel argues that the relationship between brother and sister constitutes a relationship of diversities, because they are able to hold together the tension between difference and identity. This tension is maintained between them because they are similar, in that they come from the same family or the same blood, and they are dissimilar, in that they are sexually different. It is through this relationship that sexual difference moves into opposition and thereby becomes determinate for the ethical world of ancient Greece. This tension is maintained because they are both sexually different and united by a familial bond, but because they have no "natural" desire for each other, their difference is determinate. The maintenance of the tension between difference and identity thus follows the formal terms of diversity or *Verschiedenheit* as laid out in the *Science of Logic*.

As I argued in Chapter 2, while Hegel attempts in the *Logic* to distinguish between the determinate *Verschiedenheit* he puts to work in the eidetic structure of difference and the indeterminate *Verschiedenheit* he argues operates at the empirical level, he cannot ultimately separate the two. Or rather, he both does and does not succeed in this separation. This is due to the constitutive exclusion of multiple negativity, the internally multiple and excessive *Verschiedenheit* upon which the eidetic form of *Verschiedenheit* relies but cannot recognize. Derrida's analysis implies that the excessive *Verschiedenheit* of the brother/sister relationship, and of the sister especially, is constitutively excluded in the *Phenomenology*, as it is in the *Logic*. The constitutive exclusion of multiple negativity calls into question the distinction between the eidetic, the speculative, or the transcendental, on the one hand, and the empirical, contingent, or immanent, on the other. Insofar as this distinction is made on the basis of rendering a multitude of differences into sexual difference as the border between public and private, the nation and the family, constitutive exclusion calls into question its political character. Derrida's analysis of the quasi-transcendental in Hegel takes place at precisely this nexus.

The Quasi-transcendental Proper

Derrida describes the relationship between brother and sister in the Spirit chapter in the following manner:

> Brother and sister "do not desire one another." The for-(it)self of one does not depend on the other. . . . Given the generality of the struggle for recognition in the relationship between consciousnesses, one would be tempted to conclude from this that at bottom there is no brother/sister bond, there is no brother or sister. If such a relation is unique and reaches a kind of repose (*Ruhe*) and equilibrium (*Gleichgewicht*) that are refused to every other one, that is because the brother and the sister do not receive from each other their for-self and nevertheless constitute themselves as "free individualities." These for-self's recognize, without ever depending on, each other; they no more desire each other than tear each other to pieces.
> Is this possible? Does it contradict the whole system?[24]

The (quasi-transcendental) answer to both questions is yes: it contradicts the whole system and yet it is nevertheless necessary to that system. Derrida argues that the diversity that characterizes the relation between brother and sister exceeds the difference to which Hegel wishes to confine it in the relation of opposition and contradiction. At the same time, this excessive difference of diversity also makes this very movement possible: it opens the "space of possibility" for the movement into a "speculative contradiction."[25] But this can only be accomplished through what Kevin Thompson calls a "constriction" of the "diverse multiplicity of the remains."[26] This constriction is performed with an eye toward the outcome or toward the *telos*, to the infinite return of Spirit to itself. This constriction takes place even in advance of the movement to opposition, in that Hegel claims that diversity is figured already as a duality: "difference as such is already *implicitly* contradiction."[27] Difference as diversity thus works as a kind of excluded reserve or resource from which the dialectic draws to figure its movement as a logic of opposition and contradiction, but a resource that the dialectic must repress or disavow. Difference as diversity therefore has a quasi-transcendental structure and operates as the remainder: necessary but suppressed—*excluded within.*

In *Glas*, the quasi-transcendental makes its abrupt appearance in a question cut in two. The cut strikes within the word "transcendental" in the English; in the French it strikes between the words "*l'abîme jouant*" and "*un rôle quasi transcendental.*" The entire question is as follows: "And what if what cannot be assimilated, the absolute indigestible, played a fundamental role in the system, an abyssal role rather, the abyss playing an almost tran-"[28]

The question picks up, some ten or twelve pages later:

> scendental role and allowing itself to be formed above it, as a kind of effluvium, a dream of appeasement? Isn't there always an element excluded from the system that assures the system's space of possibility? The transcendental has always been, strictly, a transcategorial, what could be received, formed, terminated in none of the categories intrinsic to the system. The system's vomit. And what if the sister, the brother/sister relation represented here the transcendental position, ex-position?[29]

First, we should note that the quasi-transcendental appears under the form of a question, not as a proposition or a claim. Derrida poses this question to Hegel's *Phenomenology* directly, under the figure of Antigone, who acts as our guide through this "abrupt passage" (and to whom we will return).[30] The question, however, reverberates throughout Hegel's system because of the way in which the system is organized: each part reflects the whole, a philosophical strategy of mastery that Derrida refers to as "envelopment."[31] Because of the totality that Hegel's system represents, moreover, it is a question posed to systems-thinking and to ideologies rooted in totality in general. This is the effect of the terms "always" in the above quotation: what is true for Hegel's system, the apotheosis of systems, would be true for systems as such, or for thinking organized in this way into systems.

Second, the reference to the quasi-transcendental as *transcategorial* refers ahead to a later passage, in which Derrida thinks through the transcategorial of the Hegelian *Aufhebung* in general, as repression. There he writes:

> In brief: can repression be thought according to the dialectic? Does the heterogeneity of all the counterforces of constriction (*Hemmung, Unterdrückung, Zwingen, Bezwingung, zuurückdrängen, Zurücksetzung*) always define a species of general negativity, forms of *Aufhebung*, conditions of the relief? Repression—what is imagined today, still in a very confused way, under this word—could occupy several places in regard to these re-(con)strictions: (1) within the series, the class, the genus, the gender, the type; (2) outside: no more as a case or a species, but as a completely other type; (3) outside in the inside, as a transcategorial or a transcendental of every possible re-(con)striction.[32]

The quasi-transcendental belongs to this last category, crossing boundaries and confusing categories because it is outside in the inside—excluded within any single category. In this passage, Derrida raises the possibility that *Aufhebung* takes different forms, as different conditions of relief (*relève*—the word Derrida, following Hyppolite, uses to translate *Aufhebung*). He identifies these different forms as, on the one hand, defining a general species and, on the other hand, making up a heterogeneity of all the counterforces of constriction. Here he poses the question: what is *Aufhebung*, such that it conditions the relief of contradiction; or, what is *Aufhebung* such that it is able to take all of these different forms?

The themes of pressure, torsion, impulse, constriction, restriction, and repression are all major themes in *Glas* as a whole; the term "*glas*" refers to the tolling sound made by a bell, as well as the glottal stop in the constriction of the throat.[33] "*Glas*" indicates the limit/passage of the glottis, the re(con)striction of the throat, or of the anus, or of the vagina, as well as the ambiguously fascinating and disturbing substances indicated by the limit/passage: milk, vomit, ejaculate.[34] In the '71–'72 lecture course which acts as the basis for *Glas* ("*La famille de Hegel*"), Derrida works from a more visual register, arguing that the impossible desire between the brother and the sister which should paralyze the system, interrupt the life of the concept, or "cut off its breath" instead occupies an invisible transcendental position, a "blind spot [*l'aveuglement*]—Hegel's love or desire—which organizes around it the entire visual field."[35] The glottal stop in *l'aveuglement* emphasizes the re(con)strictions at work, even within the lens of the eye, as the glottal stop in Hegel's name itself that opens *Glas* will call to mind the re(con)strictions that subtend absolute knowing.

Derrida here poses the question of the role that *Aufhebung* plays in each of these re-(con)strictions. Is negativity, the negativity on which the *Aufhebung* and thereby the dialectic relies, the same in each case? If not, is it irreducibly different in each of its operations, or does it make up a "species of general negativity"? Is there a general logic to these repressions, or do they indicate an operation that is in each case singular? What economy of difference is implied by the quasi-transcendental constriction? We get some indication of the kind of economy implied by the quasi-transcendental in the following passage: "Isn't there always an element excluded from the system that assures the system's space of possibility?"[36] Rather than indicating an economy of pure plenitude logically anterior to the restricted economy, the quasi-transcendental is somehow both produced by the system, and yet it makes that system possible. It is *both* the condition of the system *and* is conditioned by that same system: it is the condition of the system's possibility and impossibility. I will return to this issue of economy later in the chapter.

Last, there is the reference here to *role*: what if, Derrida asks, "the absolute indigestible, that which cannot be assimilated, played a fundamental role in the system, an abyssal role, rather, the abyss playing an almost tran-[cut] scendental role."[37] This passage introduces the complex question of the work of fiction in philosophy, and even more unusual, the work of theater in philosophy. Antigone is a fictional character, but more than that, she is a character in a work of drama, a role to be played; what then do we make of her performance in the *Phenomenology of Spirit*? What role is she playing there? And how ought we understand its operation, especially in a thinker like Hegel, who has demarcated distinct roles for philosophy and for what he calls merely representative or picture-thinking, such as that in aesthetics?

The idea of *Antigone* as a theater piece within a strictly philosophical work is particularly interesting, given that it introduces questions of mimesis and repetition, since plays are meant to be performed, copied with local variations, over and over again. This is probably not how Hegel understands his reference to Antigone, but this transcendental role cannot be entirely cleansed of the scent of sweat, pancake makeup, and powder on the bodies of those who have played the role. What would it mean to play a transcendental role? Not to be entirely transcendental, *but to play at being transcendental*, to step into that role, to copy it or mime it, such that the abyss could be flipped upside-down, into a dream or an effluvium? How precisely is an empirical translated into a transcendental, and what do we gain by understanding the contingent or the empirical as stepping into this transcendental as a role to be played, now by this, now by that? In other words, what do we gain by viewing the transcendental as *performative*?

Quasi-transcendental Cuts: Empirical and Transcendental

In *Glas*, Derrida interrogates the relationship between the transcendental and the empirical in the passages that suture the cut in the word "quasi-transcendental" in the passage quoted above. These suturing passages introduce the empirical women in Hegel's own life through his correspondence with or about them: Nanette Endel and the woman who was to become his wife, Marie von Tucher. A later cut in the left-hand column (in a book already cut in two, and sometimes more than that) appears this time between the "birds" and "dogs," the creatures against which the sister in the *Phenomenology* is to protect the brother through burial. The suture of this cut reproduces letters to or about Hegel's empirical sister, Christiane Hegel. This correspondence with or about Hegel's empirical "sisters" again highlights the constriction or the restriction of the empirical into the transcendental. In the lecture course, however, this work is done through the name "Antigonanette"—a name split in two, and then split again; a made-up name, but one that refers to multiple sisters, both real and fictional, both empirical and transcendental.

As for Nanette, to whom or what does this name refer? In the lecture course, Derrida writes:

> I'm not going to utter the proper name, as you might imagine. For example, I will not speak of Christiane. Christiane would be the sister of Hegel. Neither will I speak of Nanette. Nanette Endel would be a young woman who was a lodger in Hegel's family home. A remark from Bourgeois amazingly tells us that she "had inspired in Hegel a feeling bordering perhaps on love, but that the letters from Frankfurt to Nanette Endel reveal a feeling of sincere friendship" [the Bourgeois, occasionally amazing]. It will be necessary to see (if we can see anything coming from the side of the sister). Therefore I won't be interested here in [this] Nanette—I don't know of what this name is the diminutive, perhaps Christiane also, but this is far from certain; in any case it might have been. I am not interested in this Nana. Not to be vulgar—I can't be sure that you know this Nana: this is precisely the name of she who could be a sister.[38]

"Nanette" refers, then, both to Nanette Endel and perhaps to Christiane Hegel (as "Nanette" is a diminutive of Anne). Nanette also refers to Nana, as Derrida jokes—Nana being slang for my girl, my chick, my babydoll.[39] A current of desire runs beneath this—an incestuous desire for the sister that subtends the claim Hegel makes that recognition is only possible between the brother and the sister because there is no sexual desire between them. This desire must be repressed or disavowed in order for Hegel to pull off this particular *Aufhebung*, a negativity Derrida marks by means of the classic Freudian expression of repression: I will not speak of her, I will not be interested in her, I am not interested in her.[40] This "immense, impossible desire" slips from one "sister" to another—Nanette, Christiane, Nana, Antigone—but appears within the Hegelian system as a "powerful relation without desire," bringing into focus the question of the restriction of the empirical into the transcendental and the economies of difference marked by this restriction.[41]

As for Antigone, we already know her—the mad, impossible, tragic hero. But it is already more complicated than that: to which Antigone do we refer? Sophocles's Antigone? Hölderlin's? Hegel's? Are we referring to the eidetic sister of the *Phenomenology of Spirit*? Or the fictional, the theatrical, sister? Empirical or transcendental; necessary or contingent?

Leaving aside for the moment that Antigone is a character, not only of fiction but of drama, and therefore a role to be played, Antigone, the eidetic sister, has more than one brother. She has (at least) two brothers and (at least) one sister. Indeed, where is Ismene in this? And what of the circumstances of Antigone's own birth—her family's twisted, overlapping genealogy? Despite Hegel's eidetic treatment of her, Derrida writes, "Antigone's are not some parents among others."[42] Derrida concludes of Hegel that "the model he interrogates is perhaps not as empiric as might be imagined. It does not yet have the universal clarity he ascribes to it. It holds itself, like the name, between the two"—between the particular and the universal, between the empirical and the transcendental, like an orphan.[43] Certainly Hegel relies on Antigone in making the claim that, because the brother is the only source of recognition for the sister, her duty toward him is the highest, and he is therefore irreplaceable for her.[44] But, given Antigone's particular family history, how can we be sure to whom she refers as brother? Given that her father, Odysseus, is also her brother, and her brothers, Polyneices and Eteocles, are also her uncles, her speculative ethical commitments could be to any of these. Who then is irreplaceable in such a situation? By means of what constriction can we translate this empirical situation—or perhaps this singular situation—into an eidetic one?

At stake in the quasi-transcendental relation between the empirical and the transcendental is the meaning of constitutive exclusion itself: What differences make a difference, and why? How are some differences taken as necessary rather than contingent? What empirical differences are taken as transcendental, and how? How is sexual difference, for instance, in this case, taken to be definitive in determining citizenship, and how does it exclude Antigone from citizenship and render her unintelligible as a political actor? If the heart of the drama lies in Antigone taking Creon to task for denying that the city/state relies on the family, such that Creon can deny to the family its rights, what determines the particular relationship between the family and the city/state such that Creon is its leader rather than Antigone? In other words, how do we understand the constriction of empirical difference into transcendental difference?

As is indicated by the earlier suggestion of the transcendental as a *role*, these are contingent social and political conditions *playing* at transcendence. Why, for instance, is Antigone not next in line for the throne of Thebes, or her older sister? How are we even able to determine that Antigone is a woman, since she acts so manly, against her nature, as Ismene tells her, challenging the king as she does in public? Creon attests to her gender confusion.[45] Antigone's position is an empirical, contingent, social/political condition that has been translated into an eidetic one. Antigone herself differs and defers throughout the texts in which she appears: Is she woman? Is she man? Is she daughter, sister, lover, wife? Even as Antigone occupies an apparently eidetic position in Hegel's text, she slips away and becomes other than herself. Just as it is impossible to rid the transcendental role Antigone plays from its connection to all of the bodies that have voiced the character of Antigone, it is impossible to pin down this *figure* of Antigone as entirely one, unified and stable. The "empirical" sister (and "empirical" is itself already in question) and the "transcendental" sister necessarily contaminate each other; they are twin sisters sharing the same quasi-transcendentally doubled figure, whose borders shift and bend.

Quasi-transcendental would therefore mean that the distinction between the transcendental and the empirical cannot simply be assumed: while there may be a distinction, such a distinction is never absolute. Rather, it would mean that the transcendental is in some way conditioned by the empirical, or that which it conditions. The transcendental and the empirical would be mutually implicated, mutually contaminated and contaminating, and vulnerable to each other. This does not mean that they are indistinguishable. It does, however, mean that the transcendental would have to be viewed as *provisional*. It would mean that the transcendental would be a matter of *interpretation*, and that such an interpretation would need to be undertaken again and again. The quasi-transcendental contamination of the empirical and the transcendental does not settle these social and political conditions. But it does put them into *question*: meaning that they are a matter of questioning, or that the transcendental must be *questioned*, at every step, in order to discover who or what is playing the transcendental role this time. This would be a kind of endless task (unless the conditions change so absolutely as to end its necessity, which would itself be a matter of question or interpretation). It would also therefore be *historical*, as the particular contamination of transcendental and empirical indicated by the quasi-transcendental would moreover be different in different contexts, and never absolutely determinable.

The quasi-transcendental puts the transcendental into question, in that one must investigate the particular contamination of empirical and transcendental, or the particular transcendental performance, each time in each new context. If the quasi-transcendental is for that reason never fully determinable, never fully present or never fully knowable, then how is the empirical pressed into service for the speculative or squeezed into its transcendental role? What is the constriction or restriction of difference involved in such an operation? And what kind of negativity does constriction or restriction, or re(con)striction, imply? In other words, what kind of economy is sounded by the *glas*? Derrida suggests that a model for understanding this constriction is repression (although he remarks above that we understand this only in a very confused way). Christiane, Nanette, Nana, Antigone, "Antigonanette"—what economy of desire, what economy of difference, can, on the one hand, put into play such a rich slippage of one to the other, and, on the other hand, produce the closure of the dialectic at this moment, the successful sublation of two mutually opposed laws and two contradictory ethical acts? Moreover, given the lopsidedness of this contradiction due to the inequality between men and women, not only in the ancient world but also in the modern one, how exactly is this contradiction resolved? What happens to this difference, this fundamental inequality, once opposition and contradiction have been achieved? What is remaindered in this economy? What remains?

Derrida takes up this question in his examination of the economy of re(con)striction in *Glas* in his analysis of the relation between brother and sister in the *Phenomenology*. There, after the singular recognition between brother and sister, Derrida asks:

> What does Antigone do? If she does not die, she gets married. In any case, she remains, she continues to mount the family guard. After the departure of her brother toward "human law," "the sister becomes, or the wife remains, the *Vorstand* [president, directress, general] of the household and the guardian of the divine law." That, the sister becomes or the wife *remains* (*bleibt*). In this way, the two sexes overcome (*überwinden*) their natural essence (*natürliches Wesen*) and enter into their ethical signification (*sittlichen Bedeutung*), as diversities (*als Verschiedenheiten*) that the two differences (*Unterschiede*), which the ethical substance gives itself, share between them (*unter sich teilen*).[46]

Once the brother leaves the family, "the sister becomes, or the wife remains." A "remarkable phrase," as Derrida notes: what could account for the exchangeability of these positions?[47] How does a sister become? And moreover, how does a sister become a wife, especially as this was not Antigone's fate (might our eidetic sister falter a step and fail us here)? How did we begin from a position in which Hegel conceives of the sister as a unique and important role for women beyond either wife or mother, to the fundamental exchangeability of sister and wife? How do we make a sister, or a wife, or a mother? How do we squeeze out their differences such that they are the same, equally opposed to the men, the masculine, the universal, the state? How do we account for this? Under what economy?

While I keep insisting on the both/and character of constitutive exclusion, it is necessary to be more specific about the operation of the negativity and epistemology at work here. The quasi-transcendental character of constitutive exclusion gives us insight into the interrelation between ontology, epistemology, and politics, but it is difficult to see how it both secures and troubles the internal border that it draws. The trick is in the peculiar epistemology and negativity at work in constitutive exclusion. As I argued in Chapter 2, constitutive exclusion in the *Science of Logic* was effected through an epistemological "blind spot": the inclusion of a multiple negativity that the text relies upon but cannot recognize. This is a result of the temporality of constitutive exclusion: the particular re(con)striction of empirical differences into transcendental ones, the difference that makes a difference, is determined retroactively.

This retroactive character of constitutions is important for two reasons. First, it orients our attention to the past, toward analyzing past re(con)strictions of empirical and transcendental, and how they figure our political present. It orients us to a radical history of the present, or a genealogy—a method for which will be spelled out in Part Two. Second, it helps us to clarify the politics at work at the border between ontology and epistemology.

RETROACTIVE CONSTITUTION AND REMAINDER

In his essay "Declarations of Independence," Derrida argues that the Declaration of Independence has a "fabulous retroactivity" by which the United States and its people brought themselves into being through the signing of the Declaration of Independence.[48] The Declaration of Independence declares that "these United Colonies are, and of Right ought to be, Free and Independent States."[49] The signatories declare that they are "Representatives of the United States of America," and that they claim the right to declare the independence of the united colonies of America by the "Authority of the good People of these Colonies."[50] Derrida writes,

> But this people does not exist. They do *not* exist as an entity, it does *not* exist, *before* this declaration, not *as such*. If it gives birth to itself, as free and independent subject, as possible signer, this can hold only in the act of the signature. The signature invents the signer. The signer can only authorize him- or her-self to sign once he or she has come

> to the end [*parvenu au vout*], if one can say this of his or her own signature, in a sort of fabulous retroactivity . . . henceforth I have the right to sign, in truth I will already have had it since I was able to give it to myself. I will have given myself a name and an "ability" or a "power," understood in the sense of power- or ability-to-sign by delegation of signature. But this future perfect, the proper tense for this coup of right (as one would say coup of force), should not be declared, mentioned, taken into account. It's as though it didn't exist.[51]

Derrida argues here that though we act *as if* the signer predates the signature, or that there must exist a signer in order for there to be a signature, the signature in fact invents the signer through this "fabulous retroactivity." Every constitution is therefore a *reconstitution*, and every constitution is therefore retroactive, since it brings into being the very thing that it relies upon in order to establish its authority to act. The transcendental of the quasi-transcendental is therefore only retroactively established, and the constitution of constitutive exclusion is only brought into being retroactively. We act, however, as if this constitution actually possesses the power that it is given in retrospect. The retroactivity of the constitution is fabulous, therefore, in that it has a literary or a metaphorical structure, the structure of a fable.

Something similar is going on in *Glas*, in Antigone's passage from the sister to the "wife." Remember that Hegel writes there that "the sister becomes, or the wife remains, the manager of the house and the guardian of the divine law."[52] As a moment in the movement from diversity to opposition, the relationship between brother and sister represents the indifferent difference of diversity. This moment is both spiritual and natural, both determinate and indeterminate, as this immediate moment of history is determined, as Hegel claims, by the "natural" difference of sex. Spirit must free itself from nature, moving from the singular to the universal and from the natural to the ethical. The relationship between diversities develops into an opposition and then a contradiction, a progression that plays out in the greater *Logic* just as it does in this moment. The natural determination of sex develops into an opposition once the brother leaves the family, and "the sister becomes, or the wife remains" the guardian of the family. The brother becomes devoted to ethical action on behalf of the human law in the nation, and the sister then becomes devoted to ethical action on behalf of the divine law in the family. Their actions oppose each other as equally ethical and therefore as equally spiritual. Because of the immediacy of this moment—which still ties their ethical devotion to the natural determination of sex—this moment is to be overcome. It is not, however, overcome as partly masculine and partly feminine: as Derrida writes, "the opposition of noon and midnight resolves itself into noon."[53] The contradiction between man and woman and the laws that they both "represent" in this moment are resolved into abstract right in the Roman state, by laws no longer grounded in distinctions made by the contingency of nature. Derrida writes:

> The sexual difference is *overcome* when the brother departs, and when the other (sister and wife) remains. There is no more sexual difference *as natural difference*. . . . Once overcome, the sexual difference will have been only a natural diversity. The opposition between difference and qualitative diversity [*Verschiedenheit*] is a hinge of the greater Logic. Diversity is a moment of difference, an indifferent difference, an external difference, without opposition.[54]

Derrida's analysis of Hegel runs along two parallel vectors here. On the one hand, nothing accounts for the development of the sister into the wife; there is no need to account for this development since for Hegel there is no development, or if there is, it is merely a natural one, since it is simply the assumption of an already determined role rather than the self-conscious becoming that characterizes the life of the brother. The development of the sister into the wife (who remains) would be, as Hegel writes elsewhere, like that of the plant.[55] In any case, from the perspective of the nascent political body in this shape of history, the woman is produced as its remainder, the "eternal irony of the community," whose commitment to the law of singularity continually disrupts the community, but upon whom the community relies for raising sons to fight in war and for burying them. Woman is produced as that remainder whose identity is captured and ossified by her sex, as if there were no becoming between sister and wife, as if there were nothing to learning to be a wife, or a mother.[56]

On the other hand, Derrida explicitly links the relationship between brother and sister to the movement from diversity to opposition in the *Science of Logic*. Derrida implies here that Hegel can only render sexual difference as natural diversity retroactively. Thus the distinction between *determinate diversity* (diversity in its eidetic form) and *indeterminate diversity* (the contingent diversity which runs riot in nature) is decided *retroactively*, from the position of having already gone through diversity to opposition. Hegel does not give an account here of how indeterminate diversity becomes determinate, or in other words, how we are to constrict the empirical into the transcendental. Rather, the account runs the other way: opposition and contradiction retroactively condition the distinction between indeterminate and determinate diversity. That is, the re(con)striction of the radically contingent heterogeneity of natural diversity into determinate diversity on the way to opposition is determined *retroactively*. The economy of the quasi-transcendental, then, is *both* logically and temporally retroactive.

This retroactive temporality should not be unfamiliar; it is the same temporality put to use in Judith Butler's analysis of the performativity of gender. In her gloss on the argument of *Gender Trouble* in *The Psychic Life of Power*, Butler argues that "gender is performative, by which I mean that no gender is 'expressed' by actions, gestures, or speech, but that the performance of gender produces retroactively the illusion that there is an inner gender core. That is, the performance of gender retroactively produces the effect of some true or abiding feminine essence or disposition, so that one cannot use an expressive model for thinking about gender."[57] This retroactive production is the operation of the norm or the frame of gender under compulsory heterosexuality. In the case of a gender essence or sex, the relationship between cause and effect is determined retroactively: the essence produces the effect that was to be its cause. Similarly, the quasi-transcendental is produced retroactively: it does not point to either an essential gender as the basis of Antigone's exclusion from the public, nor does it point to a general economy of difference from which the restricted economy of the dialectic is drawn. Instead, these are cast retroactively. While Hegel identified the "natural determination of sex" as the root of the gendered distinction between the two laws of the ethical world, both sex and the distinction between determinate and indeterminate *Verschiedenheit* that it is meant to manage are in fact produced retroactively.

This retroactive operation of the quasi-transcendental also points to the economy at work in Hegel's account.[58] The operation here is not one of a general economy, or an empirical, contingent riot of indeterminate multiplicity that is then restricted into the speculative economy of the dialectic. The retroactive character of the operation of the quasi-transcendental indicates instead that this re(con)striction runs the other way. And, of course, the analysis of negativity in Chapter 2 implied as much. The distinction there between the supertext of negativity and the subtext of negativity in the *Science of Logic*, between determinate negation and multiple negativity, indicates an underground economy produced by the very restricted economy that it requires but cannot recognize. This underground economy of difference is remaindered from the restriction of the natural into the ethical, a restriction that retroactively cleanses the relation between sister and brother of desire. It retroactively posits nature, here in the form of the so-called natural distinction of sex, as the unproblematic ground out of which ethics and freedom emerge. It retroactively posits sex as the contingent, empirical ground out of which the necessary, transcendental matter of gender and the ethical laws to which gender is tied is wrung—while squeezing out almost all of the differences within and between Antigone and Polyneices, Antigone and Creon, Sophocles and Hegel, empirical sister and transcendental sister, sister and wife. This is not an operation of justification but of force, one that posits distinctions between empirical and transcendental, ontology and epistemology, and that represses the remaindered resources that put these distinctions into play.

The quasi-transcendental calls these very distinctions into question, and calls into question the border between them as a *political* operation. Derrida's turn to the figure of Antigonanette highlights Hegel's exclusion of women from the public sphere, from universality, and from conscious ethical action, which is rooted, so he claims, in the "natural determination" of sex. It also highlights the strangeness of the economy at work here: the valve between the ontological and the epistemological, between the transcendental and the empirical; between the multiplicity of empirical sisters and the multiplicity and mutability of Antigone herself, and the singularity of the eidetic, transcendental sister. The valve, the hinge, the *glas* both squeezes out all empirical differences within and between women into the speculative difference, or the role of sister, and squeezes all natural desire out of that role, despite the overlapping genealogy and excessive desires of "Antigonanette." Yet this valve paradoxically produces a lack of distinction between mother, sister, and wife: the sister becomes, and the wife remains—an essential, speculative incest.

While the dialectic progresses on the basis of the strict separation between determinate and indeterminate diversity, this distinction cannot be maintained. Or more accurately, it both is and is not maintained, as it is subtended by the constitutive exclusion of multiple negativity in the *Science of Logic*. Derrida's analysis of the retroactivity of constitutions shows that the quasi-transcendental is produced, just as the constitutively excluded is produced, and that moreover these are produced retroactively. The nondistinction between "sister" and "wife" (despite the fact that Antigone herself never becomes a wife) is produced retroactively from the perspective of sexual opposition. Sexual difference can thus be understood only *retroactively* as mere natural diversity. The retroactive operation of constitutive exclusion occurs within the epistemological blind spot produced in the fabulous expectation that we treat the cause as if it is the effect. The political stakes of the distinction between epistemology and ontology are located within that epistemological blind spot, as a contingent political choice is retroactively rendered necessary, as a matter of nature.

CONCLUSION

This diagnosis of the quasi-transcendental character of constitutive exclusion has several implications, resonating throughout different registers: ontological, political, and epistemological. First, on the ontological register, the complex economy of the quasi-transcendental indicates that there is not one form or kind of constitutive exclusion under which we may gather or through which we may understand all of the others. No exclusion is definitively primary or foundational. Rather, because bodies and systems are structured via multiple exclusions, constitutive exclusion functions multiply. Racial and gender differences are therefore not reducible to class differences; nor can class or gender be understood as an effect of race, nor disability an effect of gender, and so on. Thus, the multiple negativity produced by constitutive exclusion in the *Science of Logic* implies a broader plural ontology, an implication that will be explored in more detail in the Postscript to this book.

Second, on the political register, given that the body produced through constitutive exclusion is constituted multiply, it therefore requires multiple exclusions, or multiple figures against which it defines itself. Those who occupy the position of the "outside" are, however, also multiple. While a constitutively excluded figure may be rendered an absolute other in relation to one axis of exclusion, it may not along another axis. Insofar as she was a woman, Antigone was certainly produced as the excluded within the political body of ancient Thebes. However, since she was freeborn and a member of the royal family, she had an ability to appear within public or to make her claim before the king that others did not possess. For instance, she argues that she owes her duties to her brother because he was not a slave.[59] In this move, Antigone positions her brother as belonging to the polity by reinscribing the exclusion of slaves. Since constitutively excluded figures occupy multiple identity categories, those who contest their exclusion can play one aspect of their identities off others in order to effectively translate their claims from politically unintelligible to politically intelligible claims. In doing so, they can reconstitute the political body that had excluded them, but often by means of reinscribing other forms of exclusion. Moreover, the multiplicity of constitutive exclusions implies that no one is purely excluded, or purely outside. Constitutive exclusion thus forestalls the dehumanizing romanticization of oppression that treats suffering as ennobling, or reductively presumes that those who have suffered oppression or domination are incapable of inflicting it on others.

The retroactive temporality of constitutive exclusion also points us to the political operation erecting a border between ontology and epistemology. This is because the retroactive operation of constitutive exclusion depoliticizes the differences that it takes to be determinative. The critique of constitutive exclusion is thus necessarily a political critique, in that it seeks to re-politicize the exclusions by which we define ourselves. This critique operates in service of a future without constitutive exclusions; or if we find that some exclusions are necessary, a future in which such exclusions are determined democratically rather than by means of a disavowal that props up an epistemology of ignorance.

Third, on the epistemological register, this analysis of the quasi-transcendental indicates that the complex politics of these contestations are necessarily unintelligible to the body produced by constitutive exclusion, for whom the excluded figure will remain either invisible, or monstrous, threatening, and wild. The work of translation from unintelligible to intelligible political agency will indicate an epistemology at work in the structure of political agency, or a political epistemology.

Finally, the interrelation of these implications indicates a historical—or perhaps a genealogical—method. The retroactive temporality of the quasi-transcendental character of constitutive exclusion, as well as the provisionality or performativity of the transcendental it implies, orients us to the past in order to unearth the multiple exclusions that are sedimented in our political present. This gives the past to us as a kind of interminable task of translation and interpretation—a task to discover who we are, while taking seriously the limits to such knowledge, as well as a task to do justice to those upon whom we rely but who we cannot, by virtue of how we are constituted, see, hear, understand, or recognize. In other words, while the diagnosis of constitutive exclusion in Hegel and Derrida gets us a certain distance, it leaves us in need of a method by which to approach the limits of intelligible political agency. I turn to this method next, in Part Two.

PART TWO

Critique

4

Adorno's Negative Dialectics as Critical Method

Part Two of *Excluded Within* moves us from ontological-epistemological to more political-epistemological territory. We shift from conditions of possibility to conditions of contestation. The diagnosis of constitutive exclusion's operation at the border between ontology and epistemology emphasized its quasi-transcendental character, as both the condition of possibility and the condition of impossibility of the Hegelian system. The constitutive exclusion of multiple negativity establishes the distinction between the speculative and the empirical upon which Hegel's onto-logic depends. But since that multiple negativity also blurs the boundary between eidetic and empirical, it presents a challenge to it and also marks out more radical trajectories, beyond the orbit of the dialectic.

The operation of constitutive exclusion frequently condenses this multiple negativity into a singular figure—for instance, in the figure of Antigone. Rather than marking an alterity that is absolutely prior, the excluded figure is pressed into the role of the transcendental and is produced by the system of thought or political body it constitutes. However, the retroactive character of constitution renders that system or body insensible to that figure which acts as its internal limit, in that it cannot see, hear, or recognize that figure. Where the figure is recognized, it is rendered as absolutely external or prior to the constitution of the system or body its exclusion defines. It thus operates in an epistemological blind spot. In this way, these bodies and systems understand themselves to be what they are by necessity rather than by means of a contingent exclusion.

Moreover, the terms of intelligibility, recognition, and recognizability are drawn on the basis of constitutive exclusion. The constitutively excluded figure will therefore frequently appear (when and where as it does appear) as unintelligible, monstrous, wild, or mad. Constitutive exclusion thus poses a political-epistemological problem. Who or what is served by rendering some claims unintelligible as political claims, or some persons unintelligible as political agents? How do those who have been rendered politically unintelligible make their claims intelligible to the political body that has defined itself on the basis of that very unintelligibility? How do those who stand *outside within* the terms of political agency make the contestations of their exclusions heard? And how can those inside the terms of political agency work to hear and to understand claims they are constituted not to hear or understand?

So far, I have been operating in a largely deconstructive register. While deconstructive modes of analysis are potentially politically useful, I find that they have to be *put to use*; for this, I turn to the more materialist analysis of critical theory. We have already seen that constitutive exclusion operates by means of a retroactive temporality, one that depoliticizes and naturalizes the exclusions that constitute political bodies and systems of thought. And just as a multiplicity is constitutively excluded from Hegel's system, so multiple exclusions constitute our political bodies and systems of thought—as well as our selves, insofar as we are products of these political bodies and systems of thought. Our political bodies and our political agency are sedimented with these exclusions to which we are insensate. Since constitutive exclusion erases its own trail behind it, how are we to access those exclusions within us? How do we hear the contestation of exclusions from quarters rendered politically unintelligible from the outset? How do we read for the invisible? How do we listen for the inaudible?

In Part Two (this chapter and Chapter 5), I address these problems of (un)intelligibility and interpretation by turning to critical theory as a method. Critical theory, and especially the work of Theodor Adorno, is the best tool for this task because it teaches us to read for what is *not* here but is necessary for what *is* here; the immanent critical method teaches us to search what *is* for evidence of what *could be*. In Adorno, this means reading for traces of what he calls *nonidentity*, that element upon which all thinking relies, but which has been buried under the hegemonic modes of thought that both reflect and drive real social and political conditions. In a structure similar to that of constitutive exclusion, we find nonidentity not absolutely beyond hegemonic modes of thinking, but instead buried within them. In this sense, nonidentity marks a transcendence that emerges from within the field of immanence, or a *quasi-transcendence*. Constitutive exclusion has this quasi-transcendent character, as it marks the beyond within. Insofar as the constitutively excluded figure is ambiguously both inside and outside, the *quasi-transcendental* figure is also *quasi-transcendent*. That is, it is transcendent in that it exceeds the body that constitutes itself on the basis of its exclusion, and it exceeds the terms of recognition, intelligibility, and representation that are established on the basis of this exclusion. On the other hand, this remainder is immanent, in the sense that it remains within that body, though it goes unrecognized or unintelligible there. The constitutively excluded remaindered figure is *quasi-transcendent*, since the distinction between inside and outside—the distinction between the transcendent or absolutely beyond and the immanent or absolutely within—is both established by and troubled by constitutive exclusion as its limit. The *critique* of constitutive exclusion therefore grapples with how to *read for, listen to*, or *interpret* this quasi-transcendent element.

Like many other thinkers in the tradition of the Frankfurt School, Adorno takes up a version of hegemony or ideology in his work. Under his formulation, hegemony takes the form of the reification and totalization of what he calls "the administered society," on the one hand, and identitarian thinking or instrumental rationality, on the other. Rather than simplistically reading hegemony through the framework of base and superstructure, or the politico-economic sphere and its cultural reflections, Adorno holds thought and world in dialectical tension, each reflected in the other. Despite his infamous pessimism, there are moments of escape or of flight from this totality that occasionally flash up in his text: moments when the world reminds us that it is more than what we have taken it for, or more than the reflection of the utility to which it has been reduced. These are moments when thought indicates its freedom from its conditions or indicates that difference might be something more than a remainder to be either disciplined or destroyed. These flashes are indications of what Adorno calls the nonidentical, moments of quasi-transcendence.

Part Two thus acts as a kind of hinge between the more abstract or philosophical issues taken up in Part One, and the more concrete or political theoretical issues taken up in Part Three. It treats the epistemological register, here as political-epistemological, distinguishing and bringing together the more ontological register of the preceding chapters and the more political register of the chapters that follow. Like all working hinges, this one is split into two interlaced parts: the first one belonging more to the side of the philosophical, the second belonging more to the side of the empirical (though of course the distinction between these is more heuristic than actual). Chapter 4 treats the negative and dialectical qualities of the quasi-transcendent character of nonidentity and argues that the critique of constitutive exclusion ought to be approached via a similar negative dialectical method. Chapter 5 treats the material and historical character of nonidentity and argues that the critique of constitutive exclusion is marked by what Adorno would call the preponderance of the object: that our method of interpretation must stay close to empirical conditions rather than allow itself to be pulled toward the abstract or the merely ontological. And, building on the retroactive temporality spelled out in Chapter 3, I articulate a materialist historical, or a genealogical, method appropriate to the critique of constitutive exclusion.

In this chapter, then, I argue that constitutive exclusion has a quasi-transcendent character, and I investigate this through examining the quasi-transcendence of nonidentity in Adorno's thought. First, I define the specific significance of my usage of the term "quasi-transcendence," distinguishing it from the "quasi-transcendental" character of constitutive exclusion I explored in Chapter 3. I then argue that the quasi-transcendence of nonidentity is dialectical and negative. It is dialectical in that it is not absolutely beyond, but instead marks a transcendence that emerges from immanence. It is negative in terms of the method appropriate to it: Adorno gives us a negative double strategy of ideology critique or the critique of hegemony that is useful for understanding the critique of constitutive exclusion.

At stake in this turn to critical theory is ultimately our chance at theorizing constitutive exclusion without either pressing it to assimilate into terms that are already constituted by means of these exclusions, or unconsciously repeating the operation of constitutive exclusion as we go. The dual strategy I lay out here encourages multiple tactics of reading for nonidentity, the remainder, or the constitutively excluded figure, while at the same time forestalling the risk of determining the meaning of the claims that originate from that space in advance.

TRANSCENDENCE, THE TRANSCENDENTAL, AND THE KANTIAN "BLOCK"

Transcendence is usually taken to mean that which stands outside of or beyond being or knowledge. Transcendental, by contrast, usually indicates something that acts as a condition of possibility, whether or not it lies beyond being or knowledge. Under transcendental realism, for instance, some real existing thing acts as a cause, either ontologically or epistemologically or both, and it is in this sense *transcendental*. But it is also *transcendent* in that it lies beyond our ability to know or experience it. For example, for Kant, the forms of intuition (space and time) are transcendental, in that they act as the conditions of all experience, but they are not transcendent, as they also appear within our experience. On the other hand, the Kantian *noumena* or the thing-in-itself acts as the cause or the condition of all our experience and is therefore transcendental. However, since we can have no knowledge of the thing-in-itself, because it stands outside our experience, it is also transcendent. The *noumena* may be merely an idea, but Kant claims that it is a necessary one, even though we can have no certain knowledge of it.

Adorno refers to this limit on our knowledge as the Kantian "block," and it is a vitally important aspect of Adorno's own thought, which navigates between the Kantian block and the Hegelian dialectic. For Adorno, this limit to knowledge indicates that thought is always thought *about* something: thinking points to or aims at objects, but the concepts we employ in thinking cannot fully capture those objects. To put it another way, objects do not go into concepts without a remainder. Adorno shows that instead of treating this block negatively as a kind of check on our knowledge, Kant hypostasizes the "block" and therefore falls prey to an incipient idealism.[1] Adorno argues that this ontologization of the Kantian "block," or this tendency to treat it as abstract and necessary rather than as the contingent product of historical relations, occurs in part because the "block" was unaccompanied by the dialectical understanding of the relation between the thinking subject and the objects of knowledge which Hegel was to provide.

Adorno argues that Hegel came closest to expressing in thought what he viewed as the contradictory nature of thinking under current hegemonic conditions, both in the absorption of the thinker in the object of thought and in the ability of thought to transcend its conditions. Hegel's mistake, according to Adorno, was to bring this dialectical movement to rest in an ultimate identity between thought and thing, hypostasizing or ontologizing the sliver of transcendence in the dialectic between subject and object. Hegel brought that movement to rest in a larger unity, in Spirit or in the Concept, which Adorno takes to be the subject raised to ontology. In this respect, Hegel violated that Kantian "block."

If thinking is always thinking about something, then that something can never be fully recuperated in thought. Thought thus leaves behind a remainder and, contra Hegel, cannot be absolutely adequate to the thought thing.

Adorno's name for the remainder, that which resists appropriation by thought, is *nonidentity*. Adorno calls it nonidentity in order to mark it as that difference which escapes identification with thought or with the thinking subject. As a remainder, nonidentity is a limit-concept, neither wholly conceptual nor a-conceptual. Nonidentity is thus both transcendent and immanent: *transcendent* in the sense that it exceeds both the concept and given conditions, and *immanent* in the sense that it is found within the concept and given conditions.

In Chapter 3 I argued that constitutive exclusion has a *quasi-transcendental* character; here I argue that it has a *quasi-transcendent* character. Attention to the first calls into question the relation between epistemology and ontology, and in particular the privileging of ontology over epistemology. The retroactive character of constitutive exclusion means that exclusions that are internal and a matter of choice (or a matter of force) are taken to be natural, absolutely prior or absolutely outside: a matter of ontology, not of politics. This tendency to privilege the ontological thus works against any method for the critique of constitutive exclusion. Adorno's investigation of nonidentity as quasi-transcendent emphasizes the concrete element in thinking, and so offers us both a method of reading for or listening to the constitutively excluded figure and a method of resistance to determining what comes from that figure in advance: or in other words, a method of resisting the demand to assimilate to already established parameters of intelligibility. Adorno's insistence upon the negative and the dialectical character of nonidentity are central to that method. They remind us that at any given moment, things could have been otherwise. In order for things to ever be otherwise, we must be vigilant against our own tendencies to hypostasize and to lay down further exclusions as we make our way through the critique of constitutive exclusion.

NONIDENTITY AS DIALECTICAL

For Adorno, the term "nonidentity" (or, sometimes, "nonconceptuality") indicates that which exceeds thought or resists appropriation by thought. But what is it exactly? Is it a limit-concept, a constantly receding horizon of thought? Is it an ontological principle, which acts as a cause of thinking but which can never itself be known? If nonidentity exceeds all thought and yet gives rise to it, one could easily be led to read Adorno as a transcendental realist—taking the position that nonidentity is the name for that real existing principle that acts as our condition of possibility but is entirely beyond us and which we can never know. This principle could just as well be brute nature or God, but the result is the same: nonidentity is absolutely beyond us, beyond our capacity to know, and yet acts as a cause of either our existence or our knowledge or both.

Against Transcendental Realism

Andrew Buchwalter presents the transcendental realist interpretation of Adorno in "Hegel, Adorno, and the Concept of Transcendent Critique."[2] There he argues that the transcendent element in Adorno's thought is messianic. That messianic element cannot be found in existing conditions themselves, he argues, since these immanent conditions have been so totally disfigured by ideology and identitarian thinking that they are completely beyond redemption. Instead, Buchwalter argues that any source of possible redemption, any source of hope for something better, is to be found in "a light that *shines through* the faults and fissures of the existing domain, not one generated by that domain itself. The messianic light for Adorno is not of this world."[3] Because this redemptive light shines through the cracks in existing conditions, rather than in the conditions themselves, Buchwalter concludes that "the core of Adorno's critical theory is messianic, not materialistic."[4]

If the transcendent element in Adorno's thought is not to be found in existing conditions, then how are we able to see this light from beyond shining through the fissures of the administered world? The transcendental realist position tends to be that we gain access to this messianic element through some kind of immediate experience; this experience is sometimes an experience of "untrammeled nature," but it is most usually an aesthetic experience or an experience with a work of art.[5] Such an aesthetic experience would be characterized by "the mimetic depiction of the realm of natural beauty—a harmonious realm reconciled or 'identical' with itself."[6] Artistic representations, especially those depicting natural beauty, are accorded this privilege because of their nondiscursive nature. Because the work of art gives us access to a realm beyond "human artifice"—beyond language and concepts—it presents to us a picture of a fully reconciled world that could escape the domination of concepts.

Gordon Finlayson co-signs the transcendental realist interpretation, arguing that "according to Adorno, only certain uninterpreted aesthetic experiences that are in principle not recuperable by concepts fall under the description of the nonidentical or ineffable."[7] Finlayson treats the nonidentical as ineffable and claims that our route to it is via the immediacy of "uninterpreted" aesthetic experience. In these moments of aesthetic experience, we get a sense of the object's relation to itself, independent of us as thinking, identifying subjects. This experience is the messianic, utopic, transcendent element in Adorno's thought. Buchwalter describes it as "a noumenal order which is 'beyond the mechanism of identification,' which 'lies buried beneath the universal.'"[8] On the transcendental realist reading, then, the transcendent element in Adorno's thought is a principle that stands beyond or outside experience or knowledge, since these are totalized and totally corrupted by ideology, identitarianism, or instrumental rationality. This unknowable messianic principle is, however, perceivable via nondiscursive means, especially in aesthetic depictions of nature, in which we get a sense of the object's noumenal self-relation, independent from us as subjects. Finally, that transcendent element is the real source of truth, hope for anything beyond our current ideological conditions.

The transcendental realist interpretation of Adorno misses the mark primarily because it shows insufficient appreciation for the role of the dialectic in Adorno's thought. This leads to a simple opposition between nonidentity and the concept. The transcendental realist interpretation simply opposes immanence and transcendence, the "outside" from the "inside" of a totality defined by instrumental reasoning or identity thinking.[9] It treats nonidentity as identifiable with the object, and especially with nature, and argues that the privileged mode of accessing the nonidentical realm of the object is through aesthetic experience. Instead, the dialectic between subject and object is much more complex than a simple opposition between them. Because of their dialectical relationship, nonidentity can be found in the concept just as well as in the object, or in the tension between the concept and current conditions, as in what Adorno calls the "emphatic concepts" of freedom or in metaphysical experience. So, though it is on the side of the concrete, nonidentity is not simply identifiable with the object. Finally, the lack of appreciation for the dialectic in the transcendental realist interpretation leads to a too-simplistic understanding of materialism in Adorno, one that is entirely too ontological. Whereas Buchwalter argues that nonidentity is messianic, not materialist, there is no reason that it cannot be both.

One of the most apparent problems with the transcendental realist position is that it sets up a simple opposition between concepts and experience, between a discursive realm that is totally bankrupt and a nondiscursive realm that is purely utopic. Rather than merely opposed, these two sides should be understood as mediated by each other, in dialectical tension. Their mediation would indicate that concepts play a role in aesthetic experience and, either despite or because of the fact that concepts always indicate their own debt to the nonconceptual, that redemption can come to us through concepts. While some sense of the transcendent must be maintained in Adorno's thought—since to accede to immanence would be simply to accede to given conditions—the transcendent cannot be merely opposed to the immanent in this way. If, as Adorno argues, the task of philosophy is to say the unsayable, this can only be done through language.[10] Similarly, the promise of the nonconceptual is already contained in the concept. Thus, there is a deeper dialectic between nonidentity, or the nonconceptual, and the concept. This also indicates the character of the Adornian negative dialectic, which, rather than a Hegelian affirmative dialectic, operates according to the preponderance of the object: "To change this direction of conceptuality, to give it a turn toward nonidentity, is the hinge of negative dialectics."[11]

As I noted in the introduction to this chapter, Hegel was for Adorno the philosopher who came closest to expressing in his thought what Adorno claims is the contradictory nature of things under hegemony.[12] Hegel's dialectical thinking is thus an expression of the dialectic that arises within thought, within the world, and in the confrontation of thought with its objects. Adorno writes in the introduction to *Negative Dialectics*, "The name of dialectics says no more than that objects do not go into their concepts without leaving a remainder, that they come to contradict the traditional norm of adequacy."[13] The dialectic expresses the fact that concepts are not wholly adequate to their objects, or that objects cannot be wholly appropriated by concepts. It expresses the idea that the concept always contains some moment of the nonconceptual within it, even if only negatively, in the form of a promise. Likewise, the nonconceptual contains some moment of the conceptual within it. Some element of nonidentity always escapes the concept, and dialectics allows for its expression.

At least, this is what dialectics should do. However, Adorno argues that the Hegelian dialectic fails to live up to what Hegel himself identifies as the task of dialectical thinking. Adorno critiques the Hegelian dialectic as an idealist dialectic. Though Hegel claims to submit his thinking to the object, to the contradictoriness of things as they are under current conditions, Adorno argues that he subordinates the movement of the dialectic to an idealist outcome.[14] Hegel thus uses nonidentity for the sake of absolute identity.[15] The nonidentical gives rise to the contradiction that is the life-blood of the dialectic and is what the dialectic is meant to express. Yet even as Hegel gestures toward the nonidentical in taking up the dialectic, he puts the dialectic in service to the end of absolute identity in a totalized system. The difference between these two approaches, one oriented toward identity and the other toward nonidentity, is the difference between a *positive or affirmative* dialectic and a *negative* one.

The absolute identity that Hegel ultimately forces is the identity of the world with the transcendent subject, raised to concept or spirit. It identity between the thinker and the thought thing, *forced* by the thinker. Adorno argues that in Hegel the dialectic between subject and object, like all dialectical moments in Hegel's thought, is ultimately resolved in the positing of their identity in a totalized system. The effect of this resolution is to side with the subject and to claim that everything objective or nonidentical is fully appropriable by the subject or the concept. Adorno writes, "mind's claim to independence announces its claim to domination. Once radically separated from the object, subject reduces the object to itself; subject swallows object, *forgetting how much it is object itself*."[16] What was dialectical between subject and object is covered over, forgotten, remaindered, or disavowed. What allowed for the logic of contradiction, that quasi-transcendent sliver between thought and the object of thought—nonidentity—is swallowed up. The logic at work here is as much the logic of the exchange principle or the commodity fetish as it is the Hegelian dialectic. For Adorno, the exchange principle already indicates the fungibility of objects, the stripping of their singularity or their internal multiplicity so as to make them absolutely exchangeable. This affirmative dialectic therefore takes place in a knot of forces, both theoretical and practical. In a logic perhaps first described by Marx in "On the Jewish Question," the more abstract transcendental subjects are elevated, the more actual concrete human beings are dominated.[17] Adorno ultimately describes identity-thinking as the rationality that leads to Auschwitz: the equivalence of human beings is enforced, and whatever deviates from that basic equivalence must be destroyed.

Instead, a negative dialectic, a dialectic of the preponderance of the object rather than the subject, would not force an identity between thought and the object of thought, nor coerce the reconciliation between them. It would recognize that, as Adorno writes, the subject depends upon the object more and differently than the object depends upon the subject. It would attend to contradictoriness and negativity without forcing a reconciliation or a resolution, without bringing the movement of thought to a halt: "It lies in the definition of negative dialectics that it will not come to rest in itself, as if it were total. This is its form of hope."[18] Negative dialectics is thus a form of listening.

To claim that nonidentity is some kind of absolute origin, as the transcendental realist interpretation of Adorno does—and to imply thereby that concept and object are simply opposed—is another way of bringing this movement of thought to a rest. While the preponderance of the object means attending to the inadequation between concept and object, it does not mean an absolute separation between the two. We do not think otherwise than through concepts. But it is precisely because of the mediation of concept and object that the quasi-transcendent element, nonidentity, can come to us. This is why Adorno insists on the *negativity* of the negative dialectic.

Metaphysical Experience

Rather than relying on aesthetic experience as a path to the transcendent, I want to offer briefly, as an alternative, an account of what Adorno calls *metaphysical experience*. If it is the case that the nonconceptual can be indicated through concepts, then what Adorno describes as metaphysical experience is pertinent here.[19] In his 1965 lecture course on Aristotle's metaphysics, Adorno describes what he sees as a paradox facing thought: "this nonconceptual element, this nonprinciple, which nevertheless is constitutive of, and inherent in, all philosophy, cannot appear within that realm—which, heaven knows, can only operate with concepts—except in the form of a concept."[20] Throughout this lecture course, Adorno gives an account of how Aristotle raised the nonconceptual material element that gives rise to thinking into the concept of *hyle*, or matter. In these lectures, Adorno gives a sort of genealogy of metaphysics as it develops into identitarian thinking or ideology, so it would seem that metaphysics is simply a tool of ideology for him. Despite this, Adorno insists that metaphysics possesses the power to think beyond itself and beyond ideology:

> Philosophy has the curious characteristic that, although itself entrapped, locked inside the curious glasshouse of our constitution and our language, it is nevertheless able constantly to think beyond

> itself and its limits, to think itself through the walls of its glasshouse. And this thinking beyond itself, into openness—that, precisely, is metaphysics.[21]

Here it becomes clear that the quasi-transcendent element in Adorno's thought is not the immediacy of an aesthetic experience, or a "transcendence of the given." Rather than positing a transcendent beyond language and thought, Adorno locates the transcendent element precisely within language and thought—a discursive, conceptual self-transcendence. The very force responsible for the destruction of the object is responsible for its redemption: "metaphysics can thus be defined as the exertion of thought to save what it at the same time destroys."[22]

If the quasi-transcendent element in Adorno's thought can be indicated immanently, through thought itself, despite the damage that thought has done to the world *and* itself, then how is this done? And what assurances are there that one is not destroying what one is attempting to save? The redemption of the nonconceptual through concepts is not at all guaranteed: metaphysical experience lacks all of the necessity that already defines the totally administered society. However, Adorno indicates that insofar as this quasi-transcendent element is reachable, it will paradoxically be by means of immanence, through the method of *critique and rescue*:

> On the one hand metaphysics is always, if you will, rationalistic as a critique of a conception of true, essential being-in-itself which does not justify itself before reason; but, on the other, it is always also an attempt to rescue something which the philosopher's genius feels to be fading and vanishing. There is in fact no metaphysics, or very little, which is not an attempt to save—and to save by means of concepts—what appeared at the time to be threatened precisely by concepts, and was in the process of being disintegrated, or corroded.[23]

The insistence on dialectic is important to our understanding of the quasi-transcendent element in Adorno's thought because it indicates that it is not absolutely ineffable, beyond, or absolutely other. If it were, then our relation to it would be difficult to understand: Could we ever approach or understand an ineffable beyond? Would we even need to? If the transcendent element in Adorno were absolutely other then it would seem to be no help in understanding constitutive exclusion—either in understanding the relation between the "inside" and the "outside," or the "included" and the "excluded," or in understanding how a critical stance on the immanent field of hegemony is possible. Instead, the insistence on dialectic in Adorno indicates the emergence of transcendence from within immanence, the promise of something more and other within the totality and reification of the administered world.

This dialectical approach takes the transcendent element in Adorno's thought as *quasi-transcendent*, in that it is both within and without, a transcendence that emerges from within, and yet it is disparaged, denied, or disavowed. The dialectical aspect of nonidentity is therefore useful to understanding constitutive exclusion as it helps us to better understand how what is remaindered or what is constitutively excluded lies both within and without, or is a transcendence from within immanence. That is, if we can hear claims that come to us from that space, the ability to hear the contestation of constitutive exclusion and to reconstitute politics and political agency in light of that contestation is directly tied to Adorno's critique of identitarian thinking. It requires resisting the domination and appropriation of the object, or resisting determining the meaning of the message in advance. It requires insisting on the *negativity* of negative dialectics. In other words, it requires listening.

NONIDENTITY AS NEGATIVE

As we have seen, Adorno insists on the negativity of nonidentity. This insistence constitutes a refusal to determine in advance what redemption—the uncoerced reconciliation between subject and object—will look like. Adorno's refusal of positivity—his resistance to the demand to spell out what will result from his critique—is due to his position that our thinking is thoroughly determined by current ideological or hegemonic conditions.

Adorno goes so far as to say that "the chances are that every citizen of the wrong world would find the right one unbearable; he would be too impaired for it."[24] As the world becomes further and further totalized, it becomes more and more difficult to push thought against itself and toward the nonconceptual. This leads to a problem, however, pointed out by critics such as Habermas: in totalizing reason as identitarian, Adorno undermines his own ability to critique reason.[25] That is, if Adorno is employing reason to critique reason, and if reason is wholly corrupted by instrumental reason or identity thinking, then from what position can he launch this critique? How can Adorno be sure that, in making a rational critique of reason, he is not perpetuating the very same identitarian thinking he is trying to undermine? The stakes in this question for my analysis of constitutive exclusion are very high: if what appears as intelligible to us has been so determined by the terms set out by means of constitutive exclusion, then how can we see, hear, or recognize anything beyond or outside of those terms, from within them?

This problem is laid out very effectively by Michael Theunissen, who describes the various aspects of negativity in Adorno and provides some historical perspective on the negative theories on which Adorno draws. Theunissen argues rightly that Adorno avoids Hegelian determinate negation, but then he goes on to argue that Adorno's attempt at a negative dialectic fails, as it ends up in the "remarkably uncritical repetition of the trope of the *trosas iasetai*, the saying that the wound can be healed by what first dealt it."[26] While Theunissen is correct to observe that Adorno does not argue from some standpoint beyond the reason he critiques, this is only a problem if we take reason to be as thoroughly corrupted as he does. As we have already seen, positing nonidentity as the ineffable beyond of a thoroughly corrupt reason overlooks Adorno's commitment to dialectics.

While Adorno's infamous pessimism—what Robyn Marasco calls his commitment to despair—leaves him open to that reading, I contend that this is largely a polemical strategy, since the work of critiquing identity-thinking is as much practical as it is theoretical, and there can be no guarantees that it will work.[27] However, it is that very commitment to negativity that preserves the possibility that things could be otherwise and that reason can be other than it is. While the world may be a "mansion of dogshit," there is no other world to which we may appeal.[28] It is that very contradictory, antagonistic nature of the world that paradoxically holds out promise for our survival as well as portending our destruction. It means that the world is already more and other than it is, despite its insistence otherwise. The negativity of nonidentity, of the transcendent element in Adorno's thought, is its source of hope.

The purpose of negative dialectics is the critique of reification; as ideology critique, negative dialectics aims to reveal the dynamism in the apparently fixed and static object, and this can be done only through releasing the becoming in the reified object. This is possible only because reified objects are negative, in the sense that they are more than, or other than, what they claim to be. Negative dialectics is therefore an immanent critique, undertaken for the sake of a speculative moment. That speculative moment in Adorno's thought is also negative, in the sense that it is not determined in advance, and must be achieved practically as much as theoretically. The speculative moment in Adorno's thought is taken from Hegel; however, Adorno argues that in Hegel the speculative moment comes about as a result of coercion or force: in Hegel, resolution is produced through domination.

This is the key political stake in the difference between the negative and the affirmative dialectic: because Adorno understands dialectics as "the ontology of the wrong state of things," he sees the resolution of dialectics into the Hegelian system as the result of force and domination and the elimination of the very element that gave rise to dialectics in the first place.[29] It is the fever dream of hegemony, a dream that took concrete shape in the concentration camps. Adorno critiques the Hegelian speculative moment in order to rescue it, but in a negative sense; his method must therefore be negative as well.

Adorno's Negative Double Strategy

Adorno's method of critique is characterized by a kind of double strategy. On the one hand, he treats identity thinking as if it is as absolute as it claims to be, taking absoluteness or totality to its own limits and using its own force to push it beyond or against itself, to the determinate negation of its very totality. On the other hand, Adorno highlights the cracks and fissures of identity thinking, refusing hegemony's claims to adequation and totality by gesturing toward the material grounds on which it relies. This double strategy takes place on an epistemological register, taking identity thinking's claim to totality or absoluteness as both true and untrue. Thus, on the one hand, Adorno takes identity thinking as *true*, both in the sense that it is compulsory and in the sense that the absolute is the mark within metaphysics of the hope for something more than what merely is. On the other hand, he takes identity thinking as *untrue*, since it has not yet succeeded in achieving totality by eliminating nonidentity and is constructed on the basis of the disavowal of concreteness, actual human beings, or real social processes.

Both of these strategies are negative. The first strategy pushes toward a determinate negation of totality, and the second strategy shows the negativity within the very claim to totality. Both strategies are also negative in that they refuse to identify an outcome or to determine the result in advance. In other words, both strategies refuse a certain demand for positivity, or reject the commonsensical ideological claim that if you have no alternative to offer, then you have no right to critique. To determine the outcome in advance would be merely an extrapolation of current forms of thought, which are far too damaged by instrumental rationality to trust that any outcome would be free of it. Adorno describes the first strategy in the following passage:

> Dialectics is obliged to make a final move: being at once the impression and the critique of the universal delusive context, it must now turn even against itself. The critique of every self-absolutizing particular is a critique of the shadow which absoluteness casts upon the critique; it is a critique of the fact that critique itself, contrary to its own tendency, must remain in the medium of the concept. It destroys the claim of identity by testing and honoring it; therefore, it can reach no farther than that claim. The claim is a magic circle

> that stamps critique with the appearance of absolute knowledge. It is up to the self-reflection of critique to extinguish that claim, to extinguish it in the very negation of negation that will not become a positing [*eben darin Negation der Negation, welche nicht in Position übergeht*].[30]

The negation of negation to which Adorno refers is a determinate negation; however, in this context, it does not yield positivity as it did for Hegel, but only further negativity: the destruction of the very claim to absolute knowledge in its entirety. This strategy is similar to what I described above as metaphysical experience. Because of the dialectical nature of thought, we can push thought against itself, reaching the nonconceptual by means of concepts: "The cognitive utopia would be to use concepts to unseal the nonconceptual with concepts, without making it their equal."[31] This utopic moment lies beyond the system, and yet any closed system contains the kernel of this utopic speculative moment within it. This speculative moment is negative and yet transcendent. It is not, however, an abstract or "sacrosanct" transcendence, such as that envisioned in the transcendental realist interpretation, but rather a transcendence of the particular or the concrete.[32] Insistence on the negativity of our approach to the nonidentical preserves the contingency of the outcome of critique. There can be no guarantee of success, because the only real guarantee is force. Our critique must therefore also be negative—an insistence on positivity does not lead to hearing or understanding the claims from those who contest their position as constitutively excluded but rather to forcing those claims into a language already intelligible to us: assimilation rather than reconstitution.

This speculative moment that Adorno pushes for is also found in the repressed sources of thought, thus linking it to the other strategy. Simon Jarvis describes it as an "attempt to recollect, instead of suppress, what [thought] depends on. . . . They are determinate negations of these prohibitions which make visible the experience implicitly sedimented in them."[33] Deborah Cook associates this speculative moment in Adorno with what he calls emphatic concepts, such as the concept of freedom. In the case of freedom, Adorno writes, "Freedom is only to be grasped in determinate negation, in accordance with the concrete shape of unfreedom."[34] This sense of freedom is therefore indicated most effectively by the experience of its lack. Cook argues that determinate negation, the negativity of the speculative moment, reveals only further negativity: "Suffice it to say that to negate the negative reveals that what exists is not yet what it ought to be, and what ought to be does not yet exist."[35]

The second strategy seeks to undermine identity-thinking by means of gesturing to its cracks and fissures, pointing out that it never achieves the totality it claims to have achieved. This would also be a means of gesturing negatively to the sources of thought, without attempting to appropriate them in advance, or to claim that what gives rise to thought is fully identifiable with thought itself. In several places, Adorno refers to nonidentity as having been buried, repressed, suppressed. He suggests that the work of critique is to seek out those elements that have not been "pre-digested" by identity thinking: we must direct critique toward these elements, if we are still sensitive to them. He marks these fragments by reference to the ambiguous knowledge children possess about, for instance, the significance of the dog-catcher's van or the sickly sweet smell of the abbatoir—a sense that something is deeply wrong.[36] While children may possess these fragments of knowledge in a form that is more than merely negative, adults tend to experience them only negatively. This openness to negativity is partly what is meant by metaphysical experience.[37]

This second strategy is perhaps more familiar, as it points to the failures of totality, all of the places identity-thinking has failed to colonize or to fully determine. This strategy points more emphatically to the resistances within matter and time, since hegemony must work through matter, and that working-through takes time. This side of the dual strategy is thus very close to the analysis of norms that Butler gives in her work: while iterability is built into the operation of the norm, the norm may fail, or the frame may break, precisely because it must take time. Frequently, however, simply pointing out hegemony's failures is insufficient to halting its power and may even risk colonizing spaces it had so far overlooked.

The double strategy is important for the critique of constitutive exclusion, precisely because constitutive exclusion is marked by an epistemic ambivalence, and the double strategy indicates that multiple tactics, multiple tools, and the use of hegemony's force against itself, are all useful in the work of critique.

What does this mean for our understanding of the quasi-transcendent element in Adorno's thought, and what are its implications for constitutive exclusion? First, the transcendent element is not a purely ineffable beyond, identified with the nondiscursive, immediate givenness of objects, natural or otherwise. Instead, nonidentity, that quasi-transcendent element, is marked by what Adorno calls the preponderance of the object. It is on the side of the material rather than the ideal; on the side of the concrete rather than the side of the ontological. It can be approached from the side of the subject, but only dialectically. Thus, it can be found in either the subject or the object, or in the persistent fissures between them. The variety of locations from which the quasi-transcendent can emerge within the immanent field of hegemony makes room for multiple strategies of interpretation; the dual strategy of critique is thus an appropriate method for interpreting, reading for, or listening for constitutive exclusion. Insisting on the negativity in this method is important for forestalling the coercion or assimilation of what has been constitutively excluded and thus failing to actually hear the claims that come from that quarter. It is also vital for forestalling further exclusions in any reconstitution that would be adequate as a response to constitutive exclusion while embracing contingency, and with it, failure.

Though I am arguing here that we can approach the quasi-transcendent element in Adorno's thought by means of thought itself, this element is not entirely conceptual or abstract. The quasi-transcendent element—the nonidentical—occurs both as the resistance of the object to the concept and matter to form and as the subject's resistance to current conditions in its ability to think about them. This element is approachable from both sides of the subject, so to speak—in its ability to raise itself ever so slightly above its conditions through thinking, and its ability to be reminded of and to express the alterity, finitude, and corporeality of human beings through suffering. The fragments of nonidentity, those trace transcendent elements, are therefore *concrete* rather than abstract.

That concreteness has its index first in the preponderance of the object, but it is not limited to the object alone, since the dialectic between object and subject makes the distinction between them always a particular and historical one. This shows that the quasi-transcendent element, though it may perhaps be messianic, is nevertheless also material. We can see the materialism of nonidentity when Adorno defines philosophy as the task to give expression to suffering, or when he makes reference to the nonidentical as what "concepts suppress, disparage, and discard."[38] We will find the resources for critique and the hope for redemption in what has been thrown away, degraded, abjected—in what has been remaindered. To work through what has been destroyed is the "labor of the negative" and would give the ambiguous concept of utopia in Adorno "the color of the concrete."[39]

This double strategy thus marks the double strategy of this entire project: we can approach constitutive exclusion both in reading philosophy and in reading the world. Both require a similar method of interpretation, and both are indexed by reference to the concrete rather than the ontological, the material rather than the ideal, the unintelligible rather than the intelligible. The "preponderance of the object" thus requires that we stay close to concrete conditions and exercise an epistemological humility in our methods.

CONCLUSION

The quasi-transcendent element in Adorno's thought helps us better to understand how a channel is opened between what is constitutively excluded and the immanent space defined in and through that exclusion. If what is constitutively excluded is absolutely unintelligible to the space "inside," then it seems impossible to be able to hear any claims of contestation of constitutive exclusion from within the space drawn by it. However, as the Montgomery bus boycott illustrates (as we shall see in Part Three), there must be some way to account for the reconstitution that occurred there, as a result of the "successful" contestation of exclusion. The dialectical interdependency of the ("immanent") concept and the ("transcendent") nonconceptual makes this possible.

The commitment to negativity in the quasi-transcendent element in Adorno's thought is a response to the affirmative and appropriative character of thinking, and a recognition of how what is intelligible to us is already formed in advance by hegemonic political conditions. The negativity of quasi-transcendence in Adorno is important to the critique of constitutive exclusion because it indicates that despite the fact that there is no other world and no other reason to which we may appeal, it is still possible to push our thinking against itself and to reach the promises contained in but never delivered by that thinking. The analysis of nonidentity teaches us that our method must be negative in order to forestall the impulses toward appropriating or defining what we hear in advance, according to what we already understand, according to what is already intelligible to us.

In Chapter 5, I will treat the material and historical character of the quasi-transcendent element in Adorno's thought. While the method of critique has so far been largely about the interpretative approach, the turn to the materiality and historicity of critique points that approach in the direction of the present past. While the critique of constitutive exclusion is characterized by this negative dialectical approach, the retroactive character of constitutions indicates that our political present is sedimented with a history of these exclusions. The materialist historical orientation of critical theory is therefore useful in unearthing the exclusions that have made us who we are and in our turn toward the concrete contestations of constitutive exclusion. These unearthed exclusions mark shards of radical potential buried within our polities and our political agency—traces of "alternate legality," as Butler said of Antigone. Here, we find traces of alternate political agency that can subvert and reconstitute our current political condition, if we can find a way to listen to them.

5

Materialist History and Method

In Chapter 4, I took up the dialectical and negative character of the quasi-transcendent element in Adorno's thought; in this chapter I turn toward its materialist and historical character. This side of the hinge pulls together the ontological-epistemological emphasis of Part One and the political emphasis of Part Three. It fleshes out a method of interpretation appropriate to the political-epistemological problems posed by constitutive exclusion. How can those who are excluded within contest their exclusion? If the terms of intelligibility are defined by their exclusion, how can they make their claims heard? How can those on the "outside" make their claims intelligible, and how can those on the "inside" hear them? How can we translate across that border?

A critical method rooted in negative dialectics can help us to understand claims that exceed the boundaries of intelligibility from within and to build a method that does not attempt eliminate those claims by forcing them to assimilate to already existing terms of intelligibility. Such a method is important for revealing the contingency of the current terms of political intelligibility and for preserving the contingency of any challenge to those terms. And it is important for ideology critique, of which the critique of constitutive exclusion is an example: it points to the multiple possibilities of flight from or subversion of hegemony. Negative dialectics is central to the method of critique in order to preserve the radical potential to which constitutive exclusion gestures: if the retroactive temporality of constitutive exclusion indicates that every constitution is a reconstitution, then the critique of constitutive exclusion aims at a reconstitution *without* exclusion, or if an exclusion be necessary, that it be arrived at democratically rather than disavowed.

Part One established both the multiplicity and retroactive temporality of constitutive exclusion. If constitutive exclusion is effected through a retroactive temporality that erases its traces as it goes along, and if it is multiple—if no single form of difference can serve as an origin of the others—then the political present is sedimented with multiple exclusions to which we are epistemologically blind. Using Adorno's method of approach to nonidentity, this chapter describes the materialist and historical character of the quasi-transcendent element of his thought, fleshing out the political-epistemological texture of constitutive exclusion.

NONIDENTITY AS MATERIAL

In Chapter 4, I argued that we can approach nonidentity from either the side of concepts or the side of objects. Because of its dialectical character, nonidentity does not lie beyond these, as would be consistent with a transcendental realist principle. Nonidentity is instead both within the concept and the object, and in the fissures that separate the two. However, Adorno's insistence on the preponderance of the object does not mean that nonidentity is reducible to a *facta bruta*, the mute passivity of nature that would act as a ground or a foundation.

Adorno's insistence on the "preponderance of the object" indicates that nonidentity is on the side of the concrete rather than the ontological; more specifically, Adorno argues that it is a means of marking human suffering—as an expression of the object-ness of the subject—and orienting thought as a response to that suffering. Because of the dialectical character of nonidentity, one can find it either in the excess of the object or in the excess of the subject, but this does not indicate a dogmatic materialism. Rather, it only indicates that the quasi-transcendent element would be found in different sites at different times, according to the specific conditions one is reading. In this sense, the emphasis on the object still predominates even if we must analyze the object with concepts, since concepts themselves carry with them a reference to the object. The nonidentity in the concept, the excess of the promise of a concept in relation to what it has achieved, is still identifiable as a fault in the concept. This nonidentity is indicated by a "not-yet," or by the concept's negativity relative to current conditions. The contradiction between the concept and current conditions is an insufficiency that the concept cannot yet recognize.

This insufficiency has its root in the nonidentity between concept and object. It cannot be rooted, for instance, in a more fundamental dialectic within nonidentity itself, since it is nonidentity that gives rise to dialectics. To read nonidentity or the nonconceptual as *itself* dialectical would therefore, as Anke Thyen argues, "amount to an ontologising of the non-ontological."[1] To treat nonidentity as if it were dialectical would be to posit dialectics itself as transcendent, when it is clear that the speculatively transcendent moment toward which negative dialectics pushes is a moment in which dialectics would no longer be necessary. This is because, as Adorno argues, "dialectics is the ontology of the wrong state of things. The right state of things would be free of it: neither a system nor a contradiction."[2] Dialectics is thus appropriate to this wrong state, but we must resist its ontologization; we do this through insisting that, as Thyen argues, "this nonidentical 'something' has an essentially material character."[3]

How can we think a quasi-transcendent element that is neither dialectical in itself, nor a pure ineffable beyond, but is instead rooted in an immanent, material, indeed a somatic and physical experience? Espen Hammer succinctly describes the predicament:

> What Adorno retains from the metaphysical tradition is its desire for transcendence—that is, the simple sense that "this cannot be all." The only alternative to irredeemable despair must consist in the possibility of witnessing some form of alterity or otherness capable of resisting the closure effected by formal-instrumental rationality. On the other hand, for transcendence to be possible, metaphysics must be stripped of its traditional adherence to conceptions of the ideal, the immutable, and the totalizing universal. For Adorno, this means that metaphysics must be given a materialist twist.[4]

Adorno argues that metaphysics must converge with materialism at its moment of downfall, though the two have been traditionally opposed.[5] This should come as no surprise at this point, given the dialectical nature of Adorno's thought. But what are we to make of this? How precisely is nonidentity material? And if that materiality is somehow transcendent to thought, how is it indicated by or within thought?

Transcendence Material: Suffering as the Somatic Moment in Thought

In what may be initially an overly simplistic sense, materialism means that, on the one hand, thinking depends upon existing concrete human beings, and, on the other hand, thinking is always about something, and this "something" is not reducible to thought. Simon Jarvis argues that the speculative moment of Adorno's thought is matter: therefore, the negative dialectic is undertaken for the sake of no longer forgetting, ignoring, repressing, or disavowing matter in thinking.[6]

Adorno points to physical suffering as the source of negativity, dialectics, and thus the very movement of thought.[7] Physical suffering is the somatic moment in thinking. Suffering's ability to mark thought, even as that which identitarian thinking disparages or disavows, is a kind of negative assurance of its dialectical attachment to concepts. Adorno argues that physical suffering, often marked in his work by the event of Auschwitz (though not limited to Auschwitz), forces on us what he calls a new categorical imperative: that nothing like it ever happen again.[8] According to the dialectical sense of identity, the imperative that "suffering" forces on us is, on the one hand, that we make good on the promise inherent in the concept—that this is not all there is—and, on the other hand, that we attend to the material basis of life so as to acknowledge and alleviate suffering. The experience of suffering calls us to respond with thinking that attends to the material basis of nonidentity.

I argued previously that the transcendental realist interpretation of Adorno was flawed in that it showed an insufficient appreciation for the role of the dialectic in Adorno. Given its emphasis on immediacy or givenness, it also comes quite close to a dogmatically materialist reading of nonidentity. It would not be too far from the transcendental realist interpretation to argue that while the source of all truth lies in matter, matter itself fundamentally escapes or lies beyond our ability to know it in its entirety. As Simon Jarvis describes it:

> All attempts to avoid idealist claims of the type that thought constitutes, shapes, or is identical with its objects appear to run the opposite risk of claiming access to immediacy, to a transcendence which is just the "given." In such invocations, as Hegel himself forcefully pointed out, we are effectively invited to have faith in some datum or framework for data which is sheerly given. Our knowledge of such "givens" is mistakenly thought of as being purely passive. Enquiry must simply halt before them. Dogmatic materialism of this kind is not at all free from metaphysics in the way that it supposes. When thinking comes to a halt with an abstract appeal to history, or society, or socio-historical material specificity, or any other form of givenness, it might as well stop with God. The lesson which Adorno draws is that whether thinking is really materialist is not decided by how often the word "materialism" is repeated, but by what happens in that thinking. Materialist thinking would need to ask how thinking about that which appears to escape conceptuality is even imaginable.[9]

Adorno meets this challenge of avoiding a dogmatic materialism by insisting that the materialism of nonidentity is both negative and dialectical. Though it may seem a bit oblique, the best way to explicate the materiality of the transcendence of nonidentity is through the dialectic between subject and object. Here I want to distinguish Adorno's complex understanding of materiality from the dogmatic materialism Jarvis describes above; the task is to understand the quasi-transcendent, and thus metaphysical, sense of materialism at work in Adorno. This helps us to understand dialectics as the notion that "objects do not go into their concepts without leaving a remainder," and to understand that remainder as material.[10]

The Materialist Dialectic of Subject and Object

In his essay "On Subject and Object," Adorno writes, "the primacy of the object means [rather] that the subject for its part is object in a qualitatively different, more radical sense than object, because object cannot be known except through consciousness, hence is also subject."[11] Though the object is only knowable through consciousness, it is logically prior to the subject. And although the two exist in dialectical mutual constitution, the relation between them is not equal; the difference between subject and object makes a difference.[12] This difference is precisely what identitarian thought and practice seeks to eliminate. Adorno reminds us that the subject certainly is also an object because it is somatic or physical. The prominent marker of this is the subject's suffering under totality, or under an administered world.[13] Adorno claims that the suffering of the physical subject is the very motor of the dialectic: the "consistent sense of nonidentity" to which dialectics responds is suffering.[14] This "sense of nonidentity" ensures that dialectics must never come to a rest because if it did, it would mean putting an end to the passage between the subject and the object by eliminating the objective moment of the subject and achieving full totality or radical immanence. The result of this is the death of the subject. In this sense, as Hammer notes, the world of radical immanence would be Auschwitz, in which the only available transcendence is death itself.[15]

From this we can see that the subject is not reducible to the concept, nor is the object the same as the nonconceptual (this is the mistake that the transcendental realist interpretation of nonidentity makes).[16] The subject is also an object, as the subject's suffering indicates. But the object is just as well a subject. This is because the object is already an abstraction from particular concrete things and the object is available to the subject only by means of concepts. This is also because the object has in many cases been formed by the subject. As a part of the world dominated by the preponderance of the subject, objects are shaped, disfigured, and sometimes destroyed by ideology just as much as the objective element within the subject is.

Since the example of the cherry tree in Marx's *The German Ideology*, for instance, we are reminded that what we perceive as natural, as fully independent from human culture, is already marked by culture's domination. Marx writes, "The cherry-tree, like almost all fruit-trees, was, as is well known, only a few centuries ago transplanted by commerce into our zone, and therefore only by this action of a definite society in a definite age it has become 'sensuous certainty' for Feuerbach."[17] Our perception of what is natural is almost always the result of a long history of human intervention. Thus, a painting of a scene of natural beauty (such as the one Buchwalter takes to represent nonidentity in Chapter 4) is ideological through and through: the sense of reconciliation perceived there is the false reconciliation of domination. Adorno warns us against such naïve realism when he writes, "That the object takes precedence even though indirect itself does not cut off the subject-object dialectics. Immediacy is no more beyond dialectics than is mediation."[18]

Adorno's materialism thus cannot be understood as a dogmatic gesture to immediacy or givenness, as that is just as abstractly transcendent as the ineffable other of negative theology. Negative dialectics is ideology critique, the critique of reification, and the critique of fetishism. Such critique reveals that what we understand as an object, especially the "natural" objects, is the result of a process of becoming that is hidden within that object, a becoming that for Adorno is explicitly historical.[19]

The reification of commodities and the reification of consciousness are mediated dynamics. Both objects and subjects suffer a similar deformation: a reduction to fragments or moments, to the disparaged, discarded, or disavowed nonidentical in the object, on the one hand, and to the disparaged, discarded, or disavowed nonidentical moment of spontaneity in the subject, on the other. We cannot assume, therefore, that the quasi-transcendent element will come to us through objects alone, or with immediacy or givenness: this would be a mistake, since immediacy and givenness are determined by ideological or hegemonic conditions.

So long as we remain mired in current damaged conditions, the object will continue to operate as the "terminological mask" of nonidentity, the positive cover for the dynamic materialism of that transcendent element in which it nevertheless persists.[20] The desire to give expression to suffering is itself a materialist impulse. Rather than acting as an absolute limit, the material aspect of the transcendent requires us to continue the work of critique without presuming to know its results. The work would then be to unearth the sedimented history of the object in order to liberate the possibilities buried with it. It is in this sense that Adorno argues that "Objectivity can be made out solely by reflecting, at every historical and cognitive stage, both upon what at that time is presented as subject and object, as well as upon their mediations. To this extent object is in fact 'infinitely given as a task,' as neo-Kantianism taught."[21] Insofar as constitutive exclusion operates retroactively, political agency is also given to us "infinitely as a task." The materialist character of nonidentity reminds us that this task is guided by the concrete rather than the abstract, without simply equating the concrete with the object. If the critique of constitutive exclusion must question the specific construction of political agency in the present, the retroactive structure of constitutive exclusion gives the present to us in the form of a core sample. This means that our analysis of the quasi-transcendent character of constitutive exclusion, just like the quasi-transcendent character of nonidentity, *must be historical.*

NONIDENTITY AS HISTORICAL

The materialist character of nonidentity is already implicitly historical. Matter in Adorno refers to the somatic moment in thinking, the impulse ĸ as a response to suffering. This response is the persistent sense ıere must be something more than this, that it didn't have to be this way, or that things might have been otherwise. This responsiveness of thinking is already a critique of the hegemonic temporal mode, the teleological arc of history, in which "what is" is "what had to be." As we have seen, Adorno thinks of objects as a congealed history (on the model of Marx's understanding of the commodity as congealed labor) or a historical process of becoming hidden beneath a fetish.[22] The critique of the fetish structure of objects is aimed at unlocking or unearthing repressed pieces of the object's history. This is why the object is given to us infinitely as a task. Understanding the historical character of nonidentity in Adorno thus helps us to understand the historical method of the critique of constitutive exclusion. Just as the object is given to us infinitely as a task, our own political agency is given to us as a task. The provisional character of the constitutively excluded gives to us the task of interpretation, the task of critique. This is a historical process, since, insofar as we can know our constitutions, we can know them only retrospectively.

It is worth remembering here that all of Adorno's thought can in a certain sense be summed up as a response to a particular historical event: the Holocaust. Susan Buck-Morss argues that as a result of the Holocaust, for Adorno "the present relativized the past."[23] The project of *Negative Dialectics*, as in the *Dialectic of Enlightenment*, is an attempt to account for the occurrence of Auschwitz, but explicitly not an attempt to excuse it or to appropriate it to any purpose.[24] Adorno (and Horkheimer, in the *Dialectic of Enlightenment*) reads the past in light of the present, in order to show both the teleological inevitability of the Holocaust and to show that it could have been otherwise. To ask how history could have been otherwise, as Alison Stone points out, is impossible for enlightenment thinkers, reliant as they are upon a teleological or progressive account of history: "enlightenment thinkers cannot ask whether history could have been different, as this is not a simple factual matter. Their inability to ask whether things might have turned out differently conduces to an unthinking acceptance that current social arrangements are inevitable, a 'fate' that no one can escape. And fatalism of this kind is typically a mythical form of belief."[25] This mythical fatalism reaches its height in Hegel, for whom history is the "slaughterbench" at which individuals must be sacrificed for the sake of the realization of the idea of World Spirit.[26] The systematic death of the camps both fulfills the fatalist destiny of world spirit and also puts the lie to reason in history, as Adorno argues that to insist that it all "happens for a reason" is to mock the dead.[27]

As the relativization of the past, the present had to be made to account for Auschwitz in some way. This is both possible and impossible. It is *possible* in that universal history, on the model brought to its apotheosis by Hegel, believes it can fully account for the camps, since by its logic the extermination of millions of concrete individual humans are given meaning in service to the goal of the greater freedom and perpetual peace of a (continually deferred) future abstract humanity. It is *impossible* in that the camps shatter the logic of a rational universal history. Any accounting that history claims for the excess of death and suffering in the camps is on its face both absurd and grotesque. The occurrence of Auschwitz forces the idea that it could have been otherwise, *in and through* the very enlightenment claim that history unfolds by necessity. The thesis of the *Dialectic of Enlightenment* is largely an attempt to push this double historical strategy as a method for illuminating, if not other historical possibilities (the book is much darker and its task more extreme than that), then simply the idea that things could have turned out otherwise—holding out hope that through thought and struggle, things may yet turn out otherwise.

While negative dialectics puts the lie to universal history, it does not give it up. Universal history, like metaphysics, still retains a kind of promise: it preserves the idea of humanity as a collective and thus a kernel of a hope for something better for all of us. It preserves the idea that whether we recognize it or not, we are bound together. To do away with the *promise* of universal history would be a retreat into barbarism: "History is the unity of continuity and discontinuity. Society stays alive, not despite its antagonism, but by means of it."[28]

Adorno's critique of universal history follows the double strategy outlined in Chapter 4: pushing universal history to its limits as well as reading it against the grain, looking for the disparaged, discarded, and disavowed in history. This double strategy has its basis in the notion that the teleological temporality of universal history, much like the movement of identitarian thinking itself, is constituted retroactively, through the operation of constitutive exclusion. Our approach to history must therefore be negative, as described above. Since universal history has a dialectical structure and therefore represses or disavows some elements just as it holds out a promise for something better, we must both critique and rescue the concept of universal history. We must push the concept of universal history to its extreme, as Adorno argues in "Why Still Philosophy?": "History promises no salvation and offers the possibility of hope only to the concept whose movement follows history's path to the extreme."[29]

In accordance with the double strategy, in pushing the concept of universal history to its extreme, Adorno argues that we must at the same time investigate those places where the concept seems to falter, where it is frayed or worn thin. These are those shards of history remaindered from the concept; they are the chips of messianic time described by Benjamin, who claims that the work of the historical materialist is to establish "a concept of the present as the 'time of the now,' which is shot through with chips of messianic time."[30] Benjamin famously describes messianic time as exercising a "weak force" in which the past has a claim on us.[31] This "weak force" is similar to the force Adorno argues that the reified object possesses. Again, the force is here stored up in the object, buried, sedimented, or repressed in it. Through the work of critique, we attempt to release the object from reification, or to release its becoming, by unearthing the chips of "now-time" buried within in it.

These "chips" are the nonidentical in history. They are sedimented in history, just as becoming is congealed in the object. They are neither entirely objective nor entirely subjective, but because of the dialectic between subject and object and the reliance of metaphysical experience upon current social conditions, they will be found in different places at different times. These fragments of nonidentity are sedimented or congealed in the object as repressed elements. If nonidentity is quasi-transcendent, then these "chips" are the historical quasi-transcendent. As quasi-transcendent, they stand both within and without history: they are within history as its repressed grounds. They are also outside of history, however, in the sense that these materialist "chips" are excluded from the concept of universal history. Excluded within the self-identity of the concept, these "chips" are nonidentical. Insofar as the concept of universal history constitutes itself upon the exclusion of these chips of messianic temporality, these chips are constitutively excluded by it.

Because our thinking is so determined by instrumental reasoning, however, we are always at risk of making our critique *productive*, rather than *fruitful*, as Adorno puts it. We are always at risk of determining nonidentity in advance, appropriating, distorting, or reducing it to the demands of the exchange principle by which so much of our thinking is determined. The element of chance, accident, or contingency in this approach must be preserved here. The negativity with which Adorno approaches nonidentity is an attempt to push thought against itself and toward the boundaries of thought. The success of this can never be guaranteed; this would be to risk instrumentalizing negative dialectics itself. Adorno's negative approach to materialist history thus defines a kind of methodology for releasing nonidentity without forcing its assimilation.

As a double strategy, both critique and rescue, Adorno's negative approach to history gestures toward that which the concept excludes and the rescue of what it promises. How is this useful for our conception of constitutive excluded? How are these nonidentical chips constitutively excluded? And how can the historical character of nonidentity help us to better understand how a translation is possible between what is "excluded" and what is "included," what is "inside" and what is "outside," and to see this method as a historical structure and process?

The historical character of nonidentity tells us something more about the "time" of constitutive exclusion in its retroactive character. If we are formed through constitutive exclusion, then we can only know this constitution (and the "exclusions" upon which it relies) retrospectively. However, any particular constitution is not a necessity; that things could have been otherwise is the persistent message of Adorno's historical quasi-transcendent, as it must be for our analysis of constitutive exclusion. Moreover, the retroactive character of constitutive exclusion calls

-tion the distinction between inside and outside as the distinc-tween cause and effect, condition and conditioned. This reaffirms Adorno's understanding of nonidentity as material rather than ontological: nonidentity is not a first principle but rather the retrospective identification of what has been remaindered in order to constitute us as who we are at any given moment. Adorno does not take nonidentity to be an ontological principle, just as he does not take identitarian thought to be an effect of nonidentity as a cause. Rather, nonidentity is constitutively excluded. It is what is remaindered from identitarian thinking, in that, insofar as it is ever uncovered, recognized, or acknowledged, it is done so only in particular, only retrospectively, and only in relation to current social-political conditions.

Moreover, nonidentity is produced as nonidentity by identitarian thinking: under some other form of thinking, nonidentity might "be" something else, but as we have from our position within identity thinking no direct access to any other thinking, this other possibility is marked only negatively in the form of a hope for a future free of constitutive exclusion. If negative dialectics describes the wrong state of things, still that is the best we have because negative dialectics indicates that things could always have been different. More than that, it indicates that things are already other than what they are: their negativity already points to the traces of alterity contained in the object and in totality, traces which come to us, not from the future, but from the past:

> Grayness could not fill us with despair if our minds did not harbor the concept of different colors, scattered traces of which are not absent from the negative whole. The traces always come from the past, and our hopes come from their counterpart, from that which is or was doomed; such an interpretation may very well fit the last line of Benjamin's text on *Elected Affinities*: 'For the sake of the hopeless only are we given hope.'[32]

These chips or traces give us some indication, not only of what is excluded but of who we are by means of that exclusion. Who are we by means of the constitutive exclusion of Antigone? Who are we by virtue of the children's story-book appropriation of the radicality of Rosa Parks? Who are we by virtue of our forgetting Claudette Colvin? Who are we by virtue of being unable to hear the language of the riot? What have we lost as a result of these exclusions? Who might we have been? Who might we yet become?

CONCLUSION

The critique of constitutive exclusion poses a political-epistemological problem: How do we hear claims that we are constituted not to understand? How can we translate politically unintelligible claims, not by forcing those claims to assimilate to our own language, but by reconstituting our language and our politics so as to no longer exclude those claims? The claim of Part Two of this book has been that a critical theoretical method is appropriate to this problem. This is because critical theory teaches us how to read for what is necessary to, but disavowed within, hegemony, totality, or identity-thinking, or how to read for the quasi-transcendent element that emerges from within the delimited, immanent field of politics. In the thought of Theodor Adorno, that quasi-transcendent element is nonidentity.

As we have seen, negative dialectics is undertaken for the sake of a speculative moment that points a way beyond the immanent totality of current conditions, dominated as they are by identity-thinking, instrumental reason, or ideology. That speculative moment is marked in Adorno's thought by nonidentity, or the nonconceptual. These point to a moment transcendent to those damaged immanent conditions. However, that quasi-transcendent moment it not absolutely beyond; it does not indicate an absolute difference or otherness. Instead, the dialectical aspect of nonidentity indicates that it is marked within thought, and if it can be reached, achieved, or unlocked, this must be done from within immanent conditions, or from within a thinking already determined (although not absolutely so) by identitarian thinking. The historical materialist aspect of nonidentity indicates that it lies buried in the sedimented history of objects as well as in the promise buried in the sedimented history of concepts. In his lectures on negative dialectics, Adorno suggests in that in our method of critique we should follow the example of Freud

> and concentrate on matters that have not been pre-digested by the pre-existing concepts of the prevailing philosophy and science. . . . We might say that the non-conceptual itself, when we approach it for the first time, when we grapple with it, is already mediated by concepts in a negative sense—it is the neglected, the excluded; and the fact that the concept has not granted it access tells us something about the prejudice, the *parti pris* and the obstacles imposed by the concept.[33]

While we must approach the nonconceptual through concepts, since those concepts reflect and drive our social and political experience, we will experience it only negatively, as that which has been excluded. Adorno goes on to refer to the nonconceptual as what has been socially repressed in certain objects; instrumental reason, identity thinking, or ideology thus operate through the repression of the nonidentical in the object, despite the fact of the "constitutive character of the nonconceptual."[34]

Because the quasi-transcendent element is not an ineffable, purely abstract transcendence in a world beyond or behind our own, insofar as we are still able to reach this element, we can do so only through the very same damaged thinking that has caused its repression. There is no other world, no other reason, to which we may appeal. Because of the damage that reason has done, both to itself and to the world, we must be wary to avoid appropriating or damaging that quasi-transcendent element in our method. This is the importance of negativity; negativity is the mark of the possibility of thought to work against itself. The materialist history of objects grounds the possibility of the negative dialectic, but the commitment to negativity is its source of hope. Because of that negativity, because both concept and object are already more and other than what they are, we can still hope that we may yet become more and other than what we are.

The material and historical aspects of nonidentity teach us where we may find what has been constitutively excluded—in what has been repressed, discarded, disparaged, or disavowed: in the material, the physical, or the somatic. Again, this is not a dogmatic materialism, which would be in principle no different from dogmatic idealism. Rather, on the side of the concrete rather than the ontological, it is not an origin, a foundation, or an essential principle. While the materiality of constitutive exclusion, just like the materiality of nonidentity, is difficult to describe in a negative manner, the analysis of the materiality of nonidentity shows that we must look for clues for constitutive exclusion to come in what is disparaged or disavowed as the physical or the somatic, frequently beneath the "natural."

Moreover, what seems perfectly natural or objective from within the political body drawn through constitutive exclusion often masks a historical, social, and political process. The material character of nonidentity is at some level impossible to distinguish from the historical (for good reasons) and the connection between them is particularly salient for the critique of constitutive exclusion. Because of the multiplicity and retroactive character of constitutive exclusion, we are structured by multiple constitutions, and therefore multiple exclusions, buried beneath the borders those constitutions have drawn. We are thus given not only objects as an infinite task, as Adorno suggests, but also our own political agency. That task is the work of reconstitution: not the assimilation, colonization, or elimination of exclusions but rather a reconstitution that would do justice to them, for the utopian hope of a constitution that would no longer require them.

Finally, although Adorno himself provides us with the tools to critique constitutive exclusion, he is by no means immune to it. This is indicated by the treatment of male homosexuality as it appears in his texts (lesbians are almost entirely absent from Adorno's works, though they do play a troubling symbolic role in Benjamin's work). Adorno consistently associates male homosexuality with cruelty, domination, and fascism.[35] Even if we understand this as just another means of critiquing totality, much like the rhetorical anti-Semitism employed by Marx in "On the Jewish Question," the abjection of queer masculinity upon which this strategy relies serves to reproduce and reinscribe the abjection of gay, queer, and gender nonconforming men and trans folks.[36] While Adorno gives us the tools for diagnosing, critiquing, and perhaps even subverting constitutive exclusion, it should come as no surprise that we can—and must—turn those same tools against Adorno himself. In a world constituted through multiple exclusions, we can never be certain that we ourselves are not constituted by some exclusions that remain unintelligible to us. And this is precisely the point: an ethics or a politics that takes constitutive exclusion seriously is a project that remains unfinished.

In Part Three, I turn the tools developed here to the analysis of politics more properly, in the form of three models of the *contestation* of constitutive exclusion, and I develop new tools of analysis as a result. That Adorno's own critical method is not enough to forestall the risks of installing new exclusions as we make our way is a good indication of the stakes of tarrying with, and listening to—as much as we are capable—the constitutive exclusions that structure our own political bodies and our own terms of political agency.

PART THREE

Contestation

6

Critical Models: Antigone, Rosa Parks and Claudette Colvin

Diagnosing the operation of constitutive exclusion in philosophical systems is useful for learning to see how it structures thinking, and the method of critique of constitutive exclusion is useful for better understanding how to read for it, both in the text and in the world. But this does not tell us how the multiplicity of constitutive exclusions operate, where and how the contestation of constitutive exclusion happens, and who we are—and who we could be—as a result. Both the diagnosis and the method are incomplete without searching out those flashes of now-time, as Benjamin put it, buried in the past. These flashes illuminate the present contours of political agency, the exclusions embedded in its foundations, and the possibilities for reconstitution those exclusions mark. While Part One dealt with the diagnosis of constitutive exclusion and its role in establishing and troubling the distinction between ontology and epistemology, and Part Two dealt with the critical theoretical method proper to the political epistemological problems constitutive exclusion poses, Part Three turns to three critical models of the concrete contestation of constitutive exclusion.

Following up the demand from Benjamin and Adorno in Chapter 5 that we must practice materialist history to unearth the shards of resistance sedimented in the history of the present, I offer three models of the critical contestation of constitutive exclusion drawn from three historical moments. Strange histories, no doubt: one drawn from literature, though marked by the history of its reception; two from the history of the United States, though almost entirely determined by the narrative that frames them. What is common to them all, however, is the unintelligibility of their contestations as political claims. These models offer a series of key insights into how contestation is possible, or not; what forms it might take—rebellion, intransigence, refusal, insurrection, militancy, riot; how to listen to unintelligible political claims; how to fail at that task or to refuse it; how political bodies and the terms of political agency are structured by these failures and refusals; and what the costs of contestation entail. Not quite empirical, not quite theoretical, these critical models work the dialectic between abstract and concrete, between the delimited field of politics and its excluded conditions, and give us some sense of what possibilities remain to be redeemed.

This chapter takes up three constitutively excluded figures: first, the figure of Antigone, and second the twin figures of Claudette Colvin and Rosa Parks. These figures pose the following questions: what does contestation look like? What is intelligible and what is unintelligible in these contestations, and how does that unintelligibility shore up the borders of the political bodies that exclude them but rely on them? How can we judge the "success" of a contestation, and what are its costs? What is left behind? What remains to be redeemed?

Chapter 7 treats a different sort of figure, the fractured collectivity of the 1992 Los Angeles Riots/Rebellion. Contested even at the level of its naming, this event in the political life of the United States is somehow both vivid and forgotten. Is a riot ever politically intelligible? What is the specific texture of the LA Riots/Rebellion's political unintelligibility? What claims were made in the contestation of constitutive exclusion that the

United States failed to hear? Who are we as a result of this failure, this refusal? What bearing does it have on us now?

ANTIGONE: COSTS OF TRANSLATION

The figure of Antigone has acted as the guide throughout the course of this book. And so it makes a certain sense that we should encounter her here, in the third act, to revisit her scandalous performance, but this time to pose different questions: not how does she mark constitutive exclusion, but how does she *contest* her exclusion? How is her contestation heard (if it is), and what are its costs? What about Antigone calls us back to her?

At stake here is less historiographical or dramaturgical fidelity and more the significance of modern receptions of Antigone, both in modern thought and in the resignifications of her contestation on the stage and on the page. While she marks constitutive exclusion throughout many of her modern figurations, these are different from her reception in the ancient world, which was less structured by the disavowals of exclusion than our own. Nevertheless, something about Antigone still has a hold on us. She has been read as representing the limit between life and death, or as representing the principle of feminine devotion to kinship. She somehow continues to exceed these representations and to be taken up in new ways, in new readings and performances: in Ireland, in Nazi-occupied Paris, in apartheid South Africa.[1]

Antigone never ceases to be read, however, as a figure who haunts political borders; she troubles the boundaries between politics and kinship, between state and family, and between masculine and feminine. In *Antigone's Claim* and in the essay "Bodily Confessions," Judith Butler takes up this way Antigone seems to exceed all representations of her, and indeed to call into question representation itself. Butler's interlocutors in this task are two of Antigone's most influential interpreters, Hegel and Lacan. Both of these thinkers read Antigone as either, in the case of Hegel (as we have seen) representing the principle of kinship, outside the realm of politics entirely, or, in the case of Lacan, representing the limit between politics and kinship, between life and death. Butler instead examines the ways Antigone exposes and subtends the relationship between kinship and politics in ways that point to more radical feminist and queer political possibilities. In some places, however, Butler reads Antigone too close to Hegel or Lacan, or too close to the curse she is under from her father, Oedipus. These moments tend to render Antigone more firmly beyond politics, or to reinscribe the unintelligibility of her contestation in ways that undercut the radical potential she otherwise inspires.

In the constitution of political bodies, constitutively excluded figures are relegated to a purportedly apolitical or pre-political space (the home, the social, the market, the private, the barbaric, pre-history, the state of nature, the wilderness, India, Ireland, Africa, America) that is produced through the constitution of a properly political space. Those who are relegated to these spaces are similarly rendered apolitical or pre-political, and because the terms of intelligible political agency are drawn on the exclusion of these subjects from them, any contestation of the exclusion to which they are subject is unintelligible.

As a constitutively excluded figure, Antigone is relegated to this a- or pre-political space that the political body of Thebes nevertheless both requires and includes within itself. Her exclusion from political agency grounds the distinctions upon which political agency in ancient Thebes is defined, but her inclusion within the political body and its terms of intelligible political agency poses a problem to these distinctions that must be managed. But this is only illuminated through the drama of her contestation. In her defense of her defiance of Creon's edict, Antigone mounts a passionate and moving contestation of Creon's severe restriction of the terms of political life. By defending her right to bury her brother, Antigone attempts to make an intelligible political claim. However, she can only make this claim in a language that is defined through her exclusion from it. How then can Antigone make herself understood through her appropriation of that language, an appropriation that, as Butler points out, is also a perversion?

This appropriation is risky; deadly, even—the drama of the play is structured around this risk. Antigone risks appearing as monstrous, threatening, and mad. She risks being overtaken by the very language she must use to make her claim, perverting her own aims and reinscribing Creon's authority in defining the terms of the city. She risks her own life, against Creon's attempts to reassert the boundaries of the city, foreclosing the possibilities Antigone threatens by sentencing her to a living death: consigning her as he did her brother to an indeterminate space, suspended between this world and the next, between the living and the dead.

Butler takes up these problems explicitly in *Antigone's Claim*. While her reading is rich and productive, and for the most part preserves the tension between perversion and appropriation, in some places she tends to read Antigone as being overcome by the language she appropriates, and determined almost completely by it. This leads Butler to interpret Antigone's claim as ultimately a failure, as she writes, both because "her language is not that of a survivable political agency" and because Antigone's intent is overcome by unconscious drives.[2] In these moments, Butler reads Antigone too close to the interpretations given by either Lacan or Hegel, undercutting a reading of Antigone as a political agent who is challenging her exclusion from politics. In these moments, Butler's effort to appropriate the languages of German Idealism and psychoanalysis for her own ends is in some sense reappropriated by that very language. If Antigone cannot be read as a political agent, this is due to the terms that define the political sphere through her constitutive exclusion. Closer attention to constitutive exclusion in this case shows the necessity of the vigilant preservation of the tension *between* appropriation and perversion, both within the play and beyond it. While Antigone attempts to alter the language of political agency, Antigone is ultimately not in control of her survival, much less the survival of the altered political agency that she figures. The hope for a reconstitution of political agency that her defiance inspires extends beyond the terms of the struggle for recognition, the struggle between the opposing laws of the family and the state, or the struggle between the real and the symbolic in the multiple ways Antigone is taken up to figure the contestation of constitutive exclusion in the history of reinterpretations of the play.

Butler writes that Antigone "asserts herself through appropriating . . . the authoritative voice of the one she resists, an appropriation that has within it traces of a simultaneous refusal and assimilation of that very authority."[3] In Antigone's defense of her choice to bury her brother Polyneices, Antigone responds to Creon's sovereignty with an assertion of her own sovereignty. She will not allow the deed to be separated from her. She claims the deed as her own, and in so doing, Butler argues, she commits another deed, a defiant speech-act that has the effect of completing the first deed (the burial of her brother) by publishing it, as well as doubling its criminality—a double defiance.[4] Antigone confesses to the commission of the crime: she admits that she broke the law and at the same time denies the legitimacy of that law for her. The first deed is an admission of guilt before the law while the second is a challenge to that law. Antigone doubles her defiance of the king's sovereignty by asserting her own sovereignty before him. In the context of the play, sovereignty would at least seem to mean the ability to author one's actions, whether in speech or otherwise, and to retain some kind of control over them. Contestation over the limits of sovereignty are at the center of the play's drama, as Creon's assertions of his own sovereignty become more and more absurd in the face of the unraveling conditions of Thebes. Antigone, perhaps more than anyone else, cannot take up a straightforward relation to sovereignty (as if anyone can). Her interpellation as a woman in ancient Greece would forbid her from taking up such a sovereign position. Though she is closest kin to her brothers who have both died fighting for the throne, she is forbidden from taking any part in politics, from disobeying male relatives, and certainly from arguing with the king, in public, about her rights in political matters.

Moreover, the performative conditions of ancient Greek theater underscore Antigone's exclusion: Tina Chanter reminds us that the character would be played by a man, for an audience of men.[5] There is no language of sovereignty—arguably no language at all—to which she can appeal that doesn't already belong to the king. As Butler claims, therefore, she must appropriate this language from Creon to make her case: "Her contestation takes the verbal form of a reassertion of sovereignty, refusing to dissociate the deed from her person."[6] This appropriation must also be a perversion, since Antigone takes up a position inside that from which she is meant to have been excluded and bends the language of sovereignty to her own purposes. The clearest evidence of this perversion is the gender confusion that Antigone initiates as a result of her public stance: Creon states that if Antigone is not punished, "now I am no man, but she the man."[7]

Butler argues that it is only through appropriating the language of sovereignty that Antigone can make her claim; she has no language of her own in which to express the law she follows in burying her brother, or to express her justification for her acts. She must use the language of the king. But because that language is not adequate to her justifications, that language fails her. She appears to some degree, regardless of her intentions, as incoherent and unintelligible. Butler writes that Antigone "cannot make her claim outside the language of the state, but neither can the claim she wants to make be fully assimilated by the state."[8] In instances such as these, Butler emphasizes that Antigone is appropriating the language of sovereignty not in order to claim sovereignty alone, but in order to pervert or critique it.

However, this perversion carries with it the risk of perverting Antigone's own aims, recapturing her language in the terms by which it had already excluded her. At stake seems to be the degree to which Antigone is aware of the risk she undertakes: Butler writes that "Antigone does not achieve the effect of sovereignty she apparently seeks, and her action is not fully conscious."[9] Does Antigone unconsciously allow her own aims to be overcome by the language of sovereignty she takes up? Or does she take this risk on self-consciously? Does she assimilate to this language too much, or does she use this language against itself, exposing the limits of sovereignty? The difference seems to be between sovereign self-conscious perversion of the language of sovereignty, on the one hand, and an unconscious assimilation to the language of sovereignty, on the other. However, due to the ambiguity of Antigone's position as a constitutively excluded figure, she can neither exercise self-conscious sovereign control over her own actions or language, nor can she be unconsciously appropriated by the language she must appropriate from the king. Instead, she perverts the language of sovereignty by exposing and questioning what sovereignty excludes in order to function. In this, she may not be sovereign, but neither is she thereby outside the bounds of politics.

It seems that we can never entirely read Antigone without either Hegel or Lacan peering over our shoulder. In the background of this discussion is how Antigone, by means of representing the unconscious in these two figures, has been consigned to a pre-political space. Butler critiques these readings through rethinking the role of the unconscious in politics, to think through the very political move of consigning women and kinship to this unconscious pre-political space, and then treating as politically unintelligible any contestation of that consignment. In some moments, however, Butler reads Antigone too closely to either Hegel or Lacan to be capable of any political contestation at all. Perhaps she does remain unintelligible, but this is through no fault of her own. Antigone does the best she can with what she has; if she still cannot be heard, then it is we as political agents and the terms of that agency itself that fail her, in failing to see, hear, or understand what it has excluded.

Butler implies that what matters here is Antigone's intent, and that her intent is not to pervert or to expose the limits of sovereignty but instead to claim sovereignty for herself. Because she aims at sovereignty, she fails, and her act is not entirely a conscious one. Butler argues that this is due to two factors. First, Antigone cannot control the effects of the language she must appropriate to make her claim. Second, Antigone suffers from a pervasive feeling of guilt, stemming from her attachment to her brother and her identification with her father, which unconsciously drives her to commit a crime that will bring on her the punishment she feels she deserves.

Butler argues that Antigone's justificatory speech at lines 961–971 (in which Antigone argues that she would not have broken Creon's law for a husband or a son but only for her brother) is an attempt to honor her brother's particularity, and in fact to institute a law of particularity. This attempt fails through the use of language itself, since the word *brother* is never attached to any particular human person but has a universal function, attachable to anyone. Moreover, the word as Antigone uses it is troubled by the fact that it is not at all clear to whom Antigone refers when she uses it: because of her twisting genealogy, "brother" could just as well refer to Oedipus, who is Antigone's brother as well as her father.

On the one hand, this claim is true of any claim to sovereignty that takes place in language: language always outstrips any particular sovereign intention. Moreover, it is not clear that Antigone seeks or intends sovereignty, as Butler claims. Who more than Antigone, given the history of her family, could know the ways our words and deeds compel us to travel far beyond ourselves, beyond all control? Indeed, in the opening scene of the play, Ismene recounts to Antigone the long list of horrors their family has endured, the tragic effects of the sovereign action of their father/brother, Oedipus. She ends this speech with the statement, "Extravagant action is not sensible."[10] With this, Ismene reminds both Antigone and the audience of the tragic limits to any pretension at sovereign action that have dogged Antigone's family line since Oedipus returned to Thebes.

On the other hand, it is not quite so clear that in her justificatory speech, Antigone intends to enshrine her brother in a tragic law of particularity as Butler claims. For instance, Mary Beth Mader argues that rather than attempting to preserve or to honor Polyneices's particularity, Antigone intends to disambiguate her confused familial roles and to bring an end to her incestuous line.[11] On this reading, in her justificatory speech, Antigone wishes to stabilize her brother as *only* a brother, who can be begotten only from the mother and the father, and cannot be created through yet another incestuous union. Rather than claiming to establish a new law, Mader reads Antigone's act as "an essentially restorative or reparative effort," an act that seeks to restore the broken laws of kinship and the incest taboo.[12] Antigone would then not be trying to establish a law of particularity but instead to restore the broken order that has caused so much of her family's suffering, and which Creon exacerbates with his tyrannical decree. Antigone's claim would thus be less a sovereign attempt at an impossible law and more an attempt to restore the law that her father broke and which cursed Antigone and her family line. In doing this, Antigone exposes the reliance of the political sphere upon the family and upon the political construction of gender, since it is only by virtue of her brother's death and by virtue of women's exclusion from political rule that Creon has taken the throne.

Moreover, while Antigone must appropriate the language of sovereignty, she in fact critiques that very sovereignty in her more equivocating claims. We can see this when she makes statements such as, "Who knows if in that other world this is true piety?"[13] and, "If this proceeding is good in the gods' eyes, I shall know my sin, once I have suffered."[14] Antigone could have said to the king in her confession, "This is not true piety," or "Zeus will damn you for this," but she does not. These statements show that Antigone is no longer sure (if she ever was sure) of the order for which she sacrifices her life. She commits the crime willingly, knowingly; tragically, she does not expect to be rewarded for it, even in the afterlife. She does not claim full knowledge or control over her actions because she knows by now not to expect it.

In these three respects, it is unlikely that Antigone ever sought sovereignty in any simple way. But neither is she entirely unconscious about the way she uses the language of sovereignty against itself, making a claim in a language that cannot quite express it.

The second reason that Butler gives as to why Antigone fails in her attempt to achieve a sovereign action is due to her close identification with her father, Oedipus, and the curse that his words lay on her. Butler argues that through the public confession of her crime, Antigone acts out a guilt she experienced prior to the crime, a guilt that stems from an incestuous desire for her brother, and ultimately from the curse of her own origin in Oedipus.[15] Here Butler relies on Freud's "Criminals from a Sense of Guilt," in which Freud describes patients whose feelings of pervasive and free-floating guilt cause them to commit some crime that will bring on them the punishment they already feel they deserve. Because the guilt can finally be attached to something, the patients feel relief. Butler argues that it is guilt over her incestuous desire for her brother that drives Antigone to commit her crime, a guilt that ultimately stems from her father's crimes. She writes, "Is it her own guilt for which she becomes punishable by death, or the guilt of her father? And is there any way finally to distinguish between them since they are both cursed in apparently similar ways?"[16]

Butler goes so far as to call Antigone's act a "substitution" for that of her father/brother: "In defying the state, she repeats as well the defiant act of her brother, thus offering a repetition of the defiance that, in affirming her loyalty to her brother, situates her as one who may substitute for him and, hence, replaces and territorializes him."[17] Certainly Antigone must occupy a masculinity that is improper to her in order to make her claim in the language of sovereignty. But if we read this as not a perversion but only as a substitution, we accede to the idea that Antigone cannot challenge this propriety, cannot contest what is properly masculine, what is properly sovereign, but can only and necessarily fail at achieving it. Do we not thereby end up affirming the idea that the defiance of the law, and by extension political contestation, belongs properly to the brother and never to the sister?[18]

Here it seems that Butler finally reads Antigone as far too determined by Oedipus and Polyneices, unconsciously driven by her identification with, and her attachment to, her father/brother. The effect of such a reading is to push Antigone too far to the side of unconsciously assimilating to the language or symbolic structure she must appropriate to make her claim. Rather than taking a critical stance with regard to the sovereignty of her deeds and her speech, such a reading risks erasing Antigone's act as even provisionally her own, or, perhaps, even provisionally our own. Such a reading identifies Antigone with the unconscious, an aspect it shares with both Hegel's and Lacan's readings of Antigone. It therefore also risks once again consigning Antigone to a pre-political space.

Butler is for the most part more careful than that. While placing Antigone in the position of the unconscious may remove her safely from politics for Hegel (or so he hopes; my analysis in Chapter 3 contests Hegel's security on that score), for Butler this is not the case, as part of her project is a radical rethinking of the role of the unconscious in politics, and indeed in rethinking the entire retroactive move of asserting an a- or pre-political foundation to politics. Nevertheless, it seems that under Butler's reading here, Antigone is completely unaware of what she does in attempting to follow out a sovereignty that is untenable for her, and of being led, through this identification with and attachment to her father/brother, to a death she feels she already deserves. Indeed, Butler writes that although Antigone's argument with the king "reads as guiltless defiance, it seems in fact to be a suicidal act propelled by an obscure sense of guilt."[19]

The source of Antigone's crime is not an incestuous desire for her brother, nor is it a curse she shares with her father, as Antigone finally seems to cut the circuit of that curse when she takes up her own death in suicide. Rather, the source of her crime is the scandalous *contestation of her constitutive exclusion*, or her refusal to accept the position in the symbolic order to which she was assigned. Though her position obviously stems from the positions of her father and brothers, it cannot be entirely explained by these positions. Her situation as a woman, and especially as a woman in ancient Thebes, means that the place of masculine sovereignty is closed off from her. And yet she claims that place anyway in her act of defiance, confounding the distinctions between man and woman, ruler and ruled. It is her appearance inside those positions from which she was meant to be outside that makes her criminal. If Antigone does feel a sense of guilt preceding her crime, its source is in her constitutive exclusion in the city of Thebes.

If Antigone is identified too closely with her father and brothers, if she acts primarily according to an unconscious guilt that stems from this attachment, or if she takes up a straightforward relation to the sovereign language she appropriates as a result of this attachment (which Butler goes so far as to call a substitution), then she certainly fails at any sovereign action she may intend. But moreover, it becomes difficult to read her as a political agent at all. Under these conditions, it is difficult to identify the refusal or perversion of sovereign authority that Butler argues could be read in her appropriation of sovereign language, and it seems that Antigone is undone by her claim to sovereignty in the same way that Oedipus or Creon was. It becomes more difficult to read her as challenging the radically restricted boundaries of the political as she appears within it.

Instead, closer attention to the structure and operation of constitutive exclusion challenges us to attend to those figures haunting the borders within our politics, to attend to the claims that come from those quarters, and ultimately to question what we disavow for the sake of securing our own political agency. The model of political unintelligibility figured by Antigone calls us to question the nature of the political, and the presumptions of sovereign control, at any given moment. If Creon is properly the tragic figure of the play, then the source of his tragic undoing is precisely in his certainty in his ability to know and to secure the boundaries of politics: Antigone cannot be a political subject, and she cannot therefore make a political claim. When she nevertheless does make such a claim, she is read as monstrous, transgressing the distinctions that define the boundaries of politics, and especially those of gender. Her contestation is an insurrection from within the language of sovereignty, perverting it for her own ends, and risking being overtaken by that very language—risking madness, criminality, failure, and death in making her claim.

For the most part, Butler already recognizes that Antigone's position within the excluded is a result of her act of defiance rather than the result of her identification with or loyalty to her father/brother. Or rather, for Butler they are not so different: the term "king" could refer as much to Oedipus as to Creon, and if Antigone must appropriate the language of sovereignty to make her claim, then where she defies the king, she defies the father. Where she perverts the language of the king, she perverts the language of the father. This language of the father is the curse that Lacan claims establishes the symbolic, and Butler argues that where Antigone appropriates that language to make her claim, "though she is entangled in these words, even hopelessly, they do not quite capture her."[20] Instead, if Antigone's criminality can be said to stand for anything, it stands for "the trace of an alternate legality that haunts the conscious, public sphere as its scandalous future."[21]

This "trace of an alternate legality" is precisely what is lost in Antigone's failure to effect the translation from political unintelligibility to political intelligibility. She challenges the account of sovereignty upon which Creon insists and the narrow definition of political agency circumscribed by that account of sovereignty. As Chanter puts it, "Antigone calls attention to the blindness and hypocrisy of a polity that defines its membership by precluding as worthy of full political participation those on whom it nevertheless remains dependent materially and psychically."[22] Antigone's contestation figures the radical potential—sparked for a moment—of the outside of politics, *inside*, calling into question the limits of sovereignty, authority, and politics as they are defined by means of constitutive exclusion. What this leaves to us, as readers of Antigone, as inheritors of this claim, is to listen to her demand to attend to what is excluded by our politics, to attend to those lives that are made unintelligible and unlivable by those exclusions.

Ultimately this task is borne out in the history of reproductions of the play. Within the confines of Sophocles's play, a product of a world perhaps more frank about the exclusions structuring political life than our own, Antigone's claim fails. The history of productions of *Antigone*, however, in the multiple adaptations and rearticulations and reimaginings of Antigone in a modern context, do take up and work through Antigone's claim. In these cases, the play preserves Antigone's excess, her struggle, and her perversion of the law for the sake of articulating that "alternate trace of legality" in new ways with each production, and with each thinker who works through her claim. As a model of contestation, therefore, Antigone reveals to us the difficulties in translating one's political claim into a language predicated upon its exclusion: she risks either failure or assimilation to the language of the king, shoring up his sovereign authority. Antigone also reveals the monstrosity of constitutive exclusion, the threat of which is managed through an attempt at her reification, through Antigone's literal imprisonment in stone. And we inherit from her, by means of the peculiar aesthetic possibilities of performance, a means of working through the claims that those traces of alternate legality—those chips of messianic temporality, those shards of resistance—bear on us now.

ROSA PARKS AND CLAUDETTE COLVIN: MULTIPLICITY AND STRATEGIC STRAIGHTNESS

On March 2, 1955, Claudette Colvin, a fifteen-year-old Black girl in Montgomery, Alabama, rode the city bus home from school. When the driver told her to give up her seat for a middle-aged white woman, despite the empty seats behind and beside her, Colvin refused. She was then arrested, handcuffed, kicked, and dragged off the bus by Montgomery police, who charged her with violation of the segregation statute, assault, and disorderly conduct, humiliating her and threatening her in the process. While the local Black leadership in Montgomery—including the Women's Political Council and the Montgomery chapter of the NAACP—had been looking for an opportunity to challenge segregation on Montgomery buses in the courts and in the streets, they chose not to rally the boycott around Colvin. The leader of the Women's Political Council, Jo Ann Robinson, believed Colvin was a good candidate, but the chair of the Montgomery NAACP chapter, E. D. Nixon, was concerned: Colvin came from the wrong part of town; her father drank; she was young, fierce, and outspoken; she was dark-skinned and wore her hair in cornrows. When Nixon visited Colvin's family to discuss a boycott, he discovered that she was pregnant.[23]

While Colvin and four other women were party to the lawsuit, *Browder v. Gayle*, that ended de jure segregation of the Montgomery bus system, Colvin was not chosen as the figurehead for the boycott.[24] Neither were the other plaintiffs in the Browder case, including both thirty-six-year-old Amelia Browder herself, who was arrested in April 1955, and eighteen-year-old Mary Louise Smith, who was arrested in October, all for the same crime. Instead, the boycott began the Monday after the arrest of Rosa Parks, on Thursday, December 1, 1955.

Parks's refusal to relinquish her seat on that day has been cast not as the strategic decision of a savvy political actor but as a simple act in which a dignified, middle-aged woman chose to remain seated because she was tired from a long day at work.[25] The historical—or rather, the mythological—narrative since the boycott has reenforced this version of events. For example, in his 1993 history, *The Struggle for Black Equality* (a book I read in my high school American history class, taught by Constance Holland, herself a veteran of the civil rights movement in North Carolina), Harvard Sitkoff writes, "Mrs. Rosa Parks said no. Her feet hurt. . . . Weary after her long hard day . . . she wanted to remain seated for the rest of her ride."[26] At the concert celebrating the first inauguration of President

Barack Obama in 2009, actor Samuel L. Jackson recalled Parks's role in the civil rights struggle: "There have been many foot soldiers in the quest for justice. One was an Alabama department store seamstress. In 1955, tired from her long day of work, she brought that distant hope one step closer by the simple act of refusing to move to the back of the bus."[27]

In contrast to this national hagiography, in her detailed and moving history, *At the Dark End of the Street*, Danielle McGuire gives a far richer account of Rosa Parks's political education in the struggle against sexual violence against Black women across the South throughout the 1940s and 1950s.[28] Parks's history as a political activist and organizer—and later, as a Black nationalist—was suppressed and ignored in order to secure her iconic place in history, as what McGuire refers to as the "Madonna of Montgomery."[29] Claudette Colvin, young, poor, angry, and just as much a victim of the violence and degradation of Jim Crow, on the other hand, hardly appears at all in the story of the struggle for Black civil rights in the United States. Colvin's story came to light only in the years following the death of Rosa Parks. In an interview for the *New York Times*, Colvin said, "My mother told me to be quiet about what I did. . . . She told me: 'Let Rosa be the one. White people aren't going to bother Rosa—her skin is lighter than yours and they like her.' "[30]

These two figures fall on either side of the distinction between what is intelligible and what is unintelligible as political agency. Rosa Parks acts as the translator through which what was unintelligible as political agency became intelligible, on a large scale. Her choice to stay in her seat, her arrest, and the subsequent boycott she helped to organize, in addition to the media attention to the boycott, all hastened the end of Jim Crow as the law of the South. Claudette Colvin, though she too made a stand, has remained in the background, largely unintelligible as a political agent; she was asked to remain silent about her role while the organization focused on Parks to assure the strategic success of the boycott. But what conditioned this choice and this translation from an unintelligible to an intelligible contestation? And what were its costs? Parks's success as a political agent in this instance is arguably based on the lasting national narrative of her as taking a largely *non*-political action, of simply being a respectable middle-class woman tired from a long day at work, subjected to the indignities of arrest. This narrative has rendered her less a political *subject* than a political *object*, obscuring her long history as an activist in the struggle for equality and freedom for Black people in the United States.

While the organizers of the Montgomery boycott—including Parks herself—were savvy political actors, the historical narrative we have inherited of Parks and Colvin functions to occlude this, on either side of the decision of Parks over Colvin. This is because they are constitutively excluded from the terms of intelligible political agency. That is, on the one hand, we have for the most part forgotten Claudette Colvin's role in this pivotal moment in history, and, on the other hand, we remember and understand Parks less as a political agent than as a political object—a simple, private woman who became "political" for quite ordinary personal reasons. Even while contesting one form of exclusion (that of Black Americans from equality in public life), Parks is herself constitutively excluded, along a different border. At the same time, our ability to read either Colvin *or* Parks as political agents is occluded as part of the same structure and process. Though in different ways, this structure, this process, renders *both* unintelligible as political agents.

While Parks was certainly intelligible as a political actor to those with whom she was organizing, she was unintelligible as a political agent to the larger political body of the United States. Parks was constitutively excluded by virtue of being a Black woman, in the South in particular. Through her exclusion, Montgomery, Alabama, and the United States constituted itself as a white supremacist cis-hetero-sexual-patriarchal hegemony; Parks, Colvin, and others who shared a similar accretion of shared identity categories were cast into the position of the constitutively excluded. Their contestations of that position were thus on their face unintelligible as political claims. But while she was a part of the successful effort to reconstitute the United States along new terms, that reconstitution was effected through her ability to play some axes of her identity off others, an ability that Colvin, by virtue of her different position along these axes, did not possess.[31]

This situation indicates what political scientist Cathy Cohen calls "secondary marginalization." Cohen argues that secondary marginalization emerges under advanced marginalization, when a group has achieved de jure but not de facto equality. In order to press a claim for equality or inclusion, the group then uses a politics of respectability to police the image of the group by "an indigenous process of marginalization targeting the most vulnerable in the group."[32] Cohen's theory of secondary marginalization is thus another way of revealing how intersecting identities are produced and policed within a marginalized group. While secondary marginalization describes the *structure* of exclusion within an excluded group, feminist political theorist Holloway Sparks describes the means of *contesting* exclusions through the concept of "strategic straightness."[33] Straightness is a strategy that citizens use in their struggle for standing, or a strategy to contest their exclusion. Strategic straightness contests the exclusion of one identity category by playing to other identity categories. That is, one contests one's exclusion on the basis of sexuality, for instance, by playing to one's inclusion in the basis of class or race.

Sparks argues that strategic straightness was at work in the Montgomery bus boycott to counter the segregation of Black Americans in Montgomery by relying on the figure of Rosa Parks rather than that of Claudette Colvin. In doing this, the boycott organizers portrayed themselves as respectable, hardworking, middle-class Americans. In later actions, civil rights leaders chose to portray themselves as loyal Americans by situating themselves as heterosexual and anti-communist; this was performed by de-emphasizing the role of organizer Bayard Rustin in the 1963 March on Washington, denying him time at the podium, because Rustin was an out gay man and was at one time a member of the Communist Party. Strategic straightness is a way of explaining the contestation of exclusions based on race, for instance, by playing to and reproducing exclusions based on class, gender, or sexuality. While the organizers of the Montgomery bus boycott successfully contested the constitutive exclusion of (some) citizens based on race, leading to the reconstitution of the United States as a political body, they reinscribed exclusions based on gender, class, and sexuality.

The reenforcement of these other exclusions via the politics of sexuality or secondary marginalization has made it more difficult for later citizens to contest these exclusions, as Sparks argues was the case in the United States' welfare rights movement in the 1960s and 1970s.[34] It also left plenty of room for the exclusion of Blackness outside the frame of middle-class respectability, and beyond the immediate politics of southern desegregation (we will see effects of this in Chapter 7).[35] In later work, Sparks extends this analysis to the affective register; on her account, while some expressions of anger are politically legible and legitimate, these are found on the political right (as in the Tea Party movement) and are available to women and people of color only if they perform the public script correctly. At the same time, performing the existing script correctly "likely makes it harder for performances of political anger that do not—or cannot—successfully invoke these currently legible forms of passionate patriotism to gain the same kind of political traction."[36]

Secondary marginalization and strategic straightness teach us how these exclusions, and these constitutions, function multiply. Insofar as strategic straightness relies upon the ability of excluded persons to portray themselves as "straight," while abjecting, disavowing, or dissociating themselves from or actively policing those seen as non-normal or threatening, this indicates the multiplicity of constitutive exclusion. The political body is constituted through multiple exclusions, and those who are excluded are never "purely" excluded; they stand both within and without, subjects and objects as multiply constituted as the political bodies that they occupy and haunt. The political present is therefore sedimented with the history of these multiple exclusions, indicating that political agency and intelligibility are never fully closed or delimited. The multiplicity of constitutive exclusion thus indicates that it never ultimately "works": it never pulls off the exclusion absolutely and the constitution is never final. Instead, as Butler argues, the norm or the frame usually—or perhaps always—produces the shadow of its failure.

What does the choice to organize the Montgomery bus boycott around Parks rather than Colvin tell us about constitutive exclusion? First, it tells us that constitutive exclusion functions multiply. Because Parks was able to effectively leverage her performance of gender, sexuality, and class in her contestation of the exclusion of Black folks in Montgomery, this tells us both that the body whose borders are drawn by constitutive exclusion and those who are cast in the position of exclusion are multiple. Both the "inside" and the "outside," therefore, are multiple. What then is the difference between an insider and an outsider? Given that the choice of Parks over Colvin was a savvy political strategy in its moment—with all of the risks of failure that any political choice entails—we can say that while the "outside" is multiple, the "inside" is blind to that multiplicity, and persists in its fantasy of oneness.

Constitutive exclusion thus helps us to think about age, race, class, gender, sexuality, disability, and the possible future marginalized identity categories that Butler calls "the embarrassed 'etc.'" all together.[37] It helps us better understand how these identities constitute each other and how they are reinscribed over time. In this sense, constitutive exclusion is closely related to intersectionality. But whereas intersectionality's dominant metaphor is spatial, in that it names the locations where identities meet and redefine each other, constitutive exclusion adds the dimension of time, in particular through the retroactive temporality of constitutions. This retroactive temporality indicates the *historical sedimentation* of these identities. It shows how the histories of multiple exclusions and strategic choices build upon each other, layer by layer, shaping the ground of politics on which we presently stand, but of which we are usually ignorant.

Second, where that multiplicity is not read as wildness, unruliness, as something excessive and threatening—as it was in the case of Colvin—it is *reified* as apolitical, as it was in the case of Parks. That is, the very qualities that made Parks's contestation of her exclusion a success—that very middle-class feminine respectability—made her in the national memory a woman who didn't want to give up her seat because her feet were tired from a long day at work. The unruly threat that Parks's contestation might have posed was thus managed by rendering her simply a tired, middle-aged Black woman. Of course, this reification also serves to obscure the economic blacklist and the constant threats of violence that drove her and her husband to abandon Montgomery for Detroit in 1957.

Third, these two points reveal something important about the function of unintelligibility in the construction of political agency in the United States. The structure and operation of constitutive exclusion has served to blind us to the strategy at work in the Montgomery bus boycott and in the civil rights movement as a whole.[38] This is also due to the multiple exclusions at work in this model. That is, in choosing Parks over Colvin, the boycott organizers—including Parks herself—leveraged Parks's performance of middle-class feminine respectability in order to strategically contest the constitutive exclusion of Black people as a whole. But because this very middle-class Black feminine respectability *is itself seen as apolitical or pre-political*, this made it difficult to see the choice as strategic—it occludes our ability to see it *as* a political strategy. The narrative of Parks as simply a woman tired from a long day at work made a matter of necessity out of a strategic choice, itself risky and contingent. That there even was a strategic choice between Colvin and Parks is covered over in the reconstitution in this instance and this is itself due to the work of constitutive exclusion. Because constitutive exclusion functions retroactively, it turns the contingent character of political action into a fait accompli.

Like Antigone, Parks and the other organizers of the boycott risked being overcome by the very terms of the political agency they were contesting. They made a strategic choice to challenge some specific terms of political agency, while reinscribing other terms. The strategy was thus *both* successful *and* harmful. De jure and de facto segregation of the Montgomery bus system and the daily humiliations that came with it were ended. After more than a year of organized struggle, the Black community of Montgomery won specific material and symbolic concessions and gave hope (as well as shared strategizing and funding) to those involved in similar struggles. If, however, the goal was to contest the constitutive exclusion of all Black people, this could only have been a failure, given both the multiplicity of positions Black people in Montgomery (and beyond) inhabited and the strategy of straightness at work here. Strategic straightness meant reinscribing the exclusion of Claudette Colvin, who was just as much a victim of Jim Crow as Rosa Parks, rendering her contestation and the contestations of those similarly situated—too young, too angry, too dark, too poor, too unrespectable—once again unintelligible as political claims.

And strategic straightness also meant the reification of the "respectable" Parks, domesticating her radicality, rendering a lifetime of political organizing that earned her and her husband blacklisting and death threats into a children's story about a "meek and mild" seamstress making an individual decision, whether personal or symbolic, to stay seated on the bus. An entire political and epistemological scaffolding, formal and informal, had to be constructed to respond to such an individual choice. And the actual organizing labor of turning an individual choice into a matter of collective action is covered over in the retroactive retelling of our national civil rights fable. Straightness as the strategy in contesting constitutive exclusion in this instance meant following and reinforcing a script that carefully restricts the political intelligibility of expressions of anger from women, and especially Black women—even when that anger is an entirely reasonable response to injustice, exclusion, and violence. It meant focusing on seemingly apolitical individual choices rather than collective actions, at the very same moment when, in the national script, collective political action on the part of Black people appears as riot. There are thus real costs for the success of this strategy.

CONCLUSION

Better questions than those of costs and benefits, of successes and failures, however, are necessary: What have we lost as a result of these exclusions? What might we still recover? Who are we as a result of these exclusions? Who might we have been? Who might we still yet be? These are the necessarily speculative questions that drive the *critique* and *contestation* of constitutive exclusion. The task of the critique of constitutive exclusion is to unearth the memory that it could have been otherwise, in service of the hope that it may yet be. Constitutive exclusion constructs a teleological arc of history in which what has happened must have happened, in which we possess a fully present past that has lead us to a homogenous and unambiguous present. The *critique* and *contestation* of constitutive exclusion calls this temporality into question, showing how the past is not finished, and the present is not in fact present to us. Insofar as the past is constructed through constitutive exclusion, its critique calls us to see that it could have been otherwise, and insofar as the present is constructed through constitutive exclusion, to demand that it be otherwise. Such questions are always already demands, and they do not pretend to be merely descriptive nor dispassionate. How could they be, when they concern the intelligibility of our lives and our actions—when they concern not only *what* we mean to each other, but *how*?

This is why the critique of constitutive exclusion must be allied with a materialist history. It calls for history as counter-memory, or history as critical genealogy. It is in this sense a radical history of the present.[39] The critique of constitutive exclusion acknowledges that political agency is never a delimited field, that it produces the shadow of its own failures and the shards of its redemption. No epistemology is entirely proper to it, as intelligible political agency can never itself be fully intelligible. Rather, the critique of constitutive exclusion calls us to remember that which we have never known.

7

Multiplicity and Collective Contestation in the 1992 Los Angeles Riots/Rebellion

In the spring of 1993, as colleges and universities around the United States prepared for graduation weekend, Los Angeles erupted in flames. On April 29, shortly after 3:00 PM, a jury in a Simi Valley courtroom acquitted four Los Angeles Police Department (LAPD) officers—Stacey Koon, Lawrence Powell, Timothy Wind, and Theodore Briseno—of multiple charges against them, including assault with a deadly weapon and filing a false police report. A year earlier, on March 3, 1991, these officers made a traffic stop in the San Fernando Valley after a high-speed chase and brutally beat the suspect, Rodney King, while seventeen other police officers looked on. The video captured by George Holliday, who lived near the scene of the beating, went viral, broadcast first on local television station KTLA and then on news programs around the world. Los Angeles waited for more than a year, patiently testing the hypothesis of equal protection under the law. When the four officers were acquitted the following spring, the response mounted in some quarters of the city—South Central, Pico

Union, Koreatown, Hollywood, and parts of West Los Angeles (LA) and the San Fernando Valley—went similarly viral, having been broadcast in part live in LA and replayed around the country.

The duration of the riot is a matter of dispute: it is generally agreed that it began after the verdict was announced, shortly after 3:00 PM on April 29, but the end could be marked at May 4, when the curfew was lifted, or at May 8, when the national guard troops began to pull out, or May 10, when the deployment was ended and the federalization of national guard troops lifted.[1] Depending on which you choose, 45–55 people were killed during the course of the riot;[2] 16,291 people were arrested, and an estimated $1 billion in property was damaged or lost.[3] It was the largest urban uprising in the United States since the Watts riot in 1965, which affected some of the same space but this time spread considerably beyond it.

The 1992 Los Angeles Riots/Rebellion is borne uneasily in the national memory. Earlier riots, such as those in Watts, Detroit, Chicago, or Washington, DC, produced performances of state and national self-reflection in the form of official governmental reports, such as the McCone report, commissioned after the 1965 Watts Riot, and the Kerner Report, commissioned in 1968, which concluded famously that the nation was becoming "two societies, one black, one white—separate and unequal."[4] A wealth of social science research on race, class, gender, policing, labor, and urban politics emerged from the crises of the 1960s. The response to the 1992 Los Angeles Riots was somewhat more ephemeral: a municipal plan to rebuild, managed mostly through public-private partnerships, that evaporated in about eighteen months; a municipal commission to study policing during the course of the riots, whose report was dead on arrival due to persistent rumors of the political influence shaping it in advance. The overall tenor of the response was one of confusion and refusal. One major work of political theory was produced in the wake of the beating of Rodney King and the Riots, and in his contribution to the book, editor Robert Gooding-Williams argues that "it strains credulity to deny, as many conservative and liberal pundits immediately wanted to do, that the uprising in Los Angeles was not for many an act of political protest . . . that blacks' interpretation of their and other Americans' needs might be taken seriously seems to be beyond the pale of intelligibility."[5]

My purpose in this chapter is to frame the frame of the riots: to use constitutive exclusion to interrogate the knot of forces that make up the 1992 Los Angeles Riots/Rebellion in order to understand if not *why* the riots remain unintelligible to us as a political contestation of political conditions, at least *how* this unintelligibility is produced, and what significance it bears for us now. If a riot is not taken as politically intelligible, if a riot is not read as a legitimate political contestation, why? What forces condition this reading? How is the riot outside the frame of intelligible political claims? The contestation of constitutive exclusion takes on a different shape here: rather than insurgence and ambiguity in Antigone's contestation of her exclusion, or the strategic straightness and reification in the choice of Parks over Colvin in the 1955 Montgomery bus boycott, the 1992 Los Angeles Riots/Rebellion offers up a complex collective figure. The constitutive exclusion of the rioters puts them outside the terms of intelligible political agency, rendering their contestation of their internal exclusion unintelligible as a political claim, and defining those included as reasonable, law-abiding, and respectable. If the riot is the language of the unheard, as the Reverend Dr. Martin Luther King Jr. argued in 1967, what went unheard in the 1992 Los Angeles Riots/Rebellion—and what remained unheard, such that we could continue to frame the uprisings that erupted in the allegedly "post-racial" age of Obama as, once again, politically unintelligible?

FRAMING THE RIOT

In one sense, riots might generally seem intelligible as a political claim or as the contestation of a political condition, even if they cannot be fully intelligible or fully explicable through the assumptions of individual intent that frequently accompany the notion of political agency. Riots are not new, and they have been central to several key political shifts throughout history (e.g., the Stamp Act riots, or other riots against food shortages or high prices prior to the American Revolution; or the Réveillon riot, the March on Versailles or other bread riots prior to the French Revolution). For the contemporary United States, however, riots are framed as politically unintelligible largely through the lens of race.

Race Riots

While there were local geographical and political specificities, prior to the second half of the twentieth century, race riots were typically a matter of whites containing, controlling, or destroying people of color and/or immigrants who were seen as encroaching on whiteness, whether a white neighborhood, a white woman, or a white job. In Memphis in 1866; East St. Louis in 1917; in the Red Summer of 1919, especially in Chicago; in Tulsa in 1921; in Cicero in 1951; whites attacked people of color, especially Black folks and immigrants perceived to be out of line.[6] Shifts in the postwar economy, white flight in combination with racist housing restrictions, urban poverty, lack of quality schooling, unemployment, informal racial employment restrictions, lack of quality housing—or, one could say, shifts in the consolidation of whiteness, which made it no longer necessary to guard the race line with direct force—helped to produce the conditions that led to the urban riots of the 1960s. This was exacerbated by frustration with the civil rights movement's progress in the North. These riots were frequently sparked by an instance of police violence (as in Harlem in 1964, Los Angeles in 1965, and Detroit in 1967) or by the 1968 assassination of Martin Luther King Jr. (in, for example, Chicago; Baltimore; Washington, DC; Louisville; and Pittsburgh).[7]

Local geographical and political specificities may have made riots relatively politically intelligible as contestations of exclusion in some cases. For instance, in her comparative analysis of race-based riots in Los Angeles, Chicago, and New York, Janet Abu-Lughod argues that a highly developed political organization was able to translate the Harlem riots of 1935 and 1943 into concessions from the city, including efforts to end employment discrimination and access to public housing. She writes that the concessions the Black community of New York won after the riots "were tangible evidence that protests could be partially successful in drawing attention to the plight of specific neighborhoods and in obtaining redress through the political process. The black community, through its political organization and its overt expressions of anger, met with responsiveness from the city's government in ways that minorities in Chicago and Los Angeles never elicited."[8]

A certain measure of faith in the ability of riots to contest political conditions or as lodging a political claim is reflected in the Los Angeles Riots Study conducted by the University of California at Los Angeles (UCLA) five months after the Watts riots in 1965. Its public opinion data showed that Blacks who lived within the riot zone were relatively hopeful that the Watts Rebellion would bring greater attention to the situation of Blacks in Los Angeles and in other cities throughout the country, and that this attention would bring relief. Public opinion among whites, however, showed that this hope may have been misplaced. The UCLA study conducted personal interviews with a sample of 2,070 and longer, two-hour interviews with a random sample of 585 Black residents in the curfew area during the riot. In this smaller sample, respondents who were able to identify multiple specific grievances were more likely to approve of the riot; 43 percent of male respondents and 36 percent of female respondents reported that the riot had helped the "Negro cause," while 52 percent of male respondents and 49 percent of female respondents believed that the riot had made white people more sympathetic to grievances in segregated South Central. Only 11 percent of male respondents and 12 percent of female respondents believed it had made whites less sympathetic.[9] A sampling of 600 white residents, however, found that while 79 percent of whites agreed that the riots had increased awareness of the problems facing Black Angelenos, only 19 percent believed that the riots had helped "the Negro's cause."[10]

Governmental reports also played a role in framing riots so as to render them more politically intelligible. Commissioned governmental reports were issued after the Watts uprising of 1965, for instance, "Violence in the City: An End or a Beginning?" more commonly known as the McCone Report (commissioned by the State of California). The era of 1960s reports on urban riots culminated in a 1968 federal report from the National Advisory Commission on Civil Disorders, or the Kerner Report, named after its chair, Otto Kerner.[11] The McCone report findings contradictorily blamed Black people and leaders within the community for failing to alleviate the conditions of South Central Los Angeles, and then went on to recommend several broad policy proposals (none of which were ever fully enacted) that the community of South Central could hardly have achieved on their own.[12] The Kerner Report was much more condemnatory; it cast the riots as a response to the political problem of structural racism for which white America was ultimately responsible. It found that though police frequently escalate, rather than ameliorate, racial tension, the primary response to riots has been to provide the police with more sophisticated (and simply more) weaponry. And it concluded famously that "Our nation is moving toward two societies, one black, one white—separate and unequal."[13] The strong language of the report, however, did not lead to the implementation of any of its recommendations (which included reforms in policing, housing, employment, welfare, and education). President Lyndon Johnson considered the report radioactive during a contentious election season. Nixon won the 1968 election, of course, on a law-and-order platform; in one television ad, he famously said, "We owe it to the decent and law-abiding citizens of America to take the offensive against the criminal forces that threaten their peace and security, and to build respect for law across this country."[14]

Aside from the need for an immediate response to intolerable conditions and the need to translate anger at injustice into action against it, Black residents of Los Angeles in 1965 may have had good reason to believe that the Watts rebellion could result in real policy changes. The examples of the 1935 and 1942 Harlem riots indicate that riots can be politically intelligible and that they can help to achieve real policy goals. But if by 1965 riots were already being pushed outside the frame of intelligible political contestation, the Johnson administration's shelving of the Kerner Report and the election of Nixon pushed them out entirely. Rather than being framed as a political response to a political condition, riots were framed by criminality, a matter of law and order. And this criminality was framed as a-, extra-, or non-political. This framing was effected materially through race, and through the racial spatialization of the city. If one sees what the McCone report refers to as the "urban core" as a kind of state of nature, inhabited by savages to be either punished or pitied, then this frame makes it easier to see the rioter as simply irrational, criminal, a thug, and a hoodlum—rather than an American engaging in a political protest against unjust conditions in the only way left available to him or her.[15] Reading riots as a political contestation of political conditions was thus made harder, as the riot and those who engaged in it were pushed into a space outside of or prior to politics. Within the frame, intelligible political action was defined as law-abiding, peaceable, respectable, and respectful of property. The framing of the riot as a criminal act and not a political event is how what the Kerner commission identified as a problem largely made by the police, found its solution—yet again—in more police.

Anti-Blackness as Frame

This shift in the political intelligibility of the riot corresponds to the consolidation of riots with Blackness in the 1960s. In *Riot, Strike, Riot*, Joshua Clover writes:

> Significantly, the history of race riots in the United States begins with whites disciplining insubordinate other populations. . . . By the second half of the 20th century, race riot summons images of spontaneous black violence. It is only then that the term comes to stand for riot as such. The rhetorical convergence is crude and effective. The purportedly thoughtless and natural character of the riot, lacking reason, organization, and political mediation, is aligned with the racist tradition wherein racialized subjects are figured as natural, as animalistic, irrational, immediate.[16]

This "rhetorical convergence" is perhaps nowhere clearer than in the 1992 Riots/Rebellion. Reporting for the *Village Voice* in the aftermath of the 1992 Los Angeles Riots/Rebellion, Peter Kwong called it "America's first multicultural riot"; as we will see, given its multiracial geography, this assessment makes good sense.[17] It was framed, however, by the "rhetorical convergence" of Blackness and riot that Clover describes. This rhetorical convergence coincides with a white supremacist perceptual framing that marks Blackness as contradictorily both invisible and hypervisible—both nothing and too much. Lewis Gordon gives an existential phenomenological analysis of the riot, arguing that it exemplifies the exponentiality of the illicit appearance of Black people in public.[18] In Gordon's account, in the perceptual schema of anti-Black society, "the effect is exponential, where a black translates into blacks. This exponentiality is the [aforementioned] hyper-visibility constitutive of invisibility. It is why, in spite of the many whites and lighter-skinned Hispanics/Latinos caught on videotape looting during the Los Angeles Riots/Rebellion, the portrait of the event is black."[19] Thus, despite Kwong's characterization of the riot as a multicultural affair, it is largely perceived as a "black" riot.

This framing of the Los Angeles Riots/Rebellion as essentially "black" seems to confirm the thesis of Afro-pessimism: that the political ontology of anti-Black racism, rooted in the non-being of the slave and the violence that enforced it, cannot be analogized to other forms of oppression, even as it frames or orients other oppressions. Afro-pessimist thought provides a framework through which to understand this convergence. Yet it is difficult to get one's arms around the project called "Afro-pessimism." This difficulty is for reasons both contingent and necessary to that project and school of thought. It is contingent in the sense that "Afro-pessimism" names less a school of thought than a loose amalgamation of scholars across different fields who share a common perspective and some common citations, many of whom tend not to identify with the label "Afro-pessimist."[20] It is necessary in the sense that Afro-pessimism works from a political ontology—or perhaps an anti-ontology—of race working from or against Orlando Patterson's account of slavery as social death, which treats anti-Black racism as the limit or the underside of capital, the nation, the human, and being itself, and which thus resists or flees systematization or appropriation.[21] Afro-pessimism puts forward a position of anti-Blackness as organizing all other fields of struggle, whether based on race, gender, or sexuality. [22] It posits Blackness as the limit-point to which all other points of struggle are positioned.

A standard criticism of such approaches is that by marking the ontological as political rather than outside political and social life, we are left without hope of resistance or subversion. Afro-pessimist thought is frequently accused of such intractability, and we can learn something about how to respond to such concerns by briefly taking it up here. And given that constitutive exclusion focuses on the production and marginalization of differences, including racial difference, that line of thought is additionally important for thinking about lines of escape. In Afro-pessimist thought, if anti-Blackness operates at the level of ontology, then how do we resist, subvert, or destroy it? Jared Sexton argues that those who embrace Afro-pessimism have tended to worry too much about its ontological claims and have missed their rhetorical function (despite the literary training and styles of many of its practitioners, Wilderson in particular):

> Astonishingly, all of this refuses to countenance the rhetorical dimensions of the discourse of Afro-pessimism . . . and the productive theoretical effects of the fiction it creates, namely, a meditation on a poetics and politics of abjection wherein racial blackness operates as an asymptotic approximate of that which disturbs every claim or formation of identity and difference as such. Afro-pessimism is thus not against the politics of coalition simply because coalitions tend systematically to render supposed common interests as the concealed particular interests of the most powerful and privileged elements of the alliance. Foremost, Afro-pessimism seeks, in Wilderson's parlance, "to shit on the inspiration of the personal pronoun we" . . . because coalitions require a logic of identity and difference, of collective selves modeled on the construct of the modern individual, an entity whose coherence is purchased at the expense of whatever is cast off by definition.[23]

The rhetorical function of Afro-pessimism's intervention is thus an attempt at exploding what Sexton argues is the "essentially dividual" subject of politics, which reduces every coalition to the interests of its most powerful members.

If this is the only model of the political subject available to us, then Sexton may be entirely correct. However, the critique of constitutive exclusion that I give here calls into question this essential dividuality of the political subject, revealing it to be produced through multiple disavowed constitutive exclusions. The analysis I have given of constitutive exclusion thus far points us not to an inclusion purchased through assimilation but to a reconstitution of politics defined by the acknowledgment of our mutual constitution. Sexton is correct to argue that inclusion is insufficient; because the terms of political agency are defined through this exclusion, any inclusion would require assimilation on the part of the excluded. To do justice to these traces would thus require not inclusion but *reconstitution*. But the multiplicity of exclusions, and the multiplicity of constitutions, points us to a different political ontology.

In its insistence on negativity and on pessimism, Afro-pessimism is similar to my account here of constitutive exclusion. However, whereas Afro-pessimism emphasizes the singularity of anti-Black racism, constitutive exclusion emphasizes multiplicity. Afro-pessimism thus bears a similarity to the incipient Schmittianism I see at work in many of the earlier theorizations of constitutive exclusion, placing anti-Black racism or the figure of the slave at the root of or the foundation of all other exclusions. Thus despite the fact that Afro-pessimist thinkers do tend to work through gender, sexuality, and class dynamics, the singularity of anti-Black racism tends to downplay some of the intra-group dynamics I examine in my analysis of Rosa Parks and Claudette Colvin in Chapter 6. Afro-pessimism thus lacks one half of the dialectical method I described in Part Two, in that it leaves shards of radicality buried within a singular anti-Blackness, potentially making it more difficult to avoid installing new exclusions as the critique proceeds.

The negativity in my account of constitutive exclusion paradoxically produces a multiplicity of exclusions and thus a multiplicity of positions from which resistance and subversion may originate—as well as the multiple vectors available to and reproduced through exclusion. Nevertheless, the rhetorical force of Afro-pessimism's emphasis on the singularity of anti-Black racism is effective, compelling, and theoretically productive. It also describes something undeniably true. That is, at least in the United States, seemingly other exclusions or other struggles—feminist struggles against rape and sexual assault; the struggle for gay marriage; or the reception of the 1992 Los Angeles Riots/Rebellion as a Black riot rather than "America's first multicultural riot"—are frequently organized or framed through anti-Black racism. Though I take a certain distance from Afro-pessimism, anti-Black racism plays the central role in the framing of the 1992 Los Angeles Riots/Rebellion as politically unintelligible.

In the next section, I offer an analysis of some of the moments that make up the event of the 1992 Los Angeles Riots/Rebellion that both confirm and complicate the singularity of anti-Blackness. The model of the LA Riots/Rebellion is a contest over the very meaning of riots, a contest over whether riots can make a political claim that the nation is bound to respect. The case for the unintelligibility of the LA Riots/Rebellion was made from the Oval Office, when then-president George H. W. Bush announced in the midst of the riots that "What we saw last night and the night before in Los Angeles is not about civil rights. It's not about the great cause of equality that all Americans must uphold. It's not a message of protest. It's been the brutality of a mob, pure and simple."[24]

Many other commentators on the riot rushed to join President Bush's assessment, that what was happening on the streets of South Central was not political protest. Robert Gooding-Williams argues that this is the result of a fundamental inability to think of Black Americans as fellow citizens: taking seriously Black Americans' own understanding of the political situations in which they live, and Black Americans' interpretation of their shared circumstances with white Americans, is, as he puts it, "beyond the pale of intelligibility."[25] Cornell West argues that the interpretations of the riot by both liberal and conservative political commentators were inadequate because they fail to understand that the problems of Black Americans are not "additions to or defections from American life, but rather constitutive elements to that life."[26] Though the civil rights movement resulted in a reconstitution of the United States, that reconstitution nevertheless occurred on the basis of the reinscription of the constitutive exclusion of Blackness outside the narrow confines of middle-class respectability (as successfully performed by Parks in her contestation). This eventuality is what Martin Luther King Jr. was grappling with in his 1967 speech, "The Other America," when he stated that "a riot is the language of the unheard."[27] An intense effort, both discursive and material, is thus made to ensure that the riot remains unheard. It is the very structure and process of this unhearing that the critique of constitutive exclusion as a political theoretical tool is meant to address, and those contestations that remain unheard it is made to unbury.

THE HOLLIDAY VIDEO

A terrible ambivalence marks the famous video George Holliday captured of the beating of Rodney King. On the one hand, its existence and its transmission to viewers around the world facilitated recognition that this actually happens, that this is what policing looks like in Los Angeles and in the United States. For many Black folks it was not exactly news but rather a confirmation of their own experience, a confirmation that they were not crazy, that what happened, what does happen, is real. On the other hand, the very same video was used to justify King's beating in the acquittal of the four officers. How is this possible?

Constitutive exclusion allows us a way to read this ambivalence. The violence that the state feels authorized to use against the bodies of people of color in the United States is disavowed under a color-blind law-and-order ideology that acts as a support to white supremacy by reproducing white innocence. This disavowal is an epistemology of ignorance that constitutively excludes Black and brown personhood and that renders Black and brown bodies threatening and criminal. The event of the video thus presented a momentary challenge to white innocence on a large scale.

On the other hand, the same video was used as the primary piece of evidence to acquit the four officers of excessive force. Judith Butler asks, "If racism pervades white perception, structuring what can and cannot appear within the horizon of white perception, then to what extent does it interpret in advance 'visual evidence'?"[28] Lawyers could rely on the racist structure of white perception to push back against that challenge, to the extent that one juror came away convinced that King was in "total control" of his own brutalization.[29] The Holliday video thus acted both as a challenge to and a confirmation of hegemonic white perception, siting the struggle over intelligibility at the level of perception itself. While the video offered a glimpse of the conditions that framed the unintelligibility structured by constitutive exclusion, it was not enough to break the frame. So long as racism structures white perception, technology will never be adequate as a response. This is the primary lesson of the Holliday video: while so many felt that the tape on the air was indisputable proof that King had been brutalized by the police and expected convictions as a result, the tape in the courtroom was instead used to prove the opposite: that the police perception of a threat—the threat to the public, in other words, the threat to whiteness—was correct, and their response was legitimate.[30] Constitutive exclusion does not have a technological solution: images from videotape, police body cameras, or dash cameras are all framed by the perceiver, and their truth is contestable. Even as these images give us a glimpse of the frame, and thus the possibility to frame the frame, the norm of the frame pushes back ever more insistently. Constitutive exclusion is a political problem, and any solution to constitutive exclusion can likewise only be political.

THE DEATH OF LATASHA HARLINS

Frequently forgotten in the temporal collapse that occurs with the name "Los Angeles Riots" is the murder of Latasha Harlins. Two weeks after the beating and arrest of Rodney King, on March 16, fifteen-year-old Latasha Harlins stopped by Empire Liquor Store for a bottle of orange juice. Harlins slipped the bottle into her backpack and headed to the front counter to pay. Soon Ja Du (who was filling in for her husband while he took a break), evidently believing Harlins intended to steal the juice, confronted her. She grabbed her by the sweater and started to yank off her backpack. Harlins fought back, striking the fifty-one-year-old Du in the face; she threw the orange juice back on the counter and turned to leave. Du drew a pistol from beneath the counter and shot Harlins in the back of the head, killing her instantly. The $2.00 with which Harlins meant to pay for the juice was in her hand. That November, Du was convicted of voluntary manslaughter. The maximum sentence for that crime in California at the time was sixteen years in prison; Judge Joyce Karlin sentenced Du to a suspended sentence, 5 years of probation, 400 hours of community service, and a $500 fine.

In the already sketchy memory of the Los Angeles Riots/Rebellion, the role played by Harlin's death and Du's sentence are barely remembered at all. It sparked the organization of boycotts of some Korean/Korean American owned stores in South Central neighborhoods, and it is mentioned in several rap tracks from the era, particularly by Tupac Shakur.[31] The larger forgetting of Harlins and Du in the story of the 1992 Los Angeles Riots/Rebellion marks another layer of constitutive exclusion sedimented into the history of the uprising. While the spectacle of the Holliday video in contrast to the acquittal of the officers provided an outwardly obvious context for the riots, the death of Harlins in contrast to Du's sentence provides an implicit, local, and almost private context that gestures to the multiracial context of the riots and to the role of gender and sexuality in them. In Barbara Stevenson's history of the Harlins case, she argues that Judge Karlin was persuaded by the defense attorney in the Du trial who

> used Harlin's youth and her muscular build to reverse Latasha's gender, from that of a "girl" to that of a "guy," from female (the traditional, vulnerable victim) to a male (the traditional, violent assailant). . . . She became in the mind of the court, that is, Judge Karlin's, the fearsome image of a black, male teen from South Central Los Angeles so grotesquely criminalized in contemporary urban

> society—a violent, black beast so prominent in historical depictions of blacks in American society.[32]

Thus the racialization of gender here hypermasculinizes Harlins, making her both older and a "guy." This echoes the hypermasculinization to which Rodney King was subject. In a statement during King's arrest but withheld from the jury in King's 1993 civil trial, Officer Stacey Koon described King's movements before female Highway Patrol Officer Melanie Singer as sexually threatening: "The fear was of a Mandingo sexual encounter."[33] Officer Koon, a representative of the state, responded to the suggestion of sex between a white woman and a Black man with violence—later joking that killing King was impossible, attributing to his Blackness both an idiocy and a hypermasculinity that made him both subhuman and a superhuman threat.[34] Koon invoked the state's investment in the protection of white femininity as justification—or alibi—for his brutality, a brutality justified retroactively (and thus erased *as* brutality) by attributing its cause to King's imagined brutality. In essence, Du's defense attorney made Latasha Harlins into Rodney King, extending momentarily the femininity the state sees fit to defend to Soon Ja Du.

In a move similar to the forgetting of Claudette Colvin, the forgetting of the death of Latasha Harlins occludes the role of gender in the riots. Part of the work of framing the riots as unintelligible occurs through these queer occlusions: despite the multiracial character of the riots, they were reified as Black; despite Harlins's gender presentation, both she and King are hypermasculine. This hypermasculnization of Blackness rendered King superhumanly strong, insensate to the blows he was receiving, and fully in control of the "situation" of his brutalization. The threat he posed was a specifically racialized hypermasculine threat: the fear of a "Mandingo sexual encounter," a ready-made justification for lynching. Similarly, in the course of Du's trial, Harlins was masculinized in her encounter with Du: much was made of how tall she was for her age, how strong, how her knuckles were scarred, how she was tough—"as tough as a guy at that same age."[35]

The correlation between Blackness and hypermasculinity corresponds to Lewis Gordon's analysis of the dynamic of hypervisibility, invisibility, and exponentiality in the illicit appearance of Black people in public.[36] In the case of Parks and Colvin, the threat of unruly Blackness was managed by stabilizing it and reifying it in the feminine figure of Rosa Parks. Here, however, intersections of race and class serve to work gender the other way: because of Harlins's class position, her hypervisibility masculizined her, invisibilizing her as a young woman, again retroactively attributing to her the very brutality that served as an excuse to end her life. The dynamic between hypervisibility and invisibility in what Gordon calls the "illicit appearance" of Blacks in public thus operates slightly differently along gender lines. Constitutive exclusion can help us better understand the sedimented exclusions at play in the riot, including gender, sexuality, and class. If, as Gordon argues, Black people do not possess the right to appear in public as a group in the United States, when they do appear, they appear as a hypermasculine exponential—meaning that when they appear singly, they already appear as a group; that is, illicitly. Further, the masculinized character of hypervisibility serves to mask the burden that Black women in particular bear, in losses of privacy and intimacy, in suffering sexualized violence that merits no state protection, and in suffering losses that are not marked as losses, occluded by the more public losses of Black men.[37]

THE MULTIRACIAL GEOGRAPHY OF THE RIOTS

When 911 calls started coming in from the neighborhoods in the riot zone on April 29, 1992, police did not show up for several hours. There were evidently no preparations made for possible violence after the verdict and the chief of police of Los Angeles, Darryl Gates, left few instructions to his deputy before heading to a political fundraiser in Brentwood. While television anchors and reporters watched Reginald Denny dragged from his truck and beaten at the corner of Normandie and Florence, they asked each other, "Where are the police?" Gates told media as he was leaving the fundraiser, "There are going to be situations where people are without assistance. . . . That's just the facts of life."[38] In an interview at Loyola Marymount University, former LA Mayor Richard Riordan explained that the lack of police response was due to the fact that after increased scrutiny of the police in the aftermath of the King beating, they didn't want bad publicity.[39]

While Black citizens of South Central Los Angeles were figured as constitutively excluded in the city and in the nation, they were not alone in occupying that fragmented space. The 1992 Los Angeles Riots/Rebellion were figured as Black in the national narrative, but more Latinxs than Blacks were arrested, whites were also arrested, and the Korean American community was targeted. That it was characterized as "America's first multicultural riot" has everything to do with the racial geography of the city. In this instance, the racialized spaces of South Central Los Angeles and Koreatown—in contrast to the racialization of other spaces, like Brentwood or Beverly Hills—are the very material sedimentation of these histories of exclusion. A kind of archaeology is thus necessary to unpack the multiracial geography of the 1992 Los Angeles Riots/Rebellion. This archaeological method shows how these multiple exclusions are related and interdependent, each illuminating the other, rather than organized entirely by a single overarching exclusion.

The space in which the 1992 riots occurred coincided somewhat with the zone of the 1965 Watts Riots/Rebellion but spread beyond it and affected different communities due to the demographic and economic shifts of the intervening thirty years. In his visit to Los Angeles in 1913, W. E. B. Du Bois lauded the Black community situated in South Los Angeles, along Central Avenue from downtown to Watts. This reputation and a wealth of post–World War II defense industry and manufacturing jobs made Los Angeles the western outpost of the Great Migration. Redlining, restrictive covenants, and violence kept prospective Black homebuyers out of white neighborhoods, and as defense money dried up and the plants closed, poverty and overcrowding was left behind. The LAPD under the leadership of Chief William Parker took up the work of enforcing the color line. As Joe Domanick wrote in the *LA Weekly*, "During the Watts riots,

Parker would speak the unspeakable, and say for all to hear on a local TV show what would never again—in the post–civil rights era—be so frankly uttered by a public official. 'It is estimated that by 1970,' said Parker, '45 percent of the metropolitan area of Los Angeles will be Negro; if you want any protection for your home and family . . . you're going to have to get in and support a strong police department. If you don't do that, God help you.' "[40] These were the conditions that were set off on August 11, 1965, when an LAPD officer beat and attempted to arrest Marquette Frye, his brother, and his stepmother, while a growing number of Watts neighbors watched and began to fight back.[41]

The neighborhoods that make up South Central Los Angeles (or South Los Angeles, as it is now identified on the map) changed significantly in the intervening twenty-eight years. Those Black residents and white ethnic Italian and Jewish residents who could afford to leave did, and an influx of Latinxs, largely political or economic refugees from Mexico, El Salvador, Guatemala, or Honduras, moved in. The Korean War in the 1950s and the lifting of racial quotas on immigrants from Asia in 1965 led to increased immigration to Los Angeles, and by 1990, Los Angeles was the second largest Korean city after Seoul.[42] Even well-educated Korean immigrants to Los Angeles often had little economic opportunity, but through an informal finance system among Koreans in Los Angeles called *kye*, many were able to purchase the small food and liquor stores in South Central neighborhoods left behind by their previous Jewish, Black, and Italian owners. Korean American–owned business had small profit margins; they were worked mainly by family members, but when they did hire, they often hired economically marginalized Latinx immigrants. These immigrants often worked in poor conditions for little money; they also complained of unfair rents in Korean American–owned buildings in and around Koreatown (which was populated largely by Latinxs).[43]

During the course of the riots, however, Blacks, Latinxs, and Korean Americans faced a common abandonment. Because police would not enter the riot zone, firefighters and ambulances stopped responding to calls as well, leaving fires to spread and the sick and injured on their own. Since their stores were targeted, Korean American store owners were faced with either abandoning their property or defending it themselves. The local Korean-language radio station kept listeners abreast of the situation in Koreatown, calling on those who were able to defend their shops. One of the lasting images of the riots is the image of several Korean Americans lining the roof of a strip mall, some wearing white bandanas, surveilling their surroundings with rifles.

Because the riot is framed through the dichotomy between Black and white in the United States, this obscures the role of Asian Americans in the riot. Those analyses of the riots that did explicitly treat Koreans and Korean Americans tended simply to pit them against African Americans or to blame them for the riot. Sumi Cho argues that Asian Americans served as the scapegoat in the Los Angeles Riots/Rebellion.[44] Cho argues that the model-minority thesis—the stereotype that hard-working, thrifty, intelligent Asians, aspiring to white norms, are a model other minorities ought, or are fundamentally unable, to follow—"represents a political backlash to civil rights struggles" by using Asian Americans as a way to discipline Black, Latinx, and Native Americans, especially those engaged in radical political struggle.[45] Citing Frank Chin and Jeffrey Paul Chang's 1972 essay, she refers to this "embrace" of Asian Americans by the white majority as "racist love," in that it has nothing to do with the concern for the well-being of Asian Americans but instead is used as a means of legitimating the ongoing oppression of other people of color.

Korean Americans were therefore "triply scapegoated" by the model minority thesis during the riots: first, in that they were targeted for looting and burning; second, in that they were abandoned by the LAPD so that it could protect wealthier white neighborhoods; and third, in that they were stereotyped in the media and their voices were excluded from media coverage.[46] In that coverage, Korean Americans were positioned either as the true victims and valiant defenders of property in the face of brutal, wild, criminal rioters, or as the racist exploiters of the Black community; their participation in this was largely passive, however, since mainstream media interviewed almost no Korean-speaking people. This scapegoating served to let white Americans off the hook for the abandonment of South

Central, doing the work of reinforcing the frame defining political agency as respectful of property and the law.

As Cho writes, "Korean Americans are instrumentalized in a larger public relations campaign on behalf of Euro-Americans."[47] Black people in South Central targeted Korean-owned shops because they blamed Korean Americans for the economic deprivation and racist exploitation they experienced, precisely because they were positioned between Black South Central and white Los Angeles. When white neighborhoods were threatened, however, they received police protection, while the model minorities were abandoned, just as Black Americans in South Central were. The Korean American community was devastated by the losses of the riot, and certainly some of them retained a bitterness toward their Black neighbors. Many others, however, recognized their commonality with them; they expressed this in the largest rally of Asian Americans in the United States to date, when 30,000 gathered in Ardmore Park in Koreatown before the riot had ended, in solidarity with their Black neighbors, where many marchers carried signs that said "Justice for Rodney King" and reached out to shake the hands of Black onlookers.[48]

Latinxs, as I have noted, also occupied the fragmented space of constitutive exclusion in the Los Angeles Riots/Rebellion and make up perhaps the most politically unintelligible and invisible exclusion. As an ethnic group, Latinxs made up half of those arrested during the course of the riots, whereas Black people made up about 40 percent and whites around 10 percent. Mike Hernandez, a city councilman representing the Latinx neighborhood of Pico-Union, stated in a report commemorating the twenty-fifth anniversary of the Riots/Rebellion that when he asked for the National Guard troops that had been deployed to the city to protect Pico-Union, he was sent US Immigration and Naturalization officers instead.[49] Despite Special Order 40—an LAPD rule that bars police from inquiring after a person's immigration status, with certain exceptions—more than 1,200 Latinxs were transferred to the US Immigration and Naturalization Service and deported.[50] By 1990, South Central was about half Latinx, with the Black population living mostly on the west side while Latinxs lived mostly to the east.[51] Many were recent immigrants from El Salvador,

Nicaragua, Guatemala, and Mexico, having fled either political violence or economic violence or both. The income of 30 percent was below the poverty line, and unemployment was high. They lived in some areas that had never really been rebuilt after the Watts riots in 1965, taking up residence in whatever was available at very low rent. Latinxs also made up a majority of the residents in Koreatown: Korean Americans owned about half the stores in Koreatown but made up only about 10 percent of its residents; Latinxs made up two-thirds of the residents of Koreatown, and 30 percent to 40 percent of the owners of stores destroyed in the riot.[52] Korean American–owned stores were thus targeted by Latinxs as much as by Black folks.

Most accounts of the role of Latinxs in the LA Riots/Rebellion stop there. All we have, it seems, are some sketchy statistics; there is little story. In much of the narrative of the riots, Latinxs are an afterthought or an addendum, a minimization of their role given the numbers of Latinxs who participated in or were arrested or killed during the course of the riots. What can we make of this unintelligibility in the constitutive exclusion of Latinxs in the 1992 Los Angeles Riots/Rebellion?

Part of the story must be in the (admittedly rough) distinction between Latinxs and Chicanxs in Los Angeles, since, as Cho notes, the relatively older or better-established communities of second- and third-generation immigrants, and those who never immigrated at all, were rooted in East LA; and the poorer and more recent immigrants, from Central America as well as Mexico, were in South Central and Koreatown. These distinctions rooted in class, nation of origin, and indigeneity among those identified in the larger national context as "Latinx" played a role here, as the east side stayed fairly quiet during the riot, and possible antagonisms, or possible solidarities, were played out on the streets that made up the border between predominantly Black and predominantly Latinx South Central. Latinxs and Black people in South Central had been left to fight over the last scraps of a dying economy. Given the segregation of the city, the economic abandonment of South Central following the 1965 Watts riots, and the influx of Latinxs, but hardly any Black folks, into the neighborhood, Black residents of South Central often felt that they faced tighter competition for less and less available work. On the other hand, Latinxs shared with Black folks animosity toward Korean American business owners and landlords, as they felt mistreated and exploited by them.

Latinxs were uniquely vulnerable given their situation, and as a result they are constitutively excluded and politically unintelligible in a particular manner. Their political unintelligibility is characterized less by stereotypes and cultural imperialism than by silence and invisibility. The constitutive exclusion of transnational Latinx immigrants (and some who may not have been immigrants but who lacked proper documentation) was perhaps starkest in that so many were literally thrust beyond the city by being deported. Others were constitutively excluded within the city of Los Angeles in that they were exploited economically, but they were central to the economic health of the city, the region, and the profit margins of many small, and sometimes Korean-owned, businesses; they felt they were subject to unfair rents and poor housing conditions, and due to their marginal legal status, they were much less likely to complain about these conditions. Last, they were criminalized and targeted by police. Latinxs thus had their own reasons to make common cause with their Black neighbors to target Korean-owned business and protest their targeting and harassment by police.

THE VERDICT AND THE STRUGGLE OVER THE MEANING OF THE RESPONSE

On the afternoon of April 29, after seven days of deliberation, a jury made up of nine whites, one Asian, one Latino, and one biracial man in a Simi Valley courtroom acquitted officers Briseno, Koon, Wind, and Powell of all charges in the beating of Rodney King. The venue of the decision was significant, as the defendants had requested the trial be moved from Los Angeles to Simi Valley, an LAPD stronghold.

The acquittal ties Holliday's video of King's beating (the video, not necessarily the act itself, as the video both made the beating "news" to begin with and was central in the acquittal) to the violence that unfolded in the days that followed. In the intervening thirteen months, between the video and the verdict, a great patience was exercised, an expression of faith in equality before the law, or a testing of the hypothesis of constitutive exclusion. When the courts affirmed that hypothesis, the contestation of exclusion took place in the only venue left—in the streets.

Rather than a single figure, or a pair, the 1992 Los Angeles Riots/Rebellion presents us instead with a fractured collectivity. How are we to read this? I do not claim that the critique of constitutive exclusion can render the protracted event of the riots fully intelligible. However, it can fill in the distance between "fully intelligible" and "beyond the pale of intelligibility." The Los Angeles Riots/Rebellion is unintelligible as an instance of political protest and the rioters are unintelligible as political actors as part of their constitutive exclusion, and this constitutive exclusion is negotiated primarily through race, class, and gender. The Black citizens of South Central Los Angeles are the excluded element against which the nation defines itself, but who remain within, continuing to figure the borders of citizenship, nationhood, and political agency in this country. Since their constitutive labor cannot be recognized, they cannot be understood as political agents contesting political conditions. Their unintelligibility renders them and their claims to those on the "inside" of this hegemony as criminal, wild, and destructive. The rioter is therefore part of a mob—or, by Gordon's thesis, the Black rioter *already is* the mob—irrationally "destroying their own neighborhood," a rhetorical construction that effectively renders invisible the infrastructures of racial spacing (redlining, restrictive covenants, freeways, economic abandonment, policing) that created these neighborhoods. As Gooding-Williams argues, the Black residents of South Central were treated as either the perpetrators or the victims of the conditions that fed the riots, depending on the political framing involved.[53] Similarly, Korean Americans were seen as either the victims or the heroes struggling against their Black neighbors, while Latinxs are seen (when they are seen at all) as incidental participants. All of these perspectives presume the riot as a primarily criminal event: a threatening rupture of the state of nature into the political status quo, but not itself a political protest, a statement on or an action against a shared political situation.

The constitutive exclusion of the rioter does work for those of us on the "inside" of this hegemonic frame, in that it constitutes the United States as a nation of reasonable, responsible, law-abiding citizens. The bewilderment at and the rejection of the destruction of property constructs Americans as respectful and protective of private property—over and above Black and Latinx lives. While public opinion data after the 1965 Watts Riots/Rebellion showed that many Black residents of Los Angeles believed that the riots would bring attention to and ameliorate the marginalization and oppression faced by Black people in Los Angeles and other US cities, white respondents agreed that it had raised attention, but the attention it raised was mostly bad. By 1992, the narrative had settled in, the rioter interpreted as rioting primarily for "fun and profit," gleefully stealing consumer goods and torching the building on the way out.[54] That is not to say that looting and arson did not happen; certainly they did. The fact that rioters specifically targeted Korean and Korean American owned shops, however, indicates that something more than mere irrational destruction, or the joy of getting something for nothing, was at work. Indeed, the Du's store, Empire Liquors, was one of the first to burn.

Moreover, the condemnation and in some cases the shooting of purported looters scavenging for basic necessities during Hurricane Katrina in New Orleans in 2005 should remind us that we cannot count white hegemonic perception as neutral on this score. There may be complex motives at work in looting. In his reporting for *LA Weekly* during the 1992 Riots, Rubén Martínez quotes a Chicana mother who was looting goods: "This is about trying to get something to eat for our kids. Who knows where we're going to get food, once everything has been destroyed?"[55] Indeed, during the curfew period, there were few to no shops left or open in which to buy food, diapers, or baby formula, and many residents lacked either cars or the gas to put in them during the course of the riot.

Beyond other motives for looting, we might pay closer attention to the political significance of looting itself, especially looting from stores whose owners are viewed as exploitative, racist, or profiting from the maintenance of intense segregation. After the initial riots in Ferguson, Missouri, in response to the police murder of Black teenager Michael Brown, De

Andre Smith eloquently defended looting as a political tactic in relation to specific conditions of exploitation in the St. Louis area:

> This is how they eat here, this is how they receive money. Businesses, the taxes, police stopping people, giving them tickets, taking them to court, locking them up. That's how they make money in St Louis. Right? Traffic . . . everything is about money in St. Louis, right? So when you stop their flow of income, when you stop their whole everything, their business, which they organize—they have certain things in a certain way, right? Secret society type of deal. Right? We're gonna eat and you guys are gonna starve. Gentrification—put you in a certain neighborhood by yourself, and see if you can starve in a proper way. It's not gonna happen. Not in St. Louis.[56]

Indeed, the Justice Department Report on policing in Ferguson (released the following spring as a result of the pressure exerted by the riots) confirmed the very conditions Smith describes here. It found a widespread abuse of police authority and court practices designed to extract money from its Black residents as a strategy for funding municipal government.[57] Ta-Nehisi Coates, a writer for the *Atlantic*, took this lesson from the Department of Justice Report: "White supremacy is the technology, patented in this enlightened era, to ensure that what is yours inevitably becomes mine."[58] Under these conditions, looting cannot simply be understood as irrational criminal behavior, or "fun and profit." Indeed, these perspectives shore up a strict distinction between political protest and private property, keeping us from asking after the very political conditions of ownership. At best, it keeps us from pursuing a deeper analysis of the racial technologies of profit making. At worst, it maintains the notion that property is as or more important than the lives and personhood of Black citizens. As was the case in Ferguson, the rejection of the possibility of seeing looting in the Los Angeles Riots/Rebellion in political terms serves to maintain its unintelligibility as a contestation of constitutive exclusion, and thus maintain the hegemonic white supremacist definitions of the political.

CONCLUSION

Ultimately, the immediate rejection of the possibility that the 1992 Los Angeles Riots/Rebellion could be a political response to political conditions served to reinforce the hegemonic construction of politics and of political agency in the United States, and rendered the Riots unintelligible as a contestation of constitutive exclusion. This unintelligibility covers over layers of complex operations of exclusion at work in the Riots: its geography, its gender and sexuality, its class, its multiraciality. This unintelligibility was never necessary, and it is not now necessary; just as the anti-Blackness that frames the unintelligibility of the riots is not necessary, despite its function in ensuring that riots remain the language of the unheard.

The role of the police is certainly significant in this framing. The LAPD functioned as the agents of exclusion in the case of the Black residents of South Central and the Latinx residents of Koreatown, by using Korean and Korean American residents and shopowners as a racial buffer or border population.[59] Insofar as the rioters were confined to the same spaces, this was not simply because police could easily block off streets to control the spread of the riot (a challenge in a city as freeway-dependent as Los Angeles), but because of patterns of poverty and segregation, produced through a long history of residential exclusions, criminalization, and police brutality. Because police ceased responding to calls from within the riot zone, fire and ambulance services ceased responding as well; no matter who was calling, they were all equally abandoned. At the same time, the contestation of exclusion from inside the riot zone was unintelligible as a political protest of political conditions.

The role of police in producing political unintelligibility is decisive: shifting riots from a political protest to a matter of security; rendering protestors criminals, or threats to public safety, or (under conditions of the increased militarization of policing) terrorists further serves to render political protest in almost any form unintelligible as political and to exclude those who engage in it in such a way that our terms of politics and political agency are increasingly impoverished.

When the encampments of the Occupy Movement in Zuccotti Park, Oakland, Los Angeles, and many other places around the country were described as threats to public health—or when police in these cities expressed concerns with the drug use, theft, and sexual assault they hoped to produce by treating the encampments as a free zone, directing what they saw as potential criminals to the encampments and then refusing calls from those inside the encampments for protection—these spaces were effectively *de-politicized*, and the police response was predetermined. When the Baltimore police department's media relations unit posted a fabricated public notice in advance of planned protests against the killing of Freddie Gray in April 2016 that criminal gangs in Baltimore had declared a truce in order to unify their forces against the Baltimore Police Department, this had the effect of de-politicizing the protest in advance, rendering it merely a security matter. When marginalized and oppressed people fight back against intolerable political conditions in the streets and are rendered "thugs," criminals, or terrorists, and not as political agents making a political critique of political conditions, constitutive exclusion is at work.[60] The political unintelligibility of the riot, especially that produced by the police and through the frame of anti-Blackness, may be the lasting legacy of the Los Angeles Riots/Rebellion.

Postscript

In March of 2003, I left my job as a receptionist at a downtown law office in Chicago to join several friends and several thousand strangers to protest the US military bombardment and invasion of Iraq. The protest was filled with all kinds of people: young and old, moms pushing strollers, aging hippy types, gay liberation activists, the committed and the curious. That afternoon we skirted the riot gear–outfitted Chicago police officers and marched up Lake Shore Drive (LSD), shutting down rush hour traffic for an angry and joyful stroll up the scenic artery as night fell on the city.

We convened at the top of the hairpin turn on LSD, in a park just in front of the Drake hotel, while we contemplated what came next. A group of fellow protesters near the front began to chant "We just want to shop! We just want to shop!" making a move to head back downtown via Michigan Avenue, the "Magnificent Mile" shopping district of Chicago. At this point, however, it became clear that we were blocked by police who had caught up with us, in cars, on horseback, on motorcycles, and on foot. Silence fell over the crowd while we waited to see what was happening next. We were being kettled: police issued an order to disperse while forming a perimeter to keep us from leaving. More than 700 people would be arrested that night—the largest mass arrest in the city's history—and shipped off in flex cuffs and paddy wagons to Area 2 police headquarters, a notorious jail facility in the south side of the city (which had been the site of numerous acts of torture and violence perpetrated by Chicago police under the orders of police commander Jon Burge).

My friends and I had managed to escape down an alleyway after convincing some police that we were only interested in finding a bathroom. We made it home, exhausted yet energized. On the television, we watched open-mouthed as the cops closed in on the protestors we left behind. A live reporter on the scene stated that he had witnessed people who had not taken part in the protest, people who had just exited a restaurant and stepped out into the street, being arrested and tossed in the back of a paddy wagon. The news anchor told the reporter in no uncertain terms that because the police had issued an order to disperse, those arrested had failed to comply and so were obviously criminal. Incredulous, the reporter repeated what he had just told the anchor: that he had seen people who were in no way involved with the protest arrested. The anchor asked whether the protestors had weapons, such as bats and clubs; the reporter replied that they carried signs and placards.

It felt for the first time that I was seeing something true spoken beneath the lie. I saw a new face of power in the newsman asserting a lie that flew in the face of the account of his own reporter; I saw that reporter respond with astonished disbelief in what he was hearing from his own anchor. There was something real and true happening here. It was one of my first lessons of the Iraq War, one that I held onto, as it helped to make sense of the upside-down world I had just discovered I lived in.

The aftermath of September 11 introduced me to this peculiar sensation of being down the rabbit hole: the feeling that my perceptions about what was real and what was not, my understandings about what was true and what was not, my certainty that I was being lied to no longer bore any resemblance to the perceptions, understandings, and certainties of most of my peers and the nation at large. Rather than something hypothetical or abstract, epistemology became a dizzying daily experience, with real material consequences: fear, war, death. It was a hard education. But I have come to know it as a vital one, one that opened me up to the ways many others understand themselves to have been subject to a crazy-making contradictory sense of what is true and not, what is real and not. Most important, it has led me to understand the political uses of epistemology, the real political work done through rendering some claims unintelligible, and the rendering of some people unintelligible as political agents. The need to make sense of this, where it comes from and why and how it happens—as well as how to subvert, resist, or change it—drives the analysis of this book.

Constitutive exclusion is the conceptual tool I've developed to do this work of understanding and contesting the structure and process of political unintelligibility. I've developed the concept of constitutive exclusion throughout this book in order to better understand the construction of political bodies and political agency. I argue that, on the one hand, constitutive exclusion establishes political bodies and secures the agency of political subjects. On the other hand, constitutive exclusion makes any such secure establishment, either of political bodies or political agency, impossible. The difference between these is repression or disavowal—a not seeing, or a not knowing, built into the very definition of the political body or the concept of political agency. This is what makes constitutive exclusion a fundamentally political-epistemological problem. The language of a specifically *political* epistemology points to a sort of theoretical upgrade to feminist philosophies that focus on *social* epistemology. Social epistemologists argue that knowledge is socially situated. But I emphasize the political rather than the social, and my approach—informed by feminist and queer theory—takes up gender as a political system and thus treats political agency as gendered. My approach is also informed by critical philosophies of race and critical race theories that take up white supremacy as a political system and thus treat political agency as raced.

If it is the case that constitutive exclusion presents us with a political epistemological problem, it would seem to be an intractable one, since the hegemonic political ontology under which we operate requires us to not hear some claims as political claims. Rather than referring us to a space beyond or before politics, however, constitutive exclusion describes the border drawn between ontology and epistemology as itself a political operation, one that marks off the delimited space of hegemonic politics from its excluded, yet internal, conditions. The multiplicity of constitutive exclusion points us to a different political ontology, however: given the multiplicity of exclusions that shape the present political field and the political agency that it animates, the analysis of constitutive exclusion points us to a pluralist political ontology. As I argued in the previous chapters, to do justice to the exclusions on which our politics is founded would require not inclusion on the model of assimilation but rather reconstitution—the redemption of those shards of radicality left buried beneath and within us. While the analyses of constitutive exclusion that hew toward ontology typically flee into the abstract, the pluralist political ontology I envision here is instead rooted in the concrete. It is a way to account for the material resources for reconstitution, resources that revolutionize our very abilities to hear claims formerly unintelligible to us as political claims to which we must attend or for which we are responsible.

To draw the outlines of this pluralist political ontology, I want to briefly highlight two approaches to multiplicity, one from the side of the theoretical and one from the side of the practical (though the distinction between these is hardly a distinction at all). The first is from women of color feminist thought: from Audre Lorde and from María Lugones. The second is from the Black Lives Matter movement.

Popular educator and feminist philosopher María Lugones fleshes out a political ontology in keeping with the multiplicity indicated by constitutive exclusion in her book *Pilgrimages/Peregrinajes*. Lugones writes, "I am incomplete and unreal without other women. I am profoundly dependent on others without having to be their subordinate, their slave, their servant."[1] *Pilgrimages/Peregrinajes* is, among other things, a protracted contestation of white feminism, contesting its hegemony by calling out the ways white women block identification with women of color and thus refuse their own plural selves. At the risk of falling into the very traps Lugones identifies as the ones that white feminists frequently fall into, such as fleeing into theory when white feminism's racism is called out by women of color, and separating the theoretical tools of Latina feminism from the liberatory purpose for which they were crafted, I want to argue that the pluralist ontology and the interdependency without domination that she develops in *Pilgrimages/Peregrinajes* is significant for the development of a political ontology appropriate to the political epistemology I have articulated above, one that would upend from within and from below a political agency formed through constitutive exclusion and point us to a future without it.

In her essay "On the Logic of Pluralist Feminism," Lugones makes a distinction between what she identifies as the logic of purity and the logic of multiplicity. The logic of multiplicity she likens to emulsion, or to the combined mixing and separation in the making of mayonnaise. Under this logic, "the social world is complex and heterogeneous and each person is multiple, nonfragmented, embodied."[2] The logic of purity she likens to separating an egg yolk from the egg white, in which the goal is a total separation of the two. According to the logic of purity, she argues, "the social world is both unified and fragmented, homogeneous, hierarchically ordered. Each person is either fragmented, composite, or abstract and unified—not exclusive alternatives. Unification and homogeneity are related principles of ordering the social world. Unification requires a fragmented and hierarchical ordering. Fragmentation is another guise of unity, both in the collectivity and in the individual."[3] Both logics organize the world in real material ways, but the logic of purity is the hegemonic political logic, one recognizable to us as a result of the analysis in Part One. To interpret multiplicity as fragmentation/unity requires the production of a perspective from which to capture totality; this requires the production of a viewpoint that is one-dimensional, abstract, and ahistorical.[4] The logic of unity requires more than mere interpretation, however: it requires actual domination, such that it can "order people's lives and psyches."[5] This domination functions through a radical self-deception on the part of those privileged in the logic of unity. This privilege is produced by the labor of others—women, the poor, people of color, queers—who are rendered fragmentary, who are remaindered, and whose labor cannot be recognized.[6]

Lugones's account of the logics of purity and multiplicity bear a close affinity to the account of constitutive exclusion I have described in *Excluded Within*. Her aims are different from my own: they begin from a different place, a place from which mestiza consciousness analyzes the incoherency and contradictoriness of those subjects ruled by the logic of unity and totality with a wary, watchful eye, sometimes with laughter, sometimes with what she will call "duplicitous perception." She is not concerned with translating the claims of the logic of multiplicity into the language of the logic of fragmentation/unity.[7] She is more interested in articulating the resources and modes of resistance to what she refers to as intermeshed oppressions. However her methods—confrontation, multilinguality, the mixing of traditional epistemological analysis and the deep practical wisdom of the kitchen—flesh out a mode of listening for what one is constituted not to hear. The pluralist ontology Lugones lays out in *Pilgrimages/Peregrinajes* articulates one way of thinking both the hegemonic form of politics and the excluded resources for subverting it, at the same time.

Audre Lorde's pluralist ontology lies in the background of her visionary feminism, but it frames some of her most significant interventions. In her essay, "On the Uses of Anger," Lorde calls out the racism of white feminism, which she argues is partially effected through displacing a shared anger at racism onto Black feminists such as herself. Rather than refusing that anger and abdicating responsibility for oppressing others by taking refuge in the self-righteousness of one's own oppression, she challenges us:

> I am a lesbian woman of Color whose children eat regularly because I work in a university. If their full bellies make me fail to recognize my commonality with another woman of Color whose children do not eat because she cannot find work, or who has no children because her insides are rotted from home abortions; if I fail to recognize the lesbian who chooses not to have children, the woman who remains closeted because her homophobic community is her

> only life support, the woman who chooses silence instead of another death, the woman who is terrified lest my anger trigger the explosion of hers; if I fail to recognize them as other faces of myself, then I am contributing not only to each of their oppressions but also to my own. . . . I am not free while any woman is unfree, even when her shackles are very different from my own. And I am not free as long as one person of Color remains chained. Nor is any one of you.[8]

Lorde gives us a pluralist ontology that is complex and concrete. While in much of the rest of the speech she takes white feminists to task for their racism in refusing to acknowledge difference, here she models an ethics and a politics of difference that is rooted in a pluralist ontology. She views women who are different from herself as faces of herself, taking responsibility for women whose differences she has failed to recognize. This responsibility is rooted in a notion of the self as shaped by multiplicity, a self with many faces, some of which go unrecognized. This failure results in an unconscious continuation of conditions of oppression, even as one struggles against one's own oppression. So Lorde gives us a model of pluralist ontology that results not in an assimilationist inclusion that would leave the hegemonic political field largely unchanged, but rather a conception of plural or multiple political agency that is revolutionary and abolitionist. It finds the resources for revolutionizing our politics and our political agency in that very multiplicity, for the purposes of ending the exclusions that continue to shape them. This pluralist political ontology is available to us, however, only by listening: Lorde challenges her audience to give up the fear and guilt they use as a defense against hearing the insight in the anger they share with her at racism. Only by being able to hear anger can we learn to use the resources of our differences rather than rendering difference merely deviance in relation to the "mythical norm"—or, in Lugones's language, the logic of purity—that organizes our lives. Thus her pluralist political ontology is a way to account for the resources for reconstituting both our politics and our selves and is in service to a revolutionary political epistemological practice to accomplish this reconstitution.

This pluralist political ontology of both critique and resistance is evidenced in the political theory and practice of Black Lives Matter (BLM). This movement began in Oakland in the summer of 2013 the night after a jury in Florida acquitted George Zimmerman for the murder of Trayvon Martin. After a protest action in Oakland, Alicia Garza posted "A Love Note to Black People" on Facebook, saying "Our Lives Matter, Black Lives Matter." Her friend Patrice Cullors reposted this with the hashtag #BlackLivesMatter. The two women, together with Opal Tometi, all three of them veteran organizers, began to think about how to connect social media campaigns with on-the-ground organizing efforts. These came to fruition in the aftermath of the police killing of Michael Brown in Ferguson, Missouri, the next summer; a group of activists, including Cullors and Darnell Moore, brought a busload of activists to Ferguson to give assistance to local organizing in response to Michael Brown's killing. Careful attention to the particular needs of local organizations, in combination with the intensified attention to this effort brought by social media, sparked actions across the country in protest of the killing of Michael Brown and in solidarity with Ferguson. Similar actions were sparked nationwide in response to the murders of Eric Garner, Freddie Gray, Sandra Bland, Lacquan Macdonald, Rekia Boyd, Alton Sterling, and Philando Castile. While national media made efforts to position each victim of police violence in relation to their presumed criminality, Black Lives Matter chapters and allied organizations worked to mark each loss as a full loss, including many others that never made national headlines, especially the murders of trans women of color.

BLM has always operated on the basis of queer black feminist principles, and its organizers—a loose collective of affiliated chapters, rather than a hierarchical organization in the traditional vein of the civil rights movement—have always sought to center the experiences of the most marginalized. Garza writes, "Black Lives Matter affirms the lives of Black queer and trans folks, disabled folks, Black-undocumented folks, folks with records, women and all Black lives along the gender spectrum. It centers those who have been marginalized within Black liberation movements. It is a tactic to (re)build the Black liberation movement."[9] Acknowledging the ways that Black Lives Matter both builds on and moves beyond previous anti-racist struggles, Garza writes, "Progressive movements in the United States have made some unfortunate errors when they push for unity at the expense of really understanding the concrete differences in context, experience, and oppression. In other words, some want unity without struggle."[10]

Black Lives Matter—along with organizations in solidarity with #BLM, such as BYP100, Assata's Daughters, the Movement for Black Lives, and We Charge Genocide—offer a direct response to the politics of respectability that featured in the contestation of the constitutive exclusion in the model of the Montgomery bus boycotts in Chapter 6. While that model leveraged a strategy of straightness to advance its political goals, Black Lives Matter operates contrary to this model, emphasizing those most marginalized rather than those most accommodating to the hegemonic status quo. Black Lives Matter and allied organizations, in their theory and practice, seek to unearth the radical potential that the strategy of strategic straightness left buried in Claudette Colvin. Their strategy recognizes the multiplicity of exclusions on which the constitution of the polity and political agency relies. It counters them by centering the experience of those most marginalized by hegemonic conditions and insisting on the political agency of those for whom other venues for political contestation are closed. It insists on rendering intelligible the political claims of those most politically unintelligible, unearthing the radical potentiality buried in the overlapping constitutive exclusions of our polity. And it insists on doing so in the venues still open to such contestations, taking on the risks of unintelligibility where they are most solidified: in refusal, in disruption, in the street.

Black Lives Matter's insistence on centering the most marginalized is a practice of the contestation of constitutive exclusion in its very multiplicity. It recognizes the multiplicity of constitutions, and it works from the most marginalized of these overlapping or intermeshing exclusions. It faces the unified, self-identical construction of the polity and of political agency with its own fantasy, claiming the plurality of its construction through rescuing the multiplicity of the exclusions that define its construction. And it pushes us to listen to what we have refused to hear, to see what we have refused to face, redeeming the shards of radical potential buried under the collective figure of the rioter, the criminal.

The work of Black Lives Matter and of María Lugones and Audre Lorde echo the pluralist ontology suggested by the critique of constitutive exclusion. We have made ourselves plural, already, without recognizing it or knowing it—or rather, some of "us" already recognize it and know it, without "us" listening, without "us" hearing. A pluralist political ontology would break the spell of the hegemonic political epistemology and thus would mean working through the lessons drawn from the analysis of the models of contestation sketched above. How can we recognize our condition of interdependency? How can we create a world of interdependency without domination? How can we become less certain? How can we read for that particular absence necessary to the presence we hear, see, recognize as already intelligible? How can we listen to those claims that are unintelligible to us as political claims? How can we re-orient our ways of knowing, such that, when we hear a claim that seems unintelligible to us as a political claim, we listen carefully, with the faith that what we are hearing may tell us something important about who we are? Even if, especially if, rather than requiring the assimilation of those challenges to our own idiom, we are required to translate ourselves, *we are required to reconstitute the we of our selves*, as a result?

The question of the "we" has haunted this project. As a work about our political constitution, this ought to be the case. Lugones, Lorde, and #BLM teach us that the question of the "we" is even more complex. A pluralist ontology puts into question the very constitution of that "we": how is a "we" made? Is it produced on an additive model—an "I," plus an "I," plus an "I" equals a "we"? Is it intersectional—a "we" produced by a network of "I"s, crisscrossing each other, amplifying or resignifying the selves located at the intersections of identities articulated in and through discourse? Is it an assemblage—a "we" that is an amalgamation of more or less sticky identities, articulated through time? If, as I have argued, we currently live under a conception of the "we" that is articulated through the production of various others who cannot belong to this we, and who are yet nevertheless crucial to its existence, a pluralist ontology might chart a path out of this intolerable not seeing, not hearing, this intolerable epistemology of ignorance.

A pluralist political ontology would do this by positing an I that is already a we, in ways that these I/we's cannot fully articulate, in ways that these I/we's do not fully control or understand. It would thus require an epistemic humility rather than certainty, a careful listening to what is dismissed as "crazy," an understanding that insofar as we have "the brutality of a mob, pure and simple," that this mob is neither pure nor simple, as *we are* also this mob. It would require the understanding that there are "I"s that are "we"s that are not defined by "us," or that have nothing to do with this "us" that "we" are—in the overlapping texture of this "we," some parts would be here, some parts would not be here, without any parts being eclipsed or erased or, as Audre Lorde put it, plucked out. It would require an adoption of an attitude of intolerance toward the intolerable. It would require the faith of the faithless, of the kind that would sustain real material work; it would require vigilance. To become an I that is already a we, to become radically dependent on each other in ways that are not reducible to being a subordinate or a slave, to be vulnerable to each other—that is, to become what we are, *to become what we have already become*, retroactively—would be a becoming worthy of the name.

NOTES

CHAPTER 1

1. Sophocles, "Antigone," in *Sophocles I*, ed. Richmond Lattimore, trans. David Grene (Chicago: University of Chicago Press, 1991). In recent years there has been a resurgent interest in Antigone in political and feminist philosophy. See Tina Chanter and Sean D. Kirkland, *The Returns of Antigone: Interdisciplinary Essays* (Albany: State University of New York Press, 2014); Bonnie Honig, *Antigone, Interrupted* (Cambridge: Cambridge University Press, 2013); Tina Chanter, *Whose Antigone? The Tragic Marginalization of Slavery* (Albany: State University of New York Press, 2011); S. E. Wilmer and Audrone Zukauskaite, *Interrogating Antigone in Postmodern Philosophy and Criticism* (New York: Oxford University Press, 2010); Fanny Söderbäck, *Feminist Readings of Antigone* (Albany: State University of New York Press, 2012); Cecilia Sjöholm, *The Antigone Complex: Ethics and the Invention of Feminine Desire* (Stanford, CA: Stanford University Press, 2004); Judith Butler, *Antigone's Claim: Kinship Between Life and Death* (New York: Columbia University Press, 2000); J. Peter Euben, *Corrupting Youth: Political Education, Democratic Culture, and Political Theory* (Princeton, NJ: Princeton University Press, 1997); George Steiner, *Antigones* (New Haven, CT: Yale University Press, 1996).
2. Jean Anouilh, *Antigone: A Play* (New York: Samuel French, 2002); Athol Fugard, John Kani, and Winston Ntshona, *Statements* (New York: Theatre Communications Group, 1974); Seamus Heaney, *The Burial at Thebes: A Version of Sophocles' Antigone* (New York: Macmillan, 2014).
3. Brooks Barnes, "From Footnote to Fame in Civil Rights History," *New York Times*, November 26, 2009, sec. Books, http://www.nytimes.com/2009/11/26/books/26colvin.html; Meghan Cox Gurdon, "'Claudette Colvin,'" *Wall Street Journal*, November 21, 2009, sec. Life & Style, http://www.wsj.com/articles/SB10001424052748704204304574545643701327028.
4. While both the NAACP and the Women's Political Council seemed to agree on the strategy of contesting segregation in the courts, there is evidence that the Women's Political Council pushed for the more radical—and more risky—boycott strategy. Jo Ann Robinson, *Montgomery Bus Boycott and the Women Who Started It: The*

Memoir of Jo Ann Gibson Robinson, ed. David J. Garrow (Knoxville: University of Tennessee Press, 1987).

5. Barnes, "From Footnote to Fame in Civil Rights History."
6. I adopt this ambivalence explicitly in my usage of "riots/rebellion," following Lewis Gordon in his 2012 essay, "Of Illicit Appearance: The L.A. Riots/Rebellion as a Portent of Things to Come " (*Truthout*, http://www.truth-out.org/news/item/9008-of-illicit-appearance-the-la-riots-rebellion-as-a-portent-of-things-to-come). The contestation over the language to describe what happened in the streets is marked in the only major work of political thought to take up the riots, Robert Gooding-Williams's 1992 *Reading Rodney King/Reading Urban Uprising* (New York: Routledge, 1993), whose essays' titles treat the event variably as an uprising, a rebellion, and a "riot" (quotation marks included). As if confirming Gordon's thesis, this contestation at the level of language itself has been repeated as the country grappled with riots/rebellions in Ferguson and in Baltimore. See Robin D. G. Kelley, "Baltimore and the Language of Change." *Los Angeles Times*, May 4, 2015; and Karen Grigsby Bates, "Is It an Uprising or is It a Riot? Depends on Who's Watching." *Morning Edition*, National Public Radio, April 30, 2015.
7. Luce Irigaray, "The Eternal Irony of the Community," in *Speculum of the Other Woman*, trans. Gillian C. Gill (Ithaca, NY: Cornell University Press, 1985), 214–26.
8. Kimberlé Crenshaw, "Mapping the Margins: Intersectionality, Identity Politics, and Violence against Women of Color," *Stanford Law Review* 43, no. 6 (July 1, 1991): 1241–99, doi:10.2307/1229039. Intersectionality was first coined by Kimberlé Crenshaw, though her articulation of the concept comes from a long history of Black feminist thought on the inter-relatedness or overlapping of multiple identities, oppressions, or exclusions. See also Audre Lorde, "Age, Race, Class and Sex: Women Redefining Difference," in *Sister Outsider: Essays and Speeches* (New York: Ten Speed Press, 2012); Combahee River Collective, "A Black Feminist Statement," in *All the Women Are White, All the Blacks Are Men, But Some of Us Are Brave: Black Women's Studies*, ed. Gloria Hull, Patricia Bell Scott, and Barbara Smith (New York: Feminist Press, 1982); Angela Y. Davis, *Women, Race, and Class* (New York: Vintage Books, 2011); bell hooks, *Feminist Theory: From Margin to Center*, 2nd ed. (Cambridge, MA: South End Press, 2000); Patricia J. Williams, *The Alchemy of Race and Rights* (Cambridge, MA: Harvard University Press, 1991).
9. I use the terms "blind" and "blind spot" advisedly, with qualifications and reservations. Many disability theorists and activists have pointed out that the term "blind spot," even when applied to epistemology, is ableist insofar as it presumes sightedness as a universal condition, and a world designed with sighted people in mind. I understand the blind spot in reference to constitutive exclusion as a metaphor for the structural blind spot in all seeing—a blind spot that is both absent and present, a blind spot that is essential to sight but cannot itself be seen. Thus, even sight itself is predicated upon blindness; "ability" is thus predicated upon "disability." Whether this works theoretically, however, does nothing to alleviate the real material oppressions those labeled "disabled" experience in a world that presumes a fantastical fullness of ability and that operates according to a "mythical norm" that disavows the range of conditions of disability that we all do or will experience

as part of our lives. And however I intend the usage of this term, it still risks perpetuating the very sorts of exclusions, oppressions, and dominations this analysis is meant to uncover and destroy.

10. Chantal Mouffe, *The Return of the Political* (London: Verso, 2005). While Derrida himself does not seem to develop such a concept, this understanding of deconstruction comes down to us from the work of Henry Staten, one of Derrida's early English-language translators. See Henry Staten, *Wittgenstein and Derrida* (Lincoln: University of Nebraska Press, 1984).
11. Ernesto Laclau and Chantal Mouffe, *Hegemony and Socialist Strategy: Towards a Radical Democratic Politics* (London: Verso, 2001); Mouffe, *The Return of the Political*; Ernesto Laclau, *New Reflections on the Revolution of Our Time* (London: Verso, 1990).
12. Mouffe, *The Return of the Political*, 85.
13. Laclau, *New Reflections on the Revolution of Our Time*.
14. Several theorists rely on this Laclauian and Mouffian notion of the constitutive outside or constitutive exclusion. For instance, see Urs Stäheli, "Competing Figures of the Limit: Dispersion, Transgression, Antagonism, Indifference," in *Laclau: A Critical Reader*, ed. Simon Critchley and Oliver Marchart (New York: Routledge, 2004), 226–39; Colin Koopman, "Democracy Both Liberal and Radical: Political Agency in Dewey and Laclau and Mouffe," in *Persuasion and Compulsion in Democracy*, ed. Jacquelyn Kegley and Krzysztof Piotr Skowronski (Lanham, MD: Lexington Books, 2015), 85–106; Rafi Youatt, "Power, Pain, and the Interspecies Politics of Foie Gras," *Political Research Quarterly* 65, no. 2 (June 1, 2012): 346–58.
15. See especially the work of the following: M. Johanna Meehan, ed., *Feminists Read Habermas: Gendering the Subject of Discourse* (New York: Routledge, 1995); Joan B. Landes, "The Public and the Private Sphere: A Feminist Reconsideration," in *Feminism, the Public and the Private*, ed. Joan B. Landes (New York: Oxford University Press, 1998), 135–63; Amy Allen, "The Public Sphere: Ideology and/or Ideal?," *Political Theory* 40, no. 6 (2012): 822–29; Jodi Dean, *Solidarity of Strangers: Feminism after Identity Politics* (Berkeley: University of California Press, 1996).
16. Carole Pateman, *The Sexual Contract* (Cambridge: Polity, 1988); Nancy Fraser, "What's Critical about Critical Theory? The Case of Habermas and Gender," *New German Critique*, no. 35 (April 1, 1985): 97–131; Iris Marion Young, *Inclusion and Democracy* (New York: Oxford University Press, 2002); Jürgen Habermas, *The Structural Transformation of the Public Sphere: An Inquiry into a Category of Bourgeois Society* (Cambridge, MA: MIT Press, 1991).
17. Dean, *Solidarity of Strangers*, 79.
18. Alison Stone, "Unthought Nature: Reply to Penelope Deutscher and Mary Beth Mader," *Differences* 19, no. 3 (January 1, 2008): 150–57.
19. Penelope Deutscher, "'Women and So On,'" *Symposium: Canadian Journal of Continental Philosophy* 11, no. 1 (2007): 101–19; Penelope Deutscher, "Conditionalities, Exclusions, Occlusions," in *Rewriting Difference: Luce Irigaray and "the Greeks,"* ed. Elena Tzelepis and Athena Athanasiou (Albany: State

University of New York Press, 2010); Lynne Huffer, *Are the Lips a Grave? A Queer Feminist on the Ethics of Sex* (New York: Columbia University Press, 2013).

20. Judith Butler, *Bodies That Matter: On the Discursive Limits of "Sex"* (New York: Routledge, 1993).
21. Lee Edelman, "Against Survival: Queerness in a Time That's Out of Joint," *Shakespeare Quarterly* 62, no. 2 (2011): 148–69. See also Lee Edelman, *No Future: Queer Theory and the Death Drive* (Durham, NC: Duke University Press, 2004).
22. Jared Sexton, *Amalgamation Schemes: Antiblackness and the Critique of Multiracialism* (Minneapolis: University of Minnesota Press, 2008).
23. Judith Butler, *Frames of War: When Is Life Grievable?* (New York: Verso, 2010).
24. Butler, *Frames of War*, 5.
25. See also Butler's brief discussion of the performativity of recognition in Judith Butler, *Notes toward a Performative Theory of Assembly* (Cambridge, MA: Harvard University Press, 2016), 5–6.
26. Charles Taylor et al., *Multiculturalism: Examining the Politics of Recognition*, ed. Amy Gutmann, expanded paperback edition (Princeton, NJ: Princeton University Press, 1994); Axel Honneth, *The Struggle for Recognition: The Moral Grammar of Social Conflicts* (Cambridge, MA: MIT Press, 1996); Nancy Fraser and Axel Honneth, *Redistribution or Recognition? A Political-Philosophical Exchange* (London: Verso, 2003); Young, *Inclusion and Democracy*.
27. Luce Irigaray, *This Sex Which Is Not One* (Ithaca, NY: Cornell University Press, 1985).
28. Patchen Markell, *Bound by Recognition* (Princeton, NJ: Princeton University Press, 2003), 5. This democratic paradox of sovereignty is also the subject of Danielle Allen's *Talking to Strangers*. See Danielle Allen, *Talking to Strangers: Anxieties of Citizenship since Brown v. Board of Education* (Chicago: University of Chicago Press, 2009).
29. Glen Sean Coulthard, *Red Skin, White Masks: Rejecting the Colonial Politics of Recognition* (Minneapolis: University of Minnesota Press, 2014), 40.
30. Butler, *Frames of War*, 3.
31. Butler, *Frames of War*, 10–11.
32. Lynne Huffer, "Foucault's Fossils: Life Itself and the Return to Nature in Feminist Philosophy," in *Anthropocene Feminism*, ed. Richard Grusin (Minneapolis: University of Minnesota Press, 2017), 65–88.
33. Elizabeth Grosz, *Time Travels: Feminism, Nature, Power* (Durham, NC: Duke University Press, 2005); Hasana Sharp, *Spinoza and the Politics of Renaturalization* (Chicago: University of Chicago Press, 2011); Karen Barad, *Meeting the Universe Halfway: Quantum Physics and the Entanglement of Matter and Meaning* (Durham, NC: Duke University Press, 2007).
34. Michel Foucault, *The History of Sexuality*, Vol. 1: *An Introduction*, trans. Robert Hurley (New York: Vintage, 1990).
35. Honig, *Antigone, Interrupted*; Miriam Leonard, "Freud and Tragedy: Oedipus and the Gender of the Universal," *Classical Receptions Journal* 5, no. 1 (2013): 63–83.
36. Sina Kramer, "Judith Butler's 'New Humanism': A Thing or Not a Thing, and So What?," *philoSOPHIA* 5, no. 1 (Winter 2015): 25–40.

37. Judith Butler, "Contingent Foundations: Feminism and the Question of 'Postmodernism,'" in *Feminist Contentions: A Philosophical Exchange*, ed. Seyla Benhabib et al. (New York: Routledge, 1994), 6.
38. Butler, "Contingent Foundations," 9.
39. Butler, *Bodies That Matter*, 53.
40. I use 'Latinx' to denote men, women, and gender nonconforming Latino or Hispanic persons. Following Joel Olson's usage in *The Abolition of White Democracy*, I capitalize Black but not white, in order to emphasize their assymetry: while white denotes a political category, Black also denotes that as well as a cultural identity. See Joel Olson's *The Abolition of White Democracy* (Minneapolis: University of Minnesota Press, 2004), xviii–xix.

CHAPTER 2

1. Kimberly Hutchings and Tuija Pulkkinen, "Introduction," in *Hegel's Philosophy and Feminist Thought: Beyond Antigone?* (New York: Palgrave Macmillan, 2010), 4.
2. The "open" readings of Hegel tend to be of two types: those that argue that Hegel is an anti-metaphysical thinker or one who has no metaphysics, and those that read Hegel's metaphysics as relatively open. The anti- or non-metaphysical readings of Hegel tend to focus on a particular aspect of thought and to de-emphasize its systematicity. These readings treat Hegel's social or political thought (for instance, Fred Dallmayr) or Hegelian accounts of subjectivity and the sociality of reason (for instance, Terry Pinkard or Robert Brandom), and they tend to focus on the *Phenomenology* or the *Philosophy of Right* rather than the *Science of Logic*. Those readings that affirm a metaphysics in Hegel but interpret it as an open one tend to treat *negativity* as the metaphysics of the Hegelian system rather than logical categories, absolute knowledge, or the idea, though they do not shy away from the *Logic*. These interpretations are informed by poststructural or critical theoretical critiques of Hegel as a closed system. These accounts of negativity tend to characterize it as historical, responsive, and productive (for instance, Jean-Luc Nancy, Angelica Nuzzo, or Andrew Haas). The closed reading of Hegel takes Hegelian philosophy as representative of—or perhaps the apotheosis of—totality, the metaphysics of presence, identitarian thinking, authoritarianism, or totalitarianism (for instance, in Karl Popper). While these tend to focus primarily on Hegel's social and political thought, Rolf-Peter Horstmann offers a more attenuated and more metaphysical version. Horstmann defends an interpretation of Hegel's thought as a monistic ontology and criticizes 'open' interpretations of Hegel rooted in the *Phenomenology* or the *Philosophy of Right* as a blueprint for social constructivism or a kind of epistemic relativism that is possible only by denying the systematicity of Hegel's thought, since Hegel repudiates these positions elsewhere in his system. Fred R. Dallmayr, *G W F Hegel: Modernity and Politics* (New York: Rowman & Littlefield, 1993); Terry Pinkard, *Hegel's Phenomenology: The Sociality of Reason* (Cambridge: Cambridge University Press, 1994); Robert Brandom, *Tales of the Mighty Dead: Historical Essays in the Metaphysics of Intentionality* (Cambridge, MA: Harvard University Press, 2002). Jean-Luc Nancy, *Hegel: The Restlessness of the Negative* (Minneapolis: University of Minnesota Press, 2002); Angelica Nuzzo,

"Dialectic as a Logic of Transformative Processes," in *Hegel: New Directions*, ed. Katerina Deligiorgi (New York: Routledge, 2014), 85–103; Andrew Hass, *Hegel and the Art of Negation: Negativity, Creativity and Contemporary Thought* (London: I. B.Tauris, 2013); Karl R. Popper, *The Open Society and Its Enemies*, Vol. 2: *Hegel, Marx, and the Aftermath*, 5th rev. ed. (Princeton, NJ: Princeton University Press, 1971). Rolf-Peter Horstmann, "Hegel's Phenomenology of Spirit as an Argument for a Monistic Ontology," *Inquiry* 49, no. 1 (February 1, 2006): 103–18, doi:10.1080/00201740500497530; Rolf-Peter Horstmann, "Substance, Subject and Infinity: A Case Study of the Role of Logic in Hegel's System," in *Hegel: New Directions*, ed. Katerina Deligiorgi (New York: Routledge, 2014), 69–84.

3. Jean Hyppolite, *Logic and Existence*, trans. Len Lawlor and Amit Sen (Albany: State University of New York Press, 1997); Jean Hyppolite, *Logique et existence: essai sur la logique de Hegel* (Paris: Presses Universitaires de France, 1961). *Logique et existence*, as well as Hyppolite's seminars on Hegel, influenced a generation of readings of Hegel in France.
4. Hyppolite, *Logic and Existence*, 7.
5. Hyppolite, *Logic and Existence*, 5.
6. "Epistemology of ignorance" refers to a branch of social epistemology that holds that racism in general and anti-Black racism in particular operates by means of a not-knowing or an "inverted epistemology" at the heart of white supremacy. See Shannon Sullivan and Nancy Tuana, eds., *Race and Epistemologies of Ignorance* (Albany: State University of New York Press, 2007); Charles Mills, *The Racial Contract* (Ithaca, NY: Cornell University Press, 1997).
7. Catherine Malabou, *The Future of Hegel: Plasticity, Temporality, and Dialectic* (New York: Routledge, 2005); Catherine Malabou, *L'avenir de Hegel: plasticité, temporalité, dialectique* (Paris: Vrin, 1996).
8. Georg Wilhelm Friedrich Hegel, *Science of Logic*, trans. A. V. Miller (Amherst, MA: Humanity Books, 1998); Georg Wilhelm Friedrich Hegel, *Wissenschaft Der Logik*, Bd. I (Frankfurt-am-Main: Suhrkamp, 1986), 56 and 52, respectively. References to the *Science of Logic* will take the following form: *SL/WL*I, English/German.
9. *SL/WL*I, 54/38. Georg Wilhelm Friedrich Hegel, *Phenomenology of Spirit*, trans. A.V. Miller (New York: Oxford University Press, 1977); G. W. F. Hegel, *Phänomenologie Des Geistes* (Hamburg: Felix Meiner Verlag, 1952), 54 and 38; 36–37 and 48, respectively.
10. Jean Hyppolite, *Genesis and Structure of Hegel's* "Phenomenology of Spirit," ed. Samuel Cherniak and John Heckman (Evanston, IL: Northwestern University Press, 1979).
11. Stephen Houlgate, *The Opening of Hegel's Logic: From Being to Infinity* (West Lafayette, IN: Purdue University Press, 2006); Stephen Houlgate, *Freedom, Truth and History: An Introduction to Hegel's Philosophy* (New York: Routledge, 1991).
12. *SL/WL*I, 74/74.
13. *SL/WL*I, 75/75.

14. "Distanced nearness" refers to Adorno, and specifically to aphorism 54 of *Minima Moralia*. I will turn to Adorno's thought in Chapter 4. Theodor W. Adorno, *Minima Moralia: Reflections on a Damaged Life*, trans. E. F. N. Jephcott (London: Verso, 2005).
15. *SL/WLI*, 553/216, 553/217, and 553/217, respectively.
16. *SL/WLI*, 553/217.
17. Hegel, *Science of Logic*; Georg Wilhelm Friedrich Hegel, *Wissenschaft Der Logik*, Bd. II (Frankfurt-am-Main: Suhrkamp, 1986), 602 and 276. References to the *Science of Logic* will take the following form: *SL/WL*II, English/German.
18. *SL/WL*II, 602/276.
19. *SL/WL*II, 601/274.
20. *SL/WL*II, 602/274; emphasis in original.
21. *SL/WL*II, 603/277.
22. *SL/WL*II, 603/277.
23. *SL/WL*II, 602/276; emphasis in original.
24. *SL/WL*II, 605/280.
25. *SL/WL*II, 843/573; emphasis in original.
26. *SL/WL*II, 413/41; emphasis in original.
27. *SL/WL*II, 417/47.
28. *SL/WL*II, 418/48.
29. *SL/WL*II, 419/48.
30. *SL/WL*II, 419/49.
31. *SL/WL*II, 420/50.
32. *SL/WL*II, 421/51.
33. *SL/WL*II, 421/52.
34. *SL/WL*II, 431/64.
35. *SL/WL*II, 431/65.
36. Hyppolite, *Logic and Existence*, 109.
37. *SL/WL*II, 422/53.
38. *SL/WL*II, 422/53.
39. *SL/WL*II, 422/53; translation my own.
40. *SL/WL*II, 422/53.
41. *SL/WL*II, 607–8/282.
42. *SL/WL*II, 608/283.
43. María Lugones, *Pilgrimages/Peregrinajes: Theorizing Coalition against Multiple Oppressions* (Lanham, MD: Rowman & Littlefield, 2003).
44. *SL/WL*II, 422/53.
45. *SL/WL*II, 422/53 and 423/53, respectively.
46. *SL/WL*II, 607/282. Here Hegel associates *Verschiedenheit* with *Mannigfaltigkeit*, the Kantian manifold of presentations; however, rather than positing a distinction between them, he seems to use the terms interchangeably, which our translator (Miller) reproduces by presenting them both under the name of "variety."
47. Karin de Boer, *On Hegel: The Sway of the Negative* (London: Palgrave Macmillan, 2010), 127.

48. de Boer, *On Hegel*, 201.
49. Julia Kristeva, *Revolution in Poetic Language* (New York: Columbia University Press, 1984); José Esteban Muñoz, *Cruising Utopia: The Then and There of Queer Futurity* (New York: New York University Press, 2009). See also Sina Kramer, "On Negativity in *Revolution in Poetic Language*," *Continental Philosophy Review* 46, no. 3 (August 14, 2013): 465–79, doi:10.1007/s11007-013-9272-y.

CHAPTER 3

1. Jacques Derrida, "*La famille de Hegel, Séance 12*" (Lecture Notes. Jacques Derrida Papers. MS-C01, n.d.), 12, Box 11, Folders 5–9, Special Collections and Archives, UC Irvine Libraries, Irvine, California. All translations my own. The 1971–72 course on Hegel laid the groundwork for Derrida's analysis of Hegel in his 1974 work, *Glas*.
2. Derrida, "*La famille de Hegel, Séance 12*."
3. Geoffrey Bennington describes the quasi-transcendental as "roughly: what makes it possible for a letter to arrive at its destination necessarily includes the possibility that it might go astray; this necessary possibility means that it never completely arrives; or, what makes it possible for a performative to be brought off 'happily' necessarily includes the possibility of recitation outside the 'correct' context; this necessary possibility means that it is never completely happy" (355–56). Geoffrey Bennington, "Deconstruction and the Philosophers (The Very Idea)," in *Jacques Derrida*, ed. Zeynep Direk and Lawlor (New York: Routledge, 2002). As the paleonym Derrida develops in his analysis of Hegel in the 1971–72 lecture course and his 1974 text *Glas*, the quasi-transcendental brings into focus an array of issues: the relation, and contamination, between the empirical and the transcendental, the question of the unconditional and the conditioned, the question of the "inside" and the "outside," the question of the border, the question of logical priority, causality, or anteriority, the question of what is properly philosophical, and of propriety itself.
4. This analysis is centered primarily on *Glas* rather than on "*La famille de Hegel*" because, like many of Derrida's lecture courses, it served as an outline for *Glas* (at least its Hegel column); it covers many of the same themes, though it does so through different methods. The main difference between the two is the inclusion of Hegel's correspondence in *Glas* as a way to think through the relation between the empirical and the transcendental "sisters" in Hegel. The term "Antigonanette" in "*La famille de Hegel*" does the same work, but the mode of analysis Derrida employs in *Glas* is richer.
5. Jacques Derrida, *Glas* (Lincoln: University of Nebraska Press, 1986); Jacques Derrida, *Glas* (Paris: Éditions Galilée, 1974). It is conventional to cite *Glas* in the following manner: by column, either left or right (150L or 121R) and occasionally by inter-column (146Ra or 146Rb). References in this text will follow this convention, in addition to referencing the French. They appear as follows: (*Glas*, English/French).
6. For success at such an impossible task, see Gayatri Chakravorty Spivak, "Glas-Piece: A Compte-Rendu," *Diacritics* 7, no. 3 (1977): 22–43; C. Sartillot, "Herbarium,

Verbarium: The Discourse of Flowers," *Diacritics* 18, no. 4 (1988): 68–81; Sean Gaston, *Starting with Derrida* (London: Bloomsbury Academic, 2008). See also the companion volume to the English translation of *Glas*, the *Glassary*: John P. Leavey Jr., *Glassary: "Sounding the Unconscious"* (Lincoln: University of Nebraska Press, 1986).

7. *Glas*, 142L/161L. Without getting too speculative too quickly, I am forced to stop and wonder at the repercussions of this phrase in ears constituted to hear, in English, in the United States, something quite particular in this phrase: the middle passage. What lies buried there, what sets this ringing, this time not from below the earth or from within the rock, but from beneath the surface of the Atlantic ocean? Or rather, how does the middle passage subtend the very idea of the United States itself?
8. The theme of the limit/passage is especially important in essays such as "Tympan," "The Pit and the Pyramid" and "Structure, Sign and Play in the Discourse of the Human Sciences." Jacques Derrida, "Tympan," in *Margins of Philosophy* (Chicago: University of Chicago Press, 1982), ix–xxix; Jacques Derrida, "The Pit and the Pyramid: Introduction to Hegel's Semiology," in *Writing and Difference* (Chicago: University of Chicago Press, 1978), 69–108; Jacques Derrida, "Structure, Sign and Play in the Discourse of the Human Sciences," in *Writing and Difference*, trans. Alan Bass (Chicago: University of Chicago Press, 1978), 278–94.
9. Hegel further develops his philosophy of history in his lecture courses on it; there he places Africa before ancient Greece in terms of the development of Spirit out of nature and into history. Because Hegel viewed African peoples as entirely determined by nature, Africa is not included in the movement of history but is instead described as permanently pre-historic. This inclusion of Africa and African peoples at the beginning of the movement of history in order in effect to *exclude* them from history mirrors the quasi-transcendental historical beginning here in the Spirit chapter. Derrida takes up the problem of Africa in Hegel's philosophy of history elsewhere in *Glas*; it plays a significant part in his analysis of the fetish and fetishism. Georg Wilhelm Friedrich Hegel, *Lectures on the Philosophy of World History*, ed. Johannes Hoffmeister and Duncan Forbes, trans. Hugh Barr Nisbet (Cambridge: Cambridge University Press, 1975).
10. Georg Wilhelm Friedrich Hegel, *Spirit: Chapter Six of Hegel's Phenomenology of Spirit*, trans. Hegel Translation Group, Toronto, Ont. (Indianapolis, IN: Hackett, 2001); G.W.F. Hegel, *Phänomenologie des Geistes* (Hamburg: Felix Meiner Verlag, 1952). All references to the Spirit chapter appear as (*Spirit*, English/German). *Spirit*, 15/326.
11. *Spirit*, 16/327.
12. *Spirit*, 10/320.
13. *Spirit*, 15/326.
14. *Spirit*, 15/326.
15. *Spirit*, 15/326.
16. *Spirit*, 15/326.
17. If it were simply that the relationship that Hegel describes here ended with the ancient world—in which sex is determined by nature, which in turn determines

the unconscious singularity and ethical devotion to the family on the part of woman, and the self-conscious universality and ethical devotion to the state on the part of man—this might not be so interesting, either to Derrida or to us. However, despite the progression of Spirit throughout history, Hegel's assessment of the way nature determines sexual difference, particularly for women, seems not to have changed much from the world of ancient Greece to the world of nineteenth-century Germany. Cf. Georg Wilhelm Friedrich Hegel, *Elements of the Philosophy of Right*, trans. Allen W. Wood (Cambridge: Cambridge University Press, 1991), 207 (*Zusatz*, section 166).

18. Jacques Derrida, "*La famille de Hegel, Séance 13*" (Lecture Notes. Jacques Derrida Papers. MS-C01, n.d.), 11, Box 11, Folders 5–9, Special Collections and Archives, The UC Irvine Libraries, Irvine, California.
19. *Spirit*, 14–15/325.
20. *Spirit*, 14–15/325.
21. *Spirit*, 15/326.
22. *Spirit*, 16/327.
23. *Glas*, 167–8L/189L.
24. *Glas*, 149L/168–69L.
25. *Glas*, 162La/183La.
26. Kevin Thompson, "Hegelian Dialectic and the Quasi-Transcendental in *Glas*," in *Hegel after Derrida*, ed. Stuart Barnett (New York: Routledge, 2002), 258.
27. Thompson, "Hegelian Dialectic."
28. *Glas*, 151L/171L.
29. *Glas*, 162L/183L.
30. *Glas*, 142L/161L.
31. Derrida, "Tympan," xx.
32. *Glas*, 191L/214L.
33. *Glas*, 119L/136L. Sound and aurality in philosophy is a major theme of "Tympan" as well, as a way to counter the supposed directness of vision in philosophy, as a way to mark the complex corporeal interpretation involved in language, as a way to meditate on the role of the air that mediates our voices, and as a way to mark what is absent from the page as a condition of the text.
34. Especially (across the page in the Genet column of *Glas*) the "glue" of the little tube of "mentholated vaseline," the object for which the narrator of Genet's *Our Lady of the Flowers* is arrested in a raid in a park popular for cruising. Genet's narrator described the little tube of mentholated Vaseline as "the very sign of abjection . . . utterly vile" yet "extremely precious to me" (*Glas*, 144R/163R). The ambivalence indicated by abjection here, making the tube of Vaseline both hideous and fascinating, also indicates the negativity at work in constitutive exclusion. This is developed best by Julia Kristeva. See Julia Kristeva, *Powers of Horror* (New York: Columbia University Press, 1982).
35. "We have been fascinated—like Hegel—by Antigone and by the irreducible brother-sister relationship, as it was apparently inadmissible in the Hegelian systematic. We are fallen, suspended, therefore, as before such a powerful relation without desire, which is just as well to say a desire so immense and impossible that it could not live

and that should overturn, paralyze or exceed the Hegelian system, or else interrupt definitively the life of the concept, to cut off its breath, or else, which would amount to the same thing, to support the system from a repressed [*refoulé*] or unthought outside which would be remaindered as the space of possibility, as its transcendental, absolutely invisible, like a blind spot [*l'aveuglement*]—Hegel's love or desire—which organizes around it the entire visual field, permitting us to see everything up close, permitting all sight-reading, save for this blind focal point [*foyer optique*] which resembles an infinite wound that cannot close itself." Derrida, "*La famille de Hegel, Séance 13*," 1.

36. *Glas*, 162L/183L.
37. *Glas*, 151L/171L–162L/183L.
38. Derrida, "*La famille de Hegel, Séance 12*," 9.
39. My thanks to Yves Hersant for letting me in on the joke.
40. Sigmund Freud, "Negation [*Verneinung*]," in *The Standard Edition of the Complete Psychological Works of Sigmund Freud*, ed. James Strachey, vol. 19 (1923–25): The Ego and the Id and Other Works, 24 vols. (London: Hogarth, 1961), 234–39.
41. Derrida, "*La famille de Hegel, Séance 13*," 1.
42. *Glas*, 165L/186L.
43. *Glas*, 165L/186L.
44. *Glas*, 165L/186L.
45. "Now I am no man, but she the man" (*Antigone*, line 528). Sophocles, "Antigone." Butler pays special attention to Antigone's gender confusion in *Antigone's Claim*.
46. *Glas*, 167L/189L.
47. Derrida, "*La famille de Hegel, Séance 13*," 3.
48. Jacques Derrida, "Declarations of Independence," *New Political Science* 7, no. 1 (June 1, 1986): 7–15, doi:10.1080/07393148608429608; Jacques Derrida, "*Déclarations D'indépendance*," in *Otobiographies: L'enseignement de Nietzsche et la politique du nom propre* (Paris: Galilée, 1984), 13–32.
49. "The Declaration of Independence," *National Archives and Records Administration*, accessed October 18, 2010, http://www.archives.gov/exhibits/charters/declaration_transcript.html.
50. "The Declaration of Independence."
51. Derrida, "Declarations of Independence"; Derrida, "*Déclarations D'indépendance*," 10/16.
52. *Spirit*, 16/327.
53. *Glas*, 169L/191L.
54. *Glas*, 167 8L/189L
55. "In this sense, the human female, who has not developed the difference or the opposition, holds herself nearer the plant. The clitoris nearer the cryptogam"; "'The difference between man and woman is that of animal and plant.'" *Glas*, 114/127 and 191L/214L, respectively. Derrida refers here to Hegel's *Philosophy of Right, Zusatz* to section 166. See also Laura Werner, who argues that Hegel's analysis in the *Phenomenology* is entirely gendered, and Alison Stone, who argues that Hegel's theory of gender is metaphysical rather than biological, and thus permeates his system. Laura Werner, "The Gender of Spirit: Hegel's Moves and Strategies," in *Hegel's Philosophy and Feminist Thought: Beyond Antigone?*, ed. Kimberly Hutchings and

Tuija Pulkkinen (New York: Palgrave Macmillan, 2010), 195–209; Alison Stone, "Matter and Form," in *Hegel's Philosophy and Feminist Thought: Beyond Antigone?*, ed. Kimberly Hutchings and Tuija Pulkkinen (New York: Palgrave Macmillan, 2010), 211–32.

56. Luce Irigaray, "The Eternal Irony of the Community," in *Speculum of the Other Woman*, trans. Gillian C. Gill (Ithaca, NY: Cornell University Press, 1985).
57. Judith Butler, *The Psychic Life of Power: Theories in Subjection* (Stanford, CA: Stanford University Press, 1997), 144.
58. For more on the economy of the quasi-transcendental, see Sina Kramer, "Derrida's 'Antigonanette': On the Quasi-Transcendental." *Southern Journal of Philosophy* 52, no. 4 (December 2014): 521–51.
59. See the analysis of the marginalization of slavery in the history of interpretations of Antigone by Tina Chanter in *Whose Antigone*?

CHAPTER 4

1. Adorno does this work in his lectures on Kant's *Critique of Pure Reason*, and also in *Negative Dialectics*. Theodor W. Adorno, *Kant's Critique of Pure Reason (1959)*, ed. Rolf Tiedemann (Stanford, CA: Stanford University Press, 2001); Theodor W. Adorno, *Nachgelassene Schriften. Abteilung IV: Vorlesungen:* Band 4: *Kants "Kritik der reinen Vernunft,"* ed. Rolf Tiedemann, 2nd ed. (Frankfurt am Main: Suhrkamp, 1995); Theodor W. Adorno and E. B. Ashton, *Negative Dialectics* (New York: Continuum, 2007); Theodor W. Adorno, *Negative Dialektik* (Frankfurt-am-Main: Suhrkamp, 1975). Hereafter *Negative Dialectics* will be cited as *ND*, English/German.
2. Andrew Buchwalter, "Hegel, Adorno and the Concept of Transcendent Critique," *Philosophy and Social Criticism* 12, no. 4 (1987): 297–328.
3. Buchwalter, "Hegel, Adorno and the Concept of Transcendent Critique," 303; emphasis in original.
4. Buchwalter, "Hegel, Adorno and the Concept of Transcendent Critique," 303.
5. For "untrammeled nature," see Espen Hammer's chapter on metaphysics in *Adorno: Key Concepts*. While in other respects a complex account of Adorno in relation to metaphysics, the idea that aesthetic experience gives us access to a kind of "untrammeled nature" is problematic for reasons that I will treat in Chapter 5. Espen Hammer, "Metaphysics," in *Theodor Adorno: Key Concepts*, ed. Deborah Cook (New York: Routledge, 2008), 74.
6. Buchwalter, "Hegel, Adorno and the Concept of Transcendent Critique," 306.
7. James Gordon Finlayson, "The Theory of Ideology and the Ideology of Theory: Habermas Contra Adorno," *Historical Materialism* 11, no. 2 (2003): 174.
8. Buchwalter, "Hegel, Adorno and the Concept of Transcendent Critique," 305. Buchwalter refers here to *Negative Dialectics,* pages 406 and 318, respectively.
9. This interpretation of Adorno's thought is broadly in keeping with Habermas's reading of Adorno, especially in his "*Nachwort*" to the 1986 edition of *Dialektik der Aufklärung*, as well as in other pieces. While I don't have space to engage that interpretation directly, it should be noted that while Habermas's interpretation of Adorno has been the dominant one in English-language scholarship on Adorno,

that interpretation is problematic in several respects, not least of all in its insufficient regard for the negative dialectic between immanence and transcendence. There is a series of recent works both accounting for and countering the dominance of the Habermasian reading of Adorno. See Jürgen Habermas, "Nachwort von Jürgen Habermas," in *Dialektik Der Aufklärung* (Frankfurt-am-Main: Fischer, 1986), 128–76; Robert Hullot-Kentor, "Back to Adorno," in *Theodor Adorno: Critical Evaluations in Cultural Theory*, ed. Simon Jarvis, 2006.; Espen Hammer, *Adorno and the Political* (New York: Routledge, 2005); Simon Jarvis, *Adorno: A Critical Introduction* (New York: Routledge, 1998).

10. Theodor W. Adorno, *Philosophische Terminologie*, BD.1 (Frankfurt am Main: Suhrkamp, 1997), 88. English translation in Ulrich Plass, *Language and History in Theodor W. Adorno's Notes to Literature* (New York: Routledge, 2007), 23. This of course does not foreclose the possibility of other, non-philosophical routes to nonidentity, but simply that nonidentity can be approached from philosophy, by means of language and concepts.
11. *ND*, 12/24.
12. *ND*, 144/148.
13. *ND*, 5/16–17.
14. Theodor W. Adorno, *Hegel: Three Studies* (Cambridge, MA: MIT Press, 1994), 37.
15. Adorno, *Hegel*, 147.
16. Theodor W. Adorno, *Critical Models: Interventions and Catchwords* (New York: Columbia University Press, 2013), 246; emphasis mine.
17. Karl Marx, "On the Jewish Question," in *The Marx Engels Reader*, ed. Robert Tucker, 2nd ed. (New York: Norton, 1978), 26–52.
18. *ND*, 398/406.
19. We might also note that while it would be a worthwhile task to investigate the relation between aesthetic experience and metaphysical experience, the presumption the transcendental realists are working from is that aesthetic experience is itself somehow a non-conceptual experience, and this presumption is already seriously flawed. In fact, Deborah Cook argues that "Adorno explicitly rejects the equation of nonidentity thinking with a nondiscursive, nonrepresentational aesthetic absorption in objects when he argues that negative dialectics must not break its link with language." Deborah Cook, "From the Actual to the Possible: Nonidentity Thinking," *Constellations* 12, no. 1 (2005): 27.
20. Theodor W. Adorno, *Metaphysics: Concept and Problems*, ed. Rolf Tiedemann and Edmund Jephcott (Stanford, CA: Stanford University Press, 2002), 43.
21. Adorno, *Metaphysics*, 68.
22. Adorno, *Metaphysics*, 20.
23. Adorno, *Metaphysics*, 19.
24. *ND*, 352/345.
25. A great resource for the debate between Habermas and Adorno on the subjects of totality, reason, and critique is Deborah Cook's *Adorno, Habermas, and the Search for a Rational Society*. There Cook is right to point out that Adorno does not reject reason entirely but instead gives a historical critique of reason, in order point out that reason could have taken a different course, and may yet still be

able to. I will take up the historical aspect of nonidentity in Chapter 5. Deborah Cook, *Adorno, Habermas and the Search for a Rational Society* (New York: Routledge, 2012).

26. Michael Theunissen, "Negativity in Adorno," in *Theodor Adorno: Critical Evaluations in Cultural Theory*, ed. Simon Jarvis (New York: Routledge, 2006), 187; Michael Theunissen, "Negativität Bei Adorno," in *Adorno-Konferenz 1983*, ed. Jürgen Habermas and Ludwig von Friedeburg (Frankfurt-am-Main: Suhrkamp, 1983), 41–65.
27. Robyn Marasco, *The Highway of Despair: Critical Theory after Hegel* (New York: Columbia University Press, 2015).
28. *ND*, 366/359.
29. *ND*, 11/22.
30. *ND*, 406/397–8.
31. *ND*, 10/21.
32. *ND*, 17/29.
33. Simon Jarvis, "The Coastline of Experience-Materialism and Metaphysics in Adorno," *Radical Philosophy* 85 (1997): 15.
34. *ND*, 231/230; translation my own.
35. Deborah Cook, "A Response to Finlayson," *Historical Materialism* 11, no. 2 (2003): 192. See also Cook, "From the Actual to the Possible."
36. *ND*, 366/359.
37. Adorno's revaluation of the knowledge of children can be seen as unduly idealist or naïve; I think however that it is not meant to be taken literally, in the sense that children are free of the constraints of instrumental rationality and can therefore have some kind of immediate experience of wrong life as wrong. Clearly Adorno himself is haunted by these images of something gravely wrong as an adult; I would venture that many of us retain memories that act as turning points in our acculturation—having been met with blank indifference or laughter at our claims that something is unjust or wrong, for instance. Though I do not have space to investigate this possibility here, this suggests a potentially feminist and anti-racist valuation of naïveté as a critical concept, given that naïveté or immaturity with regard to political matters is often assigned to children, to women, and to people of color.
38. *ND*, 10/21.
39. Theodor W. Adorno, *History and Freedom: Lectures 1964–1965* (London: Polity, 2006), 253.

CHAPTER 5

1. Anke Thyen, "Dimensions of the Nonidentical," in *Theodor Adorno: Critical Evaluations in Cultural Theory*, ed. Simon Jarvis (New York: Routledge, 2006), 202.
2. *ND*, 11/22.
3. Thyen, "Dimensions of the Nonidentical," 209.
4. Hammer, 2008, 67.
5. *ND* 400/408; *ND* 358/365.
6. Jarvis, *Adorno*. As Anke Thyen puts it, "The ineliminable [*Nichthintergehbarkeit*] ontic residue in our concepts calls for a philosophical thinking that strives to do

justice to objects as they are experienced, while avoiding the typical dangers of a reductionist empiricism." Thyen, "Dimensions of the Nonidentical," 215.

7. *ND*, 202–3/202–3.
8. *ND*, 365/358.
9. Jarvis, "The Coastline of Experience-Materialism and Metaphysics in Adorno," 7–8.
10. *ND*, 5/16–7.
11. Adorno, *Critical Models*, 249.
12. *ND*, 183/184.
13. *ND*, 202–204/202–203.
14. *ND*, 5/16–17.
15. Espen Hammer, "Metaphysics," in *Theodor Adorno: Key Concepts*, ed. Deborah Cook (New York: Routledge, 2008), 66.
16. This "mistake" could be read as truth in the sense that this reduction of the subject to the concept and the object to the nonconceptual, the simple opposition between them, and eventually the elimination of the object is the truth of the epistemology of the wrong state of things.
17. Karl Marx, *The German Ideology*, ed. C. J. Arthur (New York: International Publishers, 2007), 62.
18. *ND*, 186/187.
19. Theodor W. Adorno, *Lectures on Negative Dialectics: Fragments of a Lecture Course 1965/1966* (Cambridge: Polity, 2008), 175.
20. *ND*, 192/193.
21. Adorno, *Critical Models*, 253.
22. Adorno, *Lectures on Negative Dialectics*, 175.
23. Susan Buck-Morss, *Origin of Negative Dialectics* (New York: Free Press, 1979), 52.
24. Max Horkheimer and Theodor W. Adorno, *Dialectic of Enlightenment: Philosophical Fragments*, trans. Edmund Jephcott (Stanford, CA: Stanford University Press, 2002).
25. Alison Stone, "Adorno and Logic," in *Theodor Adorno: Key Concepts*, ed. Deborah Cook (New York: Routledge, 2008), 51.
26. Georg Wilhelm Friedrich Hegel, *Reason in History: A General Introduction to the Philosophy of History*, trans. Robert S. Hartmann (Upper Saddle River, NJ: Prentice Hall, 1997), 27.
27. *ND*, 361/354.
28. *ND*, 320/314.
29. Adorno, *Critical Models*, 17.
30. Walter Benjamin, "Theses on the Philosophy of History," in *Illuminations* (Boston: Houghton Mifflin Harcourt, 1968), 263. I have my own reservations with the "Theses," specifically in its reliance upon gendered metaphors: for instance, the "whore" called "once upon a time" who drains historians in her historicist bordello, as opposed to the historical materialist who retains "man enough to blast open the continuum of history" (Thesis XVI). How different can any materialist history be if it relies upon the constitutive exclusion of women from history, rendering them either passive objects of imagined sexual conquests, or as the historian's succubus? How can we re-imagine history if it still relies upon a kind of phallic domination? Who then is redeemed by materialist history?

31. Benjamin, "Theses on the Philosophy of History," 254.
32. *ND*, 377–78/370–71.
33. Adorno, *Lectures on Negative Dialectics*, 71.
34. *ND*, 12/24.
35. For example: "Totality and homosexuality belong together." From "Tough Baby," section 24 of *Minima Moralia*. Adorno, *Minima Moralia*. For Adorno, homosexuality seems an exclusively masculine phenomenon. For an analysis of homosexuality (including the absence of lesbians) in Adorno's work, see Jennifer Rycenga, "Queerly Amiss: Sexuality and the Logic of Adorno's Dialectics," in *Adorno: A Critical Reader*, ed. Nigel C. Gibson and Andrew Rubin (Hoboken, NJ: Wiley, 2002), 361–78; Kevin S. Amidon, "What Happens to Countess Geschwitz? Revisiting Homosexuality in Horkheimer and Adorno," *New York Journal of Sociology* 1 (2008): 1–24.
36. The association of male homosexuality and fascist totalitarianism in Adorno's thought may be due to his particular history as a survivor of Nazi Germany. As Judith Halberstam notes in "The Anti-Social Turn in Queer Studies," the association of a particular male homosexuality and fascism results from what Herzog and Hewitt note was a masculinist homophilia within Nazism that served to tolerate male masculine homosexuality as it persecuted effeminacy and gender nonconformance in men. Judith Halberstam, "The Anti-Social Turn in Queer Studies," *Graduate Journal of Social Science* 5, no. 2 (November 2, 2008): 140–56; Dagmar Herzog, *Sex after Fascism: Memory and Morality in Twentieth-Century Germany* (Princeton, NJ: Princeton University Press, 2007); Andrew Hewitt, *Political Inversions: Homosexuality, Fascism, and the Modernist Imaginary* (Stanford, CA: Stanford University Press, 1996).

CHAPTER 6

1. See Chapter 1, fn 2.
2. Judith Butler, *Antigone's Claim: Kinship between Life and Death* (New York: Columbia University Press, 2000), 28.
3. Butler, *Antigone's Claim*, 11.
4. Of course, the deed is itself already doubled, as Polyneices was buried twice. Butler notes that the burial seems to "wander throughout the play," threatening becoming attached to the sentry who reports it, or to Ismene, or to criminals for hire, or to the gods. Carol Jacobs takes up the problem of the unintelligibility of the deed itself, a burial that the sentry reports leaves no mark in the earth that could attach it to a sovereign author, as an indication that Antigone's act is unintelligible because "it is neither an act of production nor of identification; [Antigone] occupies the place of the mother only by doing so differently." The ambiguity of this double burial allows Bonnie Honig to make an interesting case that Ismene performed the first burial, and Antigone the second; this argument is compelling in that it resolves certain dramaturgical issues in the way Antigone changes her tone toward Ismene throughout the play. Butler, *Antigone's Claim*, 7; Carol Jacobs, "Dusting Antigone," *MLN* 111, no. 5 (1996): 890–917; Bonnie Honig, "Ismene's Forced Choice: Sacrifice and Sorority in Sophocles' Antigone," *Arethusa* 44, no. 1 (2011): 29–68.

5. Tina Chanter, "Antigone's Excessive Relationship to Fetishism: The Performative Politics and Rebirth of Eros and Philia from Ancient Greece to Modern South Africa," *Symposium* 11, no. 2 (2007): 231–60, doi:10.5840/symposium200711227.
6. Butler, *Antigone's Claim*, 8.
7. Sophocles. "Antigone." In *Sophocles I*, edited by Richmond Lattimore, translated by David Grene (Chicago: University of Chicago Press, 1991), lines 528–29.
8. Butler, *Antigone's Claim*, 28.
9. Butler, *Antigone's Claim*, 77.
10. Sophocles, "Antigone," line 78.
11. Mary Beth Mader, "Antigone's Line," *Bulletin de La Société Américaine de Philosophie de Langue Française* 15, no. 1 (2005): 18–40.
12. Mader, "Antigone's Line," 25.
13. Sophocles, "Antigone," lines 574–575.
14. Sophocles, "Antigone," lines 982–983.
15. Judith Butler, "Bodily Confessions," in *Undoing Gender* (New York: Routledge, 2004), 161–73.
16. Butler, "Bodily Confessions," 170.
17. Butler, "Bodily Confessions," 168.
18. For another critique of Butler's de-politicization of Antigone, see Bonnie Honig, *Antigone, Interrupted* (Cambridge: Cambridge University Press, 2013); and Sina Kramer, "Judith Butler's 'New Humanism': A Thing or Not a Thing, and So What?," *philoSOPHIA* 5, no. 1 (Winter 2015): 25–40.
19. Butler, "Bodily Confessions," 170.
20. Butler, *Antigone's Claim*, 54.
21. Butler, *Antigone's Claim*, 40.
22. Tina Chanter, "Antigone's Political Legacies: Abjection in Defiance of Mourning," in *Interrogating Antigone in Postmodern Philosophy and Criticism*, ed. S. E. Wilmer and Audronė Žukauskaitė (New York: Oxford University Press, 2010), 24, http://www.oxfordscholarship.com/view/10.1093/acprof:oso/9780199559213.001.0001/acprof-9780199559213.
23. Danielle L. McGuire, *At the Dark End of the Street: Black Women, Rape, and Resistance—a New History of the Civil Rights Movement from Rosa Parks to the Rise of Black Power* (New York: Vintage Books, 2011), 74–75.
24. Colvin's own charges were not included in the suit that ended segregation on the Montgomery bus system because the local judge, Eugene Carter, dismissed the segregation charge and the disorderly conduct charge, and she was found guilty of assault, for which she paid a small fine, thus making a challenge impossible. Taylor Branch, *Parting the Waters: America in the King Years 1954–63*, reprint ed. (New York: Simon & Schuster, 1989), 123.
25. This was also a prominent version of the story during the fiftieth anniversary of the Montgomery bus boycott in 2005. Ms. Parks mentioned in her autobiography that though it was not her plan to get arrested, she was tired that day not from a long day at work but rather from "giving in." Rosa Parks and Jim Haskins, *Rosa Parks: My Story*, reprint edition (New York: Puffin Books, 1999), 116. Later studies

of the politics of social movements in general and the civil rights movement in particular emphasized Ms. Parks's leadership roles in the NAACP, including serving as secretary to the Montgomery chapter of the NAACP. See Aldon D. Morris, *Origins of the Civil Rights Movements* (New York: Simon and Schuster, 1986).

26. Harvard Sitkoff, *The Struggle for Black Equality*, rev. ed. (New York: Hill and Wang, 2008), 37.
27. Bob Garfield, "Tabula Rosa," *On the Media* (WNYC, July 3, 2009), http://www.onthemedia.org/story/132404-tabula-rosa/?utm_source=sharedUrl&utm_medium=metatag&utm_campaign=sharedUrl.
28. McGuire, *At the Dark End of the Street*. See also Jeane Theoharis's recent biography of Parks, the first such biography not written for children. Jeanne Theoharis, *The Rebellious Life of Mrs. Rosa Parks* (Boston: Beacon Press, 2013).
29. McGuire, *At the Dark End of the Street*, 107.
30. Brooks Barnes, "From Footnote to Fame in Civil Rights History," *New York Times*, November 26, 2009, sec. Books, http://www.nytimes.com/2009/11/26/books/26colvin.html.
31. For an argument that the civil rights movement in the United States effected a re-constitution of the United States as a political body, see Danielle Allen, *Talking to Strangers: Anxieties of Citizenship since Brown v. Board of Education* (Chicago: University of Chicago Press, 2009).
32. Cathy J. Cohen, *The Boundaries of Blackness: AIDS and the Breakdown of Black Politics* (Chicago: University of Chicago Press, 1999), 63–64.
33. Holloway Sparks, "Gender and the Politics of Democratic Disturbance in the Montgomery Bus Boycott," Western Political Science Association Annual Meeting, Vancouver, March 20, 2009. See also Holloway Sparks, "Dissident Citizenship: Democratic Theory, Political Courage, and Activist Women," *Hypatia* 12, no. 4 (October 1, 1997): 74–110. This strategy is confirmed in McGuire (*At the Dark End of the Street*), who argues that intensifying anti-communism and a more reactionary political atmosphere made the movement less likely to coalesce around the defense of poor Black women's sexuality and bodily autonomy than had earlier been the case.
34. Holloway Sparks, "You Can't Be Nice: Dissident Citizenship, Gender, and the Politics of Disturbance in the U.S. Welfare Rights Movement," Western Political Science Association Annual Meeting, San Diego, March 21, 2008; Sparks, "Gender and the Politics of Democratic Disturbance in the Montgomery Bus Boycott." These are parts of a forthcoming manuscript titled *Dissident Citizenship: Gender and the Politics of Democratic Disturbance*.
35. Another articulation of some of the effects of the politics of respectability can be found in Evelynn M. Hammonds, "Toward a Genealogy of Black Female Sexuality: The Problematic of Silence," in *Feminist Genealogies, Colonial Legacies, Democratic Futures*, ed. M. Jacqui Alexander and Chandra Talpade Mohanty (New York: Routledge, 1996), 170–82.
36. Holloway Sparks, "Mama Grizzlies and Guardians of the Republic: The Democratic and Intersectional Politics of Anger in the Tea Party Movement," *New Political Science* 37, no. 1 (2015): 45.

37. Judith Butler, *Gender Trouble: Feminism and the Subversion of Identity* (New York: Routledge, 2006), 143.
38. See Doug McAdam, *Political Process and the Development of Black Insurgency, 1930–1970* (Chicago: University of Chicago Press, 1999). In this work, McAdam surveys the literature on social movements in sociology and political science and critiques it as inadequate to explaining the civil rights movement, because these disciplines have traditionally treated the emergence of social movements as either an apolitical individual response to psychic strain, the irrational behavior of the masses, or the mobilization of a largely apolitical mass by elites for resources.
39. The references to Foucault here are entirely purposeful, though a fully argued case for Foucault as a critical theorist will have to be undertaken another time, or by someone else entirely—see, for instance, George Cicariello-Maher, *Decolonizing Dialectics* (Durham: Duke University Press, 2017).

CHAPTER 7

1. Janet Abu-Lughod, *Race, Space, and Riots* (New York: Oxford University Press, 2007), 235.
2. Abu-Lughod, *Race, Space, and Riots*, 237, fn. 40.
3. Gerald Horne, "Epilogue: The 1990s," in *Fire This Time: The Watts Uprising and the 1960s* (Charlottesville: University of Virginia Press, 1995).
4. Kerner Commission, U.S. Riot, and Tim Wicker, *Report of the National Advisory Commission on Civil Disorders* (New York: Bantam Books, 1968), 1.
5. Robert Gooding-Williams, *Reading Rodney King, Reading Urban Uprising* (New York: Routledge, 1993), 170.
6. Hannah Rosen, *Terror in the Heart of Freedom: Citizenship, Sexual Violence, and the Meaning of Race in the Postemancipation South* (Chapel Hill: University of North Carolina Press, 2009); Charles L. Lumpkins, *American Pogrom: The East St. Louis Riot and Black Politics* (Athens: Ohio University Press, 2008); William M. Tuttle, *Race Riot: Chicago in the Red Summer of 1919* (Champaign: University of Illinois Press, 1970); James S. Hirsch, *Riot and Remembrance: The Tulsa Race War and Its Legacy* (New York: Houghton Mifflin, 2002); Isabel Wilkerson, *The Warmth of Other Suns* (New York: Vintage Books, 2011).
7. Gerald Horne, *Fire This Time: The Watts Uprising and the 1960s* (Charlottesville: University of Virginia Press, 1995); Abu-Lughod, *Race, Space, and Riots.*
8. Abu-Lughod, *Race, Space, and Riots*, 146.
9. Abu-Lughod, *Race, Space, and Riots*, 217. I use the terms "male" and "female" here because these are the terms the researchers reported; I do not know how the researchers determined the sex of the respondents, nor how the researchers determined the correlation between the sex and gender of the respondents.
10. Nathan Cohen, ed., *The Los Angeles Riots: A Socio-Psychological Study* (New York: Praeger, 1970), 489.
11. McCone Commission on the Los Angeles Riots, "Violence in the City: An End or a Beginning" (Los Angeles: Governor's Commission on the Los Angeles Riots,

December 2, 1965); Kerner Commission et al., *Report of the National Advisory Commission on Civil Disorders*.

12. McCone Commission on the Los Angeles Riots, "Violence in the City: An End or a Beginning?" (Los Angeles: Governor's Commission on the Los Angeles Riots, December 2, 1965). See also Abu-Lughod, *Race, Space, and Riots*, 214.
13. Kerner Commission et al., *Report of the National Advisory Commission on Civil Disorders*, 1.
14. Julian E. Zelizer, "Is America Repeating the Mistakes of 1968?" *Atlantic*, July 8, 2016, http://www.theatlantic.com/politics/archive/2016/07/is-america-repeating-the-mistakes-of-1968/490568/.
15. Imagining the "urban core" as a kind of state of nature, or imagining black people as inhabiting a kind of state of nature, is familiar to social theorists who study the city in general, and echoes through imagery associated with Los Angeles in particular, from Ronald Reagan warning that "the jungle is waiting to take over" after the Watts riot, to LAPD officer Stacey Koons (one of the officers charged in the beating of King) referring to a domestic dispute between African Americans as something out of *Gorillas in the Mist* (quoted in Eric Avila, *Popular Culture in the Age of White Flight: Fear and Fantasy in Suburban Los Angeles* [Berkeley: University of California Press, 2004], 48). Charles Mills argues that not only is city space racialized, but that black bodies in the United States carry a kind of state of nature around with them within civil society, a threat that must be simultaneously managed and denied. Avila, *Popular Culture in the Age of White Flight*, 48; Associated Press, "Judge Says Remarks on 'Gorillas' May Be Cited in Trial on Beating," *New York Times*, June 12, 1991, sec. US, http://www.nytimes.com/1991/06/12/us/judge-says-remarks-on-gorillas-may-be-cited-in-trial-on-beating.html; Charles Mills, *The Racial Contract* (Ithaca, NY: Cornell University Press, 1997).
16. Joshua Clover, *Riot. Strike. Riot: The New Era of Uprisings* (London: Verso, 2016), 112.
17. Peter Kwong, "The First Multicultural Riots," in *Inside the Riots*, ed. Don Hazen (Los Angeles: Institute for Alternative Journalism, 1992), 89.
18. Lewis Gordon, "Of Illicit Appearance: The L.A. Riots/Rebellion as a Portent of Things to Come," *Truthout*, accessed May 7, 2015, http://www.truth-out.org/news/item/9008-of-illicit-appearance-the-la-riots-rebellion-as-a-portent-of-things-to-come.
19. Gordon, "Of Illicit Appearance," 8.
20. Frank B. Wilderson III, *Red, White & Black: Cinema and the Structure of U.S. Antagonisms* (Durham. NC: Duke University Press, 2010); Saidiya V. Hartman, *Scenes of Subjection: Terror, Slavery, and Self-Making in Nineteenth-Century America* (New York: Oxford University Press, 1997); Saidiya V. Hartman and Frank B. Wilderson, "THE POSITION OF THE UNTHOUGHT," *Qui Parle* 13, no. 2 (2003): 183–201; Ian Baucom, *Specters of the Atlantic: Finance Capital, Slavery, and the Philosophy of History* (Durham, NC: Duke University Press, 2005); Stephanie E. Smallwood, *Saltwater Slavery: A Middle Passage from Africa to American Diaspora* (Cambridge, MA: Harvard University Press, 2009); Jared Sexton, "The Social Life of Social Death: On Afro-Pessimism and Black Optimism," *InTensions*, no. 5 (Fall/Winter 2011), http://www.yorku.ca/intent/issue5/index.php; Jared

Sexton, *Amalgamation Schemes: Antiblackness and the Critique of Multiracialism* (Minneapolis: University of Minnesota Press, 2008); Jared Sexton, "People-of-Color-Blindness: Notes on the Afterlife of Slavery," *Social Text* 28, no. 2 103 (June 20, 2010): 31–56, doi:10.1215/01642472-2009-066.

21. Orlando Patterson, *Slavery and Social Death* (Cambridge, MA: Harvard University Press, 1985).
22. My thanks for a conversation with Anthony Paul Smith for this formulation of the project of Afro-Pessimism.
23. Jared Sexton, "Afro-Pessimism: The Unclear Word," *Rhizomes*, no. 29 (2016): para. 6, http://www.rhizomes.net/issue29/sexton.html.
24. "The President's Message; Excerpts from Bush's Speech on Los Angeles Riots: 'Need to Restore Order,'" *New York Times*, May 2, 1992.
25. Robert Gooding-Williams, *Reading Rodney King, Reading Urban Uprising* (New York: Routledge, 1993), 170.
26. Cornell West, "Learning to Talk of Race," in *Reading Rodney King, Reading Urban Uprising*, ed. Robert Gooding-Williams (New York: Routledge, 1993), 256.
27. Calin Gilea, *Dr. Martin Luther King, Jr at Stanford—"The Other America,"* Youtube video, 2014, 24:37, https://www.youtube.com/watch?t=604&v=m3H978KlR20.
28. Judith Butler, "Endangered/Endangering: Schematic Racism and White Paranoia," in *Reading Rodney King, Reading Urban Uprising*, ed. Robert Gooding-Williams (New York: Routledge, 1993), 15–16.
29. Butler, "Endangered/Endangering," 15.
30. On July 6, 2016, a St. Anthony, Minnesota, police officer, Jeronimo Yanez, shot and killed Philando Castile after Castile reached for his pocket to get his identification as the officer had commanded. His girlfriend, Lavish/Diamond Reynolds, began filming the encounter and posting it to Facebook Live in the immediate aftermath of the shooting. In a statement, acting St. Anthony chief Sgt. Jon Mangseth said, "There is no other threat to the public at this time." Since neither Castile nor Reynolds nor her young child in the backseat posed a threat at any time, we must pause to wonder who, exactly, Sgt. Mangseth considers the public, and how exactly Mangseth believes he and his police force are protecting them. On July17, 2014, NYPD Officer Daniel Pantaleo choked Eric Garner to death; while New York prosecutors declined to indict Pantaleo, Ramsey Orta, the man who filmed Garner's killing, will serve jail time for unrelated charges. Yanez is facing manslaughter. Camile Domonoske and Bill Chappell, "Police Stop Ends in Black Man's Death; Aftermath Is Live-Streamed on Facebook," *NPR.org*, accessed July 7, 2016, http://www.npr.org/sections/thetwo-way/2016/07/07/485066807/police-stop-ends-in-black-mans-death-aftermath-is-livestreamed-online-video. "Two Years after Eric Garner's Death, Ramsey Orta, Who Filmed Police, Is Only One Heading to Jail," *Democracy Now!*, accessed July 15, 2016, http://www.democracynow.org/2016/7/13/two_years_after_eric_garner_s. Lauren Gambino, "Eric Garner: Grand Jury Declines to Indict NYPD Officer over Chokehold Death," *Guardian*, December 3, 2014, sec. US news, https://www.theguardian.com/us-news/2014/dec/03/eric-garner-grand-jury-declines-indict-nypd-chokehold-death.

31. Tupac Shakur, *Keep Ya Head Up*, Strictly 4 My N.I.G.G.A.Z. . . . (Interscope, 1993); Tupac Shakur, *Something 2 Die 4 (Interlude)*, Strictly 4 My N.I.G.G.A.Z. . . . (Interscope, 1993); Tupac Shakur, *I Wonder If Heaven Got a Ghetto*, R U Still Down? (Remember Me) (Interscope, 1997); Tupac Shakur, *Hellrazor*, R U Still Down? (Remember Me) (Interscope, 1997); Tupac Shakur, *Thugz Mansion*, Better Dayz (Amaru, 2002). In *In Search of the Black Fantastic*, Richard Iton gives a rich account of the dialectic between the exclusion of blacks on the political level and the inclusion of blacks on the level of popular culture, and the modes of resistance and transnational solidarity they produce as a result, in what he calls the "black superpublic." See Richard Iton, *In Search of the Black Fantastic: Politics and Popular Culture in the Post-Civil Rights Era* (New York: Oxford University Press, 2010).
32. Brenda Stevenson, *The Contested Murder of Latasha Harlins: Justice, Gender, and the Origins of the LA Riots* (Oxford: Oxford University Press, 2013), 270.
33. Lou Cannon, "Ruling in King Case Hinders Prosecution: Jury Won't Hear Officer's Racial Phrase," *Houston Chronicle*, March 26, 1993, sec. A.
34. "Judge May Bar Cop's 'Mandingo' Remark from King Beating Trial," *Journal Times*, accessed May 25, 2015, http://journaltimes.com/news/national/judge-may-bar-cop-s-mandingo-remark-from-king-beating/article_e7d8efc8-1ac1-5108-b714-64a5723c2466.html.
35. Du's attorney, from the trial transcript, quoted Stevenson, *The Contested Murder of Latasha Harlins*, 270.
36. Gordon, Lewis. "Of Illicit Appearance: The L.A. Riots/Rebellion as a Portent of Things to Come." *Truthout*. Accessed May 7, 2015, http://www.truth-out.org/news/item/9008-of-illicit-appearance-the-la-riots-rebellion-as-a-portent-of-things-to-come.
37. On the loss of privacy, in particular among poor Black women subject to greater state surveillance and state control, see Dorothy Roberts, *Killing the Black Body: Race, Reproduction, and the Meaning of Liberty* (New York: Vintage Books, 1999); Imani Perry, *More Beautiful and More Terrible: The Embrace and Transcendence of Racial Inequality in the United States* (New York: New York University Press, 2011). On the loss of intimacy and on intra-racial intimate justice, see Shatema Threadcraft, "Intimate Injustice, Political Obligation, and the Dark Ghetto," *Signs* 39, no. 3 (March 2014): 735–60, doi:10.1086/674382. See also Shatema Threadcraft, *Intimate Justice: The Black Female Body and the Body Politic* (New York: Oxford University Press, 2016). On race and sexual violence, see Kimberlé Crenshaw, "Mapping the Margins: Intersectionality, Identity Politics, and Violence against Women of Color," *Stanford Law Review* 43, no. 6 (July 1, 1991): 1241–99, doi:10.2307/1229039; and Angela Y. Davis, "Rape, Racism, and the Myth of the Black Rapist," in *Women, Race, & Class* (New York: Vintage Books, 2011), 172–201. On the occlusion of police violence against Black women, see Kimberlé Crenshaw and Beth Richie, "Say Her Name: Resisting Police Brutality Against Black Women." *African American Policy Forum*. Accessed April 30, 2017, http://www.aapf.org/sayhernamereport/.
38. Marc Cooper and Greg Goldin, "Some People Don't Count," in *Inside the Riots* (Los Angeles: Institute for Alternative Journalism, 1992), 43.

39. Richard Riordan, "Former Mayor Richard Riordan in Conversation with CSLA Director Fernando Guerra" (Urban Lecture Series, Center for the Study of Los Angeles, Loyola Marymount University, Los Angeles, February 21, 2012).
40. Joe Domanick, "Police Power," in *Inside the Riots* (Los Angeles: Institute for Alternative Journalism, 1992), 23.
41. A timeline of the 1965 Watts Riot can be found in Abu-Lughod, *Race, Space, and Riots*, 204–213.
42. Abu-Lughod, *Race, Space, and Riots*, 246. See also Lou Cannon, *Official Negligence: How Rodney King and the Riots Changed Los Angeles and the LAPD* (Boulder, CO: Times Books, 1997).
43. Abu-Lughod, *Race, Space, and Riots*, 247.
44. Sumi Cho, "Korean-Americans vs. African-Americans: Conflict and Construction," in *Reading Rodney King, Reading Urban Uprising*, ed. Robert Gooding-Williams (New York: Routledge, 1993), 196–212.
45. Cho, "Korean-Americans vs. African-Americans," 203. Cho refers here to the essay "Racist Love" by Frank Chin and Jefferey Paul Chan, in *Seeing Through the Shuck*, ed. Richard Kostelanetz (New York: Ballantine Books, 1972), 65–79.
46. Cho, "Korean-Americans vs. African-Americans," 197.
47. Cho, "Korean-Americans vs. African-Americans," 206.
48. Peter Kwong, "The First Multicultural Riots," in *Inside the Riots*, ed. Don Hazen (Los Angeles: Institute for Alternative Journalism, 1993), 88–93. For more Korean and Korean-American perspectives on the riots, see Nancy Abelmann and John Lie, *Blue Dreams: Korean Americans and the Los Angeles Riots* (Cambridge, MA: Harvard University Press, 1997); Edward J. W. Park, "Community Divided: Korean American Politics in Post-Civil Unrest Los Angeles," in *Asians and Latino Americans in a Restructuring Economy: The Metamorphosis of Southern California*, ed. Marta Lopez-Garza and David R. Diaz (Stanford, CA: Stanford University Press, 2001), 273–88; Elaine Kim, "Home Is Where the Han Is: A Korean-American Perspective on the Los Angeles Upheavals," in *Reading Rodney King, Reading Urban Uprising*, ed. Robert Gooding-Williams (New York: Routledge, 1993), 215–35.
49. Meraji, Shereen Marisol. "As Los Angeles Burned, the Border Patrol Swooped In." *All Things Considered*, April 27, 2017, http://www.npr.org/sections/codeswitch/2017/04/27/525619864/as-los-angeles-burned-the-border-patrol-swooped-in.
50. Meraji, "As Los Angeles Burned, the Border Patrol Swooped In."
51. Abu-Lughod, *Race, Space, and Riots*, 241.
52. Abu-Lughod, *Race, Space, and Riots*, 241; Kwong, "The First Multicultural Riots," 1992, 89.
53. Gooding-Williams, *Reading Rodney King, Reading Urban Uprising*, 170.
54. Cf. Edward C. Banfield, *The Unheavenly City: The Nature and the Future of Our Urban Crisis* (New York: Little, Brown, 1970). In a chapter titled "Rioting Mainly for Fun and Profit," Banfield describes the (essentialized) cultural difference of the underclass, who, because they live for the moment, are unable to develop the habits that would lift them out of poverty. Banfield seems to have coined the phrase, which enjoyed a renaissance during the 2011 London riots. Public opinion research on the 2011 London riots showed that the rioters overwhelmingly saw themselves

as protesting their targeting by the police or the persistent criminalization of the young and working-class/jobless. That riot was sparked when the police killed a young black man, a twenty-four-year-old father.

55. Rubén Martínez, "Riot Scenes," in *Inside the Riots*, ed. Don Hazen (Los Angeles: Institute for Alternative Journalism, 1993), 30–34.
56. Kim Bell, "DeAndre Smith Justifies the Looting in Ferguson," *St. Louis Post Dispatch*, August 11, 2014, http://video.stltoday.com/DeAndre-Smith-justifies-the-looting-in-Ferguson-26502237.
57. United States Department of Justice, Civil Rights Division, "Investigation of the Ferguson Police Department," Government Investigation Report (Washington, DC: Department of Justice, Civil Rights Division, March 4, 2015), http://www.justice.gov/sites/default/files/opa/press-releases/attachments/2015/03/04/ferguson_police_department_report.pdf.
58. Ta-Nehisi Coates, "The Gangsters of Ferguson," *Atlantic*, March 5, 2015, http://www.theatlantic.com/politics/archive/2015/03/The-Gangsters-Of-Ferguson/386893/.
59. Falguni A. Sheth, *Toward a Political Philosophy of Race* (Albany: State University of New York Press, 2009).
60. Ben Feuerherd and Bob Fredericks, "Obama Calls Baltimore Rioters 'Criminals and Thugs,'" *New York Post*, April 28, 2015, http://nypost.com/2015/04/28/obama-calls-baltimore-rioters-criminals-and-thugs/.

POSTSCRIPT

1. María Lugones, *Pilgrimages/Peregrinajes: Theorizing Coalition against Multiple Oppressions* (Lanham, MD: Rowman & Littlefield, 2003), 83.
2. Lugones, *Pilgrimages/Peregrinajes*, 127.
3. Lugones, *Pilgrimages/Peregrinajes*, 127.
4. Lugones, *Pilgrimages/Peregrinajes*, 128.
5. Lugones, *Pilgrimages/Peregrinajes*, 127.
6. Lugones, *Pilgrimages/Peregrinajes*, 131.
7. Lugones, *Pilgrimages/Peregrinajes*, 225.
8. Audre Lorde, "On the Uses of Anger," in *Sister Outsider: Essays and Speeches* (New York: Ten Speed Press, 2012), 132–33.
9. "A Herstory of the #BlackLivesMatter Movement by Alicia Garza," *Feminist Wire*, October 7, 2014, http://www.thefeministwire.com/2014/10/blacklivesmatter-2/.
10. "A Herstory of the #BlackLivesMatter Movement."

BIBLIOGRAPHY

Abelmann, Nancy, and John Lie. *Blue Dreams: Korean Americans and the Los Angeles Riots*. Cambridge, MA: Harvard University Press, 1997.

Abu-Lughod, Janet. *Race, Space, and Riots*. New York: Oxford University Press, 2007.

Adorno, Theodor W. *Negative Dialektik*. Frankfurt-am-Main: Suhrkamp, 1975.

Adorno, Theodor W. *Critical Models: Interventions and Catchwords*. New York: Columbia University Press, 2013.

Adorno, Theodor W. *Hegel: Three Studies*. Cambridge, MA: MIT Press, 1994.

Adorno, Theodor W. *History and Freedom: Lectures 1964–1965*. Cambridge, CA: Polity, 2006.

Adorno, Theodor W. *Kant's Critique of Pure Reason (1959)*. Edited by Rolf Tiedemann. Stanford, CA: Stanford University Press, 2001.

Adorno, Theodor W. *Lectures on Negative Dialectics: Fragments of a Lecture Course 1965/1966*. Cambridge: Polity, 2008.

Adorno, Theodor W. *Metaphysics: Concept and Problems*. Edited by Rolf Tiedemann and Edmund Jephcott. Stanford, CA: Stanford University Press, 2002.

Adorno, Theodor W. *Minima Moralia: Reflections on a Damaged Life*. Translated by E. F. N. Jephcott. London: Verso, 2005.

Adorno, Theodor W. *Nachgelassene Schriften. Abteilung IV: Vorlesungen*, Band 4: *Kants "Kritik der reinen Vernunft."* Edited by Rolf Tiedemann. 2nd ed. Frankfurt am Main: Suhrkamp, 1995.

Adorno, Theodor W. *Negative Dialectics*. Translated by E. B. Ashton. New York: Continuum, 2007.

Adorno, Theodor W. *Philosophische Terminologie*, BD.1. Frankfurt am Main: Suhrkamp, 1997.

Allen, Amy. "The Public Sphere: Ideology and/or Ideal?," *Political Theory* 40, no. 6 (2012): 822–29.

Allen, Danielle. *Talking to Strangers: Anxieties of Citizenship since Brown v. Board of Education*. Chicago: University of Chicago Press, 2009.

Amidon, Kevin S. "What Happens to Countess Geschwitz? Revisiting Homosexuality in Horkheimer and Adorno." *New York Journal of Sociology* 1 (2008): 1–24.

Anouilh, Jean. *Antigone: A Play*. Translated by Jeremy Sams. Hollywood: Samuel French, 2002.

Associated Press. "Judge Says Remarks on 'Gorillas' May Be Cited in Trial on Beating." *New York Times*, June 12, 1991, sec. US. http://www.nytimes.com/1991/06/12/us/judge-says-remarks-on-gorillas-may-be-cited-in-trial-on-beating.html.

Avila, Eric. *Popular Culture in the Age of White Flight: Fear and Fantasy in Suburban Los Angeles*. Berkeley: University of California Press, 2004.

Banfield, Edward C. *The Unheavenly City: The Nature and the Future of Our Urban Crisis*. New York: Little, Brown, 1970.

Barad, Karen. *Meeting the Universe Halfway: Quantum Physics and the Entanglement of Matter and Meaning*. Durham, NC: Duke University Press, 2007.

Barnes, Brooks. "From Footnote to Fame in Civil Rights History." *New York Times*, November 26, 2009, sec. Books. http://www.nytimes.com/2009/11/26/books/26colvin.html.

Bates, Karen Grigsby. "Is It an 'Uprising' or a 'Riot'? Depends on Who's Watching." *Morning Edition*, National Public Radio, April 30, 2015. Accessed April 24, 2017. http://www.npr.org/sections/codeswitch/2015/04/30/403303769/uprising-or-riot-depends-whos-watching

Baucom, Ian. *Specters of the Atlantic: Finance Capital, Slavery, and the Philosophy of History*. Durham, NC: Duke University Press, 2005.

Bell, Kim. "DeAndre Smith Justifies the Looting in Ferguson." *St. Louis Post Dispatch*, August 11, 2014. http://video.stltoday.com/DeAndre-Smith-justifies-the-looting-in-Ferguson-26502237.

Benjamin, Walter. "Theses on the Philosophy of History." In *Illuminations*. Boston: Houghton Mifflin Harcourt, 1968.

Bennington, Geoffrey. "Deconstruction and the Philosophers (The Very Idea)." In *Jacques Derrida: Critical Assessments of Leading Philosophers*, edited by Zeynep Direk and Lawlor, Vol. 2. New York: Routledge, 2002.

Branch, Taylor. *Parting the Waters : America in the King Years 1954–63*. New York: Simon & Schuster, 1989.

Brandom, Robert. *Tales of the Mighty Dead: Historical Essays in the Metaphysics of Intentionality*. Cambridge, MA: Harvard University Press, 2002.

Buchwalter, Andrew. "Hegel, Adorno and the Concept of Transcendent Critique." *Philosophy and Social Criticism* 12, no. 4 (1987): 297–328.

Buck-Morss, Susan. *Origin of Negative Dialectics*. New York: Free Press, 1979.

Butler, Judith. *Antigone's Claim: Kinship between Life and Death*. New York: Columbia University Press, 2000.

Butler, Judith. *Bodies That Matter: On the Discursive Limits of "Sex."* New York: Routledge, 1993.

Butler, Judith. "Bodily Confessions." In *Undoing Gender*, 161–73. New York: Routledge, 2004.

Butler, Judith. "Contingent Foundations: Feminism and the Question of 'Postmodernism.'" In *Feminist Contentions: A Philosophical Exchange*, edited by Seyla Benhabib, Judith Butler, Drucilla Cornell, and Nancy Fraser, 35–57. New York: Routledge, 1994.

Butler, Judith. "Endangered/Endangering: Schematic Racism and White Paranoia." In *Reading Rodney King, Reading Urban Uprising*, edited by Robert Gooding-Williams, 15–22. New York: Routledge, 1993.

Butler, Judith. *Frames of War: When Is Life Grievable?* London: Verso, 2010.

Butler, Judith. *Gender Trouble: Feminism and the Subversion of Identity*. New York: Routledge, 2006.

Butler, Judith. *The Psychic Life of Power: Theories in Subjection*. Stanford, CA: Stanford University Press, 1997.

Cannon, Lou. *Official Negligence: How Rodney King and the Riots Changed Los Angeles and the LAPD*. Boulder, CO: Times Books, 1997.

Cannon, Lou. "Ruling in King Case Hinders Prosecution: Jury Won't Hear Officer's Racial Phrase." *Houston Chronicle*, March 26, 1993, sec. A.

Chanter, Tina. "Antigone's Excessive Relationship to Fetishism: The Performative Politics and Rebirth of Eros and Philia from Ancient Greece to Modern South Africa." Edited by Antonio Calcagno. *Symposium* 11, no. 2 (2007): 231–60. doi:10.5840/symposium200711227.

Chanter, Tina. "Antigone's Political Legacies: Abjection in Defiance of Mourning." In *Interrogating Antigone in Postmodern Philosophy and Criticism*, edited by S. E. Wilmer and Audronė Žukauskaitė, 19–47. New York: Oxford University Press, 2010.

Chanter, Tina. *Whose Antigone? The Tragic Marginalization of Slavery*. Albany: State University of New York Press, 2011.

Chanter, Tina, and Sean D. Kirkland. *The Returns of Antigone: Interdisciplinary Essays*. Albany: State University of New York Press, 2014.

Chin, Frank, and Jefferey Paul Chan. "Racist Love." In *Seeing through the Shuck*, edited by Richard Kostelanetz, 65–79. New York: Ballantine Books, 1972.

Cho, Sumi. "Korean-Americans vs. African-Americans: Conflict and Construction." In *Reading Rodney King, Reading Urban Uprising*, edited by Robert Gooding-Williams, 196–212. New York: Routledge, 1993.

Ciccariello-Maher, George. *Decolonizing Dialectics*. Durham: Duke University Press, 2017.

Clover, Joshua. *Riot. Strike. Riot: The New Era of Uprisings*. London: Verso, 2016.

Coates, Ta-Nehisi. "The Gangsters of Ferguson." *Atlantic*, March 5, 2015. http://www.theatlantic.com/politics/archive/2015/03/The-Gangsters-Of-Ferguson/386893/.

Cohen, Cathy J. *The Boundaries of Blackness: AIDS and the Breakdown of Black Politics*. Chicago: University of Chicago Press, 1999.

Cohen, Nathan, ed. *The Los Angeles Riots: A Socio-Psychological Study*. New York: Praeger, 1970.

The Combahee River Collective. "A Black Feminist Statement." In *All the Women Are White, All the Blacks Are Men, But Some of Us Are Brave: Black Women's Studies*, edited by Gloria Hull, Patricia Bell Scott, and Barbara Smith. New York: Feminist Press, 1982.

Cook, Deborah. *Adorno, Habermas and the Search for a Rational Society*. New York: Routledge, 2012.

Cook, Deborah. "A Response to Finlayson." *Historical Materialism* 11, no. 2 (2003): 189–98.

Cook, Deborah. "From the Actual to the Possible: Nonidentity Thinking." *Constellations* 12, no. 1 (2005): 21–35.

Cooper, Marc, and Greg Goldin. "Some People Don't Count." In *Inside the Riots*. Los Angeles: Institute for Alternative Journalism, n.d.

Coulthard, Glen Sean. *Red Skin, White Masks: Rejecting the Colonial Politics of Recognition*. Minneapolis: University of Minnesota Press, 2014.

Crenshaw, Kimberlé. "Mapping the Margins: Intersectionality, Identity Politics, and Violence against Women of Color." *Stanford Law Review* 43, no. 6 (July 1, 1991): 1241–99. doi:10.2307/1229039.

Crenshaw, Kimberlé, and Beth Richie. "Say Her Name: Resisting Police Brutality Against Black Women." *African American Policy Forum*. Accessed April 30, 2017. http://www.aapf.org/sayhernamereport/.

Dallmayr, Fred R. *G W F Hegel: Modernity and Politics*. Lanham, MD: Rowman and Littlefield, 1993.

Davis, Angela Y. "Rape, Racism, and the Myth of the Black Rapist." In *Women, Race, & Class*, 172–201. New York: Vintage Books, 2011.

Davis, Angela Y. *Women, Race, & Class*. New York: Vintage Books, 2011.

de Boer, Karin. *On Hegel: The Sway of the Negative*. London: Palgrave Macmillan, 2010.

Dean, Jodi. *Solidarity of Strangers: Feminism after Identity Politics*. Berkeley: University of California Press, 1996.

"The Declaration of Independence." *National Archives and Records Administration*. Accessed October 18, 2010. http://www.archives.gov/exhibits/charters/declaration_transcript.html.

Derrida, Jacques. "Déclarations D'indépendance." In *Otobiographies: L'enseignement de Nietzsche et la politique du nom propre*, 13–32. Paris: Galilée, 1984.

Derrida, Jacques. "Declarations of Independence." *New Political Science* 7, no. 1 (June 1, 1986): 7–15. doi:10.1080/07393148608429608.

Derrida, Jacques. "Différance." In *Margins of Philosophy*, 1–27. Chicago: University of Chicago Press, 1982.

Derrida, Jacques. "From Restricted to General Economy: A Hegelianism Without Reserve." In *Writing and Difference*. 2nd ed., 317–50. New York: Routledge, 2001.

Derrida, Jacques. *Glas*. Paris: Éditions Galilée, 1974.

Derrida, Jacques. *Glas*. Lincoln: University of Nebraska Press, 1986.

Derrida, Jacques. "*La famille de Hegel, Séance 12*." Lecture Notes. Jacques Derrida Papers. MS-C01, n.d. Box 11, Folders 5–9. Special Collections and Archives, UC Irvine Libraries, Irvine, California.

Derrida, Jacques. "*La famille de Hegel, Séance 13*." Lecture Notes. Jacques Derrida Papers. MS-C01, n.d. Box 11, Folders 5–9. Special Collections and Archives, UC Irvine Libraries, Irvine, California.

Derrida, Jacques. "The Pit and the Pyramid: Introduction to Hegel's Semiology." In *Writing and Difference*, 69–108. Chicago: University of Chicago Press, 1978.

Derrida, Jacques. "Structure, Sign and Play in the Discourse of the Human Sciences." In *Writing and Difference*. Translated by Alan Bass, 278–94. Chicago: University of Chicago Press, 1978.

Derrida, Jacques. "Tympan." In *Margins of Philosophy*, ix–xxix. Chicago: University of Chicago Press, 1982.

Domanick, Joe. "Police Power." In *Inside the Riots: What Really Happened, and Why It Will Happen Again*, 21–23. Los Angeles: Institute for Alternative Journalism, 1992.

Domonoske, Camile, and Bill Chappell. "Police Stop Ends in Black Man's Death; Aftermath Is Live-Streamed on Facebook." *NPR.org*. Accessed July 7, 2016. http://www.npr.org/sections/thetwo-way/2016/07/07/485066807/police-stop-ends-in-black-mans-death-aftermath-is-livestreamed-online-video.

Edelman, Lee. "Against Survival: Queerness in a Time That's Out of Joint." *Shakespeare Quarterly* 62, no. 2 (2011): 148–69. doi:10.1353/shq.2011.0015.

Edelman, Lee. *No Future: Queer Theory and the Death Drive*. Durham, NC: Duke University Press, 2004.

Euben, J. Peter. *Corrupting Youth: Political Education, Democratic Culture, and Political Theory*. Princeton, NJ: Princeton University Press, 1997.

Feuerherd, Ben, and Bob Fredericks. "Obama Calls Baltimore Rioters 'Criminals and Thugs.'" *New York Post*, April 28, 2015. http://nypost.com/2015/04/28/obama-calls-baltimore-rioters-criminals-and-thugs/.

Finlayson, James Gordon. "The Theory of Ideology and the Ideology of Theory: Habermas Contra Adorno." *Historical Materialism* 11, no. 2 (2003): 165–87.

Foucault, Michel. *The History of Sexuality*, Vol. 1: *An Introduction*. Translated by Robert Hurley. New York: Vintage, 1990.

Fraser, Nancy. "What's Critical about Critical Theory? The Case of Habermas and Gender." *New German Critique*, no. 35 (April 1, 1985): 97–131. doi:10.2307/488202.

Fraser, Nancy, and Axel Honneth. *Redistribution or Recognition? A Political-Philosophical Exchange*. London: Verso, 2003.

Freud, Sigmund. "Negation [Verneinung]." In *The Standard Edition of the Complete Psychological Works of Sigmund Freud*, edited by James Strachey, Vol. 19 (1923–25): *The Ego and the Id and Other Works*, 234–39. London: Hogarth, 1961.

Fugard, Athol, John Kani, and Winston Ntshona. *Statements*. New York: Theatre Communications Group, 1974.

Gambino, Lauren. "Eric Garner: Grand Jury Declines to Indict NYPD Officer over Chokehold Death." *Guardian*, December 3, 2014, sec. US news. https://www.theguardian.com/us-news/2014/dec/03/eric-garner-grand-jury-declines-indict-nypd-chokehold-death.

Garfield, Bob. "Tabula Rosa." *On the Media*. WNYC, July 3, 2009. http://www.onthemedia.org/story/132404-tabula-rosa/?utm_source=sharedUrl&utm_medium=metatag&utm_campaign=sharedUrl.

Garza, Alicia. "A Herstory of the #BlackLivesMatter Movement by Alicia Garza." *Feminist Wire*, October 7, 2014. http://www.thefeministwire.com/2014/10/blacklivesmatter-2/.

Gasché, Rodolphe. *Inventions of Difference: On Jacques Derrida*. Cambridge, MA: Harvard University Press, 1994.

Gasché, Rodolphe. *The Tain of the Mirror: Derrida and the Philosophy of Reflection*. Cambridge, MA: Harvard University Press, 1986.

Gaston, Sean. *Starting with Derrida*. London: Bloomsbury Academic, 2008.

Gilea, Calin. *Dr. Martin Luther King, Jr at Stanford—"The Other America."* Youtube video, 2014. https://www.youtube.com/watch?t=604&v=m3H978KlR20.

Gooding-Williams, Robert. *Reading Rodney King, Reading Urban Uprising.* New York: Routledge, 1993.

Gordon, Lewis. "Of Illicit Appearance: The L.A. Riots/Rebellion as a Portent of Things to Come." *Truthout.* Accessed May 7, 2015. http://www.truth-out.org/news/item/9008-of-illicit-appearance-the-la-riots-rebellion-as-a-portent-of-things-to-come.

Grosz, Elizabeth. *Time Travels: Feminism, Nature, Power.* Durham, NC: Duke University Press, 2005.

Gurdon, Meghan Cox. "'Claudette Colvin.'" *Wall Street Journal,* November 21, 2009, sec. Life & Style. http://www.wsj.com/articles/SB10001424052748704204304574545643701327028.

Habermas, Jürgen. "Nachwort von Jürgen Habermas." In *Dialektik Der Aufklärung,* 128–76. Frankfurt-am-Main: Fischer, 1986.

Habermas, Jürgen. *The Structural Transformation of the Public Sphere: An Inquiry into a Category of Bourgeois Society.* Cambridge, MA: MIT Press, 1991.

Halberstam, Judith. "The Anti-Social Turn in Queer Studies." *Graduate Journal of Social Science* 5, no. 2 (November 2, 2008): 140–56.

Hammer, Espen. *Adorno and the Political.* New York: Routledge, 2005.

Hammer, Espen. "Metaphysics." In *Theodor Adorno: Key Concepts,* edited by Deborah Cook, 63–75. New York: Routledge, 2008.

Hammonds, Evelynn M. "Toward a Genealogy of Black Female Sexuality: The Problematic of Silence." In *Feminist Genealogies, Colonial Legacies, Democratic Futures,* edited by M. Jacqui Alexander and Chandra Talpade Mohanty, 170–82. New York: Routledge, 1996.

Hartman, Saidiya V. *Scenes of Subjection: Terror, Slavery, and Self-Making in Nineteenth-Century America.* New York: Oxford University Press, 1997.

Hartman, Saidiya V., and Frank B. Wilderson. "THE POSITION OF THE UNTHOUGHT." *Qui Parle* 13, no. 2 (2003): 183–201.

Hass, Andrew. *Hegel and the Art of Negation: Negativity, Creativity and Contemporary Thought.* London: I. B.Tauris, 2013.

Heaney, Seamus. *The Burial at Thebes: A Version of Sophocles' Antigone.* London: Macmillan, 2014.

Hegel, Georg Wilhelm Friedrich. *Elements of the Philosophy of Right.* Translated by Allen W. Wood. Cambridge: Cambridge University Press, 1991.

Hegel, Georg Wilhelm Friedrich. *Lectures on the Philosophy of World History.* Edited by Johannes Hoffmeister and Duncan Forbes. Translated by Hugh Barr Nisbet. Cambridge: Cambridge University Press, 1975.

Hegel, Georg Wilhelm Friedrich. *Phänomenologie des Geistes.* Hamburg: Felix Meiner Verlag, 1952.

Hegel, Georg Wilhelm Friedrich. *Phenomenology of Spirit.* Translated by A.V. Miller. New York: Oxford University Press, 1977.

Hegel, Georg Wilhelm Friedrich. *Reason in History: A General Introduction to the Philosophy of History.* Translated by Robert S. Hartmann. Upper Saddle River, NJ: Prentice Hall, 1997.

Hegel, Georg Wilhelm Friedrich. *Science of Logic*. Translated by A.V. Miller. Amherst, MA: Humanity Books, 1998.

Hegel, Georg Wilhelm Friedrich. *Spirit: Chapter Six of Hegel's Phenomenology of Spirit*. Translated by Toronto Hegel Translation Group. Indianapolis: Hackett, 2001.

Hegel, Georg Wilhelm Friedrich. *Wissenschaft Der Logik*, Bd. I. Frankfurt-am-Main: Suhrkamp, 1986.

Hegel, Georg Wilhelm Friedrich. *Wissenschaft Der Logik*, Bd.II. Frankfurt-am-Main: Suhrkamp, 1986.

Herzog, Dagmar. *Sex after Fascism: Memory and Morality in Twentieth-Century Germany*. Princeton, NJ: Princeton University Press, 2007.

Hewitt, Andrew. *Political Inversions: Homosexuality, Fascism, and the Modernist Imaginary*. Stanford, CA: Stanford University Press, 1996.

Hirsch, James S. *Riot and Remembrance: The Tulsa Race War and Its Legacy*. New York: Houghton Mifflin, 2002.

Honig, Bonnie. *Antigone, Interrupted*. Cambridge: Cambridge University Press, 2013.

Honig, Bonnie. "Ismene's Forced Choice: Sacrifice and Sorority in Sophocles' Antigone." *Arethusa* 44, no. 1 (2011): 29–68.

Honneth, Axel. *The Struggle for Recognition: The Moral Grammar of Social Conflicts*. Cambridge, MA: MIT Press, 1996.

hooks, bell. *Feminist Theory: From Margin to Center*. 2nd ed. Cambridge, MA: South End Press, 2000.

Horkheimer, Max, and Theodor W. Adorno. *Dialectic of Enlightenment: Philosophical Fragments*. Translated by Edmund Jephcott. Stanford, CA: Stanford University Press, 2002.

Horne, Gerald. "Epilogue: The 1990s." In *Fire This Time: The Watts Uprising and the 1960s*. Charlottesville: University of Virginia Press, 1995.

Horne, Gerald. *Fire This Time: The Watts Uprising and the 1960s*. Charlottesville: University of Virginia Press, 1995.

Horstmann, Rolf-Peter. "Hegel's *Phenomenology of Spirit* as an Argument for a Monistic Ontology." *Inquiry* 49, no. 1 (February 1, 2006): 103–18. doi:10.1080/00201740500497530.

Horstmann, Rolf-Peter. "Substance, Subject and Infinity: A Case Study of the Role of Logic in Hegel's System." In *Hegel: New Directions*, edited by Katerina Deligiorgi, 69–84. New York: Routledge, 2014.

Houlgate, Stephen. *Freedom, Truth and History: An Introduction to Hegel's Philosophy*. New York: Routledge, 1991.

Houlgate, Stephen. *The Opening of Hegel's Logic: From Being to Infinity*. West Lafayette, IN: Purdue University Press, 2006.

Huffer, Lynne. "Foucault's Fossils: Life Itself and the Return to Nature in Feminist Philosophy." In *Anthropocene Feminism*, edited by Richard Grusin, 65–88. Minneapolis: University of Minnesota Press, 2017.

Hullot-Kentor, Robert. "Back to Adorno." In *Theodor Adorno: Critical Evaluations in Cultural Theory*, edited by Simon Jarvis. New York: Routledge, 2006.

Hutchings, Kimberly, and Tuija Pulkkinen. "Introduction." In *Hegel's Philosophy and Feminist Thought: Beyond Antigone?* New York: Palgrave Macmillan, 2010.

Hyppolite, Jean. *Genesis and Structure of Hegel's "Phenomenology of Spirit."* Edited by Samuel Cherniak and John Heckman. Evanston, IL: Northwestern University Press, 1979.

Hyppolite, Jean. *Logic and Existence*. Translated by Len Lawlor and Amit Sen. Albany: State University of New York Press, 1997.

Hyppolite, Jean. *Logique et existence: essai sur la logique de Hegel*. Paris: Presses Universitaires de France, 1961.

Irigaray, Luce. "The Eternal Irony of the Community." In *Speculum of the Other Woman*, translated by Gillian C. Gill, 214–26. Ithaca, NY: Cornell University Press, 1985.

Irigaray, Luce. *This Sex Which Is Not One*. Ithaca, NY: Cornell University Press, 1985.

Iton, Richard. *In Search of the Black Fantastic: Politics and Popular Culture in the Post-Civil Rights Era*. New York: Oxford University Press, 2010.

Jacobs, Carol. "Dusting Antigone." *MLN* 111, no. 5 (1996): 890–917.

Jarvis, Simon. *Adorno: A Critical Introduction*. New York: Routledge, 1998.

Jarvis, Simon. "The Coastline of Experience: Materialism and Metaphysics in Adorno." *Radical Philosophy* 85 (1997): 7–19.

"Judge May Bar Cop's 'Mandingo' Remark from King Beating Trial." *Journal Times*. Accessed May 25, 2015. http://journaltimes.com/news/national/judge-may-bar-cop-s-mandingo-remark-from-king-beating/article_e7d8efc8-1ac1-5108-b714-64a5723c2466.html.

Kelley, Robin D. G. "Baltimore and the Language of Change." *Los Angeles Times*, May 4, 2015. Accessed April 24, 2017. http://www.latimes.com/opinion/op-ed/la-oe-0504-kelley-baltimore-rebellion-20150504-story.html.

Kerner Commission, U. S. Riot, and Tim Wicker. *Report of the National Advisory Commission on Civil Disorders*. New York: Bantam Books, 1968.

Kim, Elaine. "Home Is Where the Han Is: A Korean-American Perspective on the Los Angeles Upheavals." In *Reading Rodney King, Reading Urban Uprising*, edited by Robert Gooding-Williams, 215–35. New York: Routledge, 1993.

Koopman, Colin. "Democracy Both Liberal and Radical: Political Agency in Dewey and Laclau and Mouffe." In *Persuasion and Compulsion in Democracy*, edited by Jacquelyn Kegley and Krzysztof Piotr Skowronski, 85–106. Lanham, MD: Lexington Books, 2015.

Kramer, Sina. "Derrida's 'Antigonanette': On the Quasi-Transcendental." *Southern Journal of Philosophy* 52, no. 4 (December 1, 2014): 521–51. doi:10.1111/sjp.12084.

Kramer, Sina. "Judith Butler's 'New Humanism': A Thing or Not a Thing, and So What?" *philoSOPHIA* 5, no. 1 (Winter 2015): 25–40.

Kramer, Sina. "On Negativity in Revolution in Poetic Language." *Continental Philosophy Review* 46, no. 3 (August 14, 2013): 465–79. doi:10.1007/s11007-013-9272-y.

Kristeva, Julia. *Powers of Horror*. New York: Columbia University Press, 1982.

Kristeva, Julia. *Revolution in Poetic Language*. New York: Columbia University Press, 1984.

Kwong, Peter. "The First Multicultural Riots." In *Inside the Riots*, edited by Don Hazen, 88–93. Los Angeles: Institute for Alternative Journalism, 1993.

Laclau, Ernesto. *New Reflections on the Revolution of Our Time*. London: Verso, 1990.

Laclau, Ernesto, and Chantal Mouffe. *Hegemony and Socialist Strategy: Towards a Radical Democratic Politics*. London: Verso, 2001.

Landes, Joan B. "The Public and the Private Sphere: A Feminist Reconsideration." In *Feminism, the Public and the Private*, edited by Joan B. Landes, 135–63. New York: Oxford University Press, 1998.

Leavey, John P. Jr. *Glassary: "Sounding the Unconscious."* Lincoln: University of Nebraska Press, 1986.

Leonard, Miriam. "Freud and Tragedy: Oedipus and the Gender of the Universal." *Classical Receptions Journal* 5, no. 1 (2013): 63–83.

Lorde, Audre. "Age, Race, Class and Sex: Women Redefining Difference." In *Sister Outsider: Essays and Speeches*. New York: Ten Speed Press, 2012: 114–123.

Lorde, Audre. "On the Uses of Anger." In *Sister Outsider: Essays and Speeches*. New York: Ten Speed Press, 2012.

Lugones, María. *Pilgrimages/Peregrinajes: Theorizing Coalition against Multiple Oppressions*. Lanham. MD: Rowman and Littlefield, 2003.

Lumpkins, Charles L. *American Pogrom: The East St. Louis Riot and Black Politics*. Athens: Ohio University Press, 2008.

Mader, Mary Beth. "Antigone's Line." *Bulletin de La Société Américaine de Philosophie de Langue Française* 15, no. 1 (2005): 18–40.

Malabou, Catherine. *L'avenir de Hegel: plasticité, temporalité, dialectique*. Paris: Vrin, 1996.

Malabou, Catherine. *The Future of Hegel: Plasticity, Temporality, and Dialectic*. New York: Routledge, 2005.

Marasco, Robyn. *The Highway of Despair: Critical Theory after Hegel*. New York: Columbia University Press, 2015.

Markell, Patchen. *Bound by Recognition*. Princeton, NJ: Princeton University Press, 2003.

Martínez, Rubén. "Riot Scenes." In *Inside the Riots*, edited by Don Hazen, 30–34. Los Angeles: Institute for Alternative Journalism, 1993.

Marx, Karl. *The German Ideology*. Edited by C. J. Arthur. New York: International Publishers, 2007.

Marx, Karl. "On the Jewish Question." In *The Marx Engels Reader*, edited by Robert Tucker, 2nd ed., 26–52. New York: Norton, 1978.

McAdam, Doug. *Political Process and the Development of Black Insurgency, 1930–1970*. 2nd ed. Chicago: University of Chicago Press, 1999.

McCone Commission on the Los Angeles Riots. "Violence in the City: An End or a Beginning." Los Angeles: Governor's Commission on the Los Angeles Riots, December 2, 1965.

McGuire, Danielle L. *At the Dark End of the Street: Black Women, Rape, and Resistance—A New History of the Civil Rights Movement from Rosa Parks to the Rise of Black Power*. New York: Vintage Books, 2011.

Meehan, M. Johanna. *Feminists Read Habermas: Gendering the Subject of Discourse*. New York: Routledge, 1995.

Meraji, Shereen Marisol. "As Los Angeles Burned, The Border Patrol Swooped In." *All Things Considered*, April 27, 2017. http://www.npr.org/sections/codeswitch/2017/04/27/525619864/as-los-angeles-burned-the-border-patrol-swooped-in.

Mills, Charles. *The Racial Contract*. Ithaca, NY: Cornell University Press, 1997.

Morris, Aldon D. *Origins of the Civil Rights Movements*. New York: Simon & Schuster, 1986.

Mouffe, Chantal. *The Return of the Political*. London: Verso, 2005.

Muñoz, José Esteban. *Cruising Utopia: The Then and There of Queer Futurity*. New York: New York University Press, 2009.

Nancy, Jean-Luc. *Hegel: The Restlessness of the Negative*. Minneapolis: University of Minnesota Press, 2002.

Nuzzo, Angelica. "Dialectic as a Logic of Transformative Processes." In *Hegel: New Directions*, edited by Katerina Deligiorgi, 85–103. New York: Routledge, 2014.

Olson, Joel. *The Abolition of White Democracy*. Minneapolis: University of Minnesota Press. 2004.

Park, Edward J. W. "Community Divided: Korean American Politics in Post–Civil Unrest Los Angeles." In *Asians and Latino Americans in a Restructuring Economy: The Metamorphosis of Southern California*, edited by Marta Lopez-Garza and David R. Diaz, 273–88. Stanford, CA: Stanford University Press, 2001.

Parks, Rosa, and Jim Haskins. *Rosa Parks: My Story*. Reprint ed. New York: Puffin Books, 1999.

Pateman, Carole. *The Sexual Contract*. Cambridge: Polity Press, 1988.

Patterson, Orlando. *Slavery and Social Death*. Cambridge, MA: Harvard University Press, 1985.

Perry, Imani. *More Beautiful and More Terrible: The Embrace and Transcendence of Racial Inequality in the United States*. New York: New York University Press, 2011.

Pinkard, Terry. *Hegel's Phenomenology: The Sociality of Reason*. Cambridge: Cambridge University Press, 1994.

Plass, Ulrich. *Language and History in Theodor W. Adorno's Notes to Literature*. New York: Routledge, 2007.

Popper, Karl. *The Open Society and Its Enemies*, Vol. 2: *Hegel, Marx, and the Aftermath*. 5th rev. ed. Princeton, NJ: Princeton University Press, 1971.

"The President's Message; Excerpts from Bush's Speech on Los Angeles Riots: 'Need to Restore Order.'" *New York Times*, May 2, 1992.

Riordan, Richard. "Former Mayor Richard Riordan in Conversation with CSLA DIrector Fernando Guerra." Interview in the Urban Lecture Series, Center for the Study of Los Angeles, Loyola Marymount University, Los Angeles, February 21, 2012.

Roberts, Dorothy. *Killing the Black Body: Race, Reproduction, and the Meaning of Liberty*. New York: Vintage Books, 1999.

Roberts, Dorothy. "Punishing Drug Addicts Who Have Babies: Women of Color, Equality, and the Right of Privacy." In *Critical Race Theory: The Key Writings That Formed the Movement*, edited by Kimberlé Crenshaw, Neil Gotunda, and Gary Peller, 384–426. New York: New Press, 1995.

Robinson, Jo Ann. *Montgomery Bus Boycott and the Women Who Started It: The Memoir of Jo Ann Gibson Robinson*. Edited by David J. Garrow. Knoxville: University of Tennessee Press, 1987.

Rosen, Hannah. *Terror in the Heart of Freedom: Citizenship, Sexual Violence, and the Meaning of Race in the Postemancipation South*. Chapel Hill: University of North Carolina Press, 2009.

Rycenga, Jennifer. "Queerly Amiss: Sexuality and the Logic of Adorno's Dialectics." In *Adorno: A Critical Reader*, edited by Nigel C. Gibson and Andrew Rubin, 361–78. Hoboken, NJ: Wiley, 2002.

Sartillot, C. "Herbarium, Verbarium: The Discourse of Flowers." *Diacritics* 18, no. 4 (1988): 68–81.

Sexton, Jared. "Afro-Pessimism: The Unclear Word." *Rhizomes*, no. 29 (2016). http://www.rhizomes.net/issue29/sexton.html.

Sexton, Jared. *Amalgamation Schemes: Antiblackness and the Critique of Multiracialism*. Minneapolis: University of Minnesota Press, 2008.

Sexton, Jared. "People-of-Color-Blindness Notes on the Afterlife of Slavery." *Social Text* 28, no. 2, 103 (June 20, 2010): 31–56. doi:10.1215/01642472-2009-066.

Sexton, Jared. "The Social Life of Social Death: On Afro-Pessimism and Black Optimism." *InTensions*, no. 5 (Fall/Winter 2011). http://www.yorku.ca/intent/issue5/index.php.

Shakur, Tupac. *Hellrazor*. Vol. R U Still Down? (Remember Me). Interscope Records, 1997.

Shakur, Tupac. *I Wonder If Heaven Got a Ghetto*. Vol. R U Still Down? (Remember Me). Interscope Records, 1997.

Shakur, Tupac. *Keep Ya Head Up*. Vol. Strictly 4 My N.I.G.G.A.Z . . . Interscope Records, 1993.

Shakur, Tupac. *Something 2 Die 4 (Interlude)*. Vol. Strictly 4 My N.I.G.G.A.Z . . . Interscope Records, 1993.

Shakur, Tupac. *Thugz Mansion*. Vol. Better Dayz. Amaru Records, 2002.

Sharp, Hasana. *Spinoza and the Politics of Renaturalization*. Chicago: University of Chicago Press, 2011.

Sheth, Falguni A. *Toward a Political Philosophy of Race*. Albany: State University of New York Press, 2009.

Sitkoff, Harvard. *The Struggle for Black Equality*. Rev. ed. New York: Hill and Wang, 2008.

Sjöholm, Cecilia. *The Antigone Complex: Ethics and the Invention of Feminine Desire*. Stanford, CA: Stanford University Press, 2004.

Smallwood, Stephanie E. *Saltwater Slavery: A Middle Passage from Africa to American Diaspora*. Cambridge, MA: Harvard University Press, 2009.

Söderbäck, Fanny. *Feminist Readings of Antigone*. Albany: State University of New York Press, 2012.

Sophocles. "Antigone." In *Sophocles I*, edited by Richmond Lattimore, translated by David Grene. Chicago: University of Chicago Press, 1991.

Sparks, Holloway. "Dissident Citizenship: Democratic Theory, Political Courage, and Activist Women." *Hypatia* 12, no. 4 (October 1, 1997): 74–110.

Sparks, Holloway. "Gender and the Politics of Democratic Disturbance in the Montgomery Bus Boycott." Paper presented at the Western Political Science Association Annual Meeting, Vancouver, March 20, 2009.

Sparks, Holloway. "Mama Grizzlies and Guardians of the Republic: The Democratic and Intersectional Politics of Anger in the Tea Party Movement." *New Political Science* 37, no. 1 (2015): 25–47.

Sparks, Holloway. "You Can't Be Nice: Dissident Citizenship, Gender, and the Politics of Disturbance in the U.S. Welfare Rights Movement." Paper presented at the Western Political Science Association Annual Meeting, San Diego, March 21, 2008.

Spivak, Gayatri Chakravorty. "Glas-Piece: A Compte-Rendu." *Diacritics* 7, no. 3 (1977): 22–43.

Stäheli, Urs. "Competing Figures of the Limit: Dispersion, Transgression, Antagonism, Indifference." In *Laclau: A Critical Reader*, edited by Simon Critchley and Oliver Marchart, 226–39. New York: Routledge, 2004.

Staten, Henry. *Wittgenstein and Derrida*. Lincoln: University of Nebraska Press, 1984.

Steiner, George. *Antigones*. New Haven, CT: Yale University Press, 1996.

Stevenson, Brenda. *The Contested Murder of Latasha Harlins: Justice, Gender, and the Origins of the LA Riots*. Oxford: Oxford University Press, 2013.

Stone, Alison. "Adorno and Logic." In *Theodor Adorno: Key Concepts*, edited by Deborah Cook, 47–62. New York: Routledge, 2014.

Stone, Alison. "Matter and Form." In *Hegel's Philosophy and Feminist Thought: Beyond Antigone?*, edited by Kimberly Hutchings and Tuija Pulkkinen, 211–32. New York: Palgrave Macmillan, 2010.

Sullivan, Shannon, and Nancy Tuana, eds. *Race and Epistemologies of Ignorance*. Albany: State University of New York Press, 2007.

Taylor, Charles, Kwame Anthony Appiah, Jürgen Habermas, Stephen C. Rockefeller, Michael Walzer, and Susan Wolf. *Multiculturalism: Examining the Politics of Recognition*. Edited by Amy Gutmann. Expanded Paperback edition. Princeton, NJ: Princeton University Press, 1994.

Theoharis, Jeanne. *The Rebellious Life of Mrs. Rosa Parks*. Boston: Beacon Press, 2013.

Theunissen, Michael. "Negativität Bei Adorno." In *Adorno-Konferenz 1983*, edited by Jürgen Habermas and Ludwig von Friedeburg, 41–65. Frankfurt-am-Main: Suhrkamp, 1983.

Theunissen, Michael. "Negativity in Adorno." In *Theodor Adorno: Critical Evaluations in Cultural Theory*, edited by Simon Jarvis. New York: Routledge, 2006.

Thompson, Kevin. "Hegelian Dialectic and the Quasi-Transcendental in *Glas*." In *Hegel after Derrida*, edited by Stuart Barnett, 239–59. New York: Routledge, 2002.

Threadcraft, Shatema. "Intimate Injustice, Political Obligation, and the Dark Ghetto." *Signs* 39, no. 3 (March 2014): 735–60. doi:10.1086/674382.

Threadcraft, Shatema. *Intimate Justice: The Black Female Body and the Body Politic*. New York: Oxford University Press, 2016.

Thyen, Anke. "Dimensions of the Nonidentical." In *Theodor Adorno: Critical Evaluations in Cultural Theory*, edited by Simon Jarvis. New York: Routledge, 2006.

Tuttle, William M. *Race Riot: Chicago in the Red Summer of 1919*. Champaign: University of Illinois Press, 1970.

"Two Years after Eric Garner's Death, Ramsey Orta, Who Filmed Police, Is Only One Heading to Jail." *Democracy Now!* Accessed July 15, 2016. http://www.democracynow.org/2016/7/13/two_years_after_eric_garner_s.

United States Department of Justice, Civil Rights Division. "Investigation of the Ferguson Police Department." Government Investigation Report. Washington, DC: Department of Justice, Civil Rights Division, March 4, 2015. http://www.justice.

gov/sites/default/files/opa/press-releases/attachments/2015/03/04/ferguson_police_department_report.pdf.

Werner, Lara. "The Gender of Spirit: Hegel's Moves and Strategies." In *Hegel's Philosophy and Feminist Thought: Beyond Antigone?*, edited by Kimberly Hutchings and Tuija Pulkkinen, 195–209. New York: Palgrave Macmillan, 2010.

West, Cornell. "Learning to Talk of Race." In *Reading Rodney King, Reading Urban Uprising*, edited by Robert Gooding-Williams, 255–60. New York: Routledge, 1993.

Wilderson, Frank B. III. *Red, White & Black: Cinema and the Structure of U.S. Antagonisms*. Durham, NC: Duke University Press, 2010.

Wilkerson, Isabel. *The Warmth of Other Suns*. New York: Vintage Books, 2011.

Williams, Patricia J. *The Alchemy of Race and Rights*. Cambridge, MA: Harvard University Press, 1991.

Wilmer, S. E., and Audrone Zukauskaite. *Interrogating Antigone in Postmodern Philosophy and Criticism*. New York: Oxford University Press, 2010.

Youatt, Rafi. "Power, Pain, and the Interspecies Politics of Foie Gras," *Political Research Quarterly* 65, no. 2 (June 1, 2012): 346–58.

Young, Iris Marion. *Inclusion and Democracy*. Oxford: Oxford University Press, 2002.

Zelizer, Julian E. "Is America Repeating the Mistakes of 1968?" *Atlantic*, July 8, 2016. http://www.theatlantic.com/politics/archive/2016/07/is-america-repeating-the-mistakes-of-1968/490568/.

INDEX